D0207637

DISENCHANTED IMAGES

THEODORE ZIOLKOWSKI

Disenchanted Images

A LITERARY ICONOLOGY

PRINCETON UNIVERSITY PRESS

Published by Princeton University Press, Princeton, New Jersey

IN THE UNITED KINGDOM:
Princeton University Press, Guildford, Surrey

Library of Congress Cataloging in Publication Data
will be found on the last printed page of this book

This book has been composed in Linotype Times Roman

Printed in the United States of America
by Princeton University Press, Princeton, New Jersey

For Yetta

Know that your words have won me at the last
To practice magic and concealed arts.
Philosophy is odious and obscure,
Both law and physic are for petty wits,
Divinity is basest of the three—
Unpleasant, harsh, contemptible, and vilde.
'Tis magic, magic, that hath ravish'd me!

Marlowe, *Doctor Faustus*

Preface

Mme du Deffand, when asked if she believed in ghosts, replied: "Non, mais j'en ai peur." I have long felt a deep and spontaneous sympathy with that wise and witty woman of the Enlightenment, whose respect for reason did not preclude a reverence for those aspects of life, inaccessible to pure rationality, that are sometimes uncritically called supernatural. My own enchantment with walking statues, haunted portraits, and magic mirrors dates back to my childhood in Montevallo, Alabama. So when I was invited to deliver the 1973 Dancy Lectures at the University of Montevallo, I could think of no topic more appropriate than the magic images to which this book is devoted. For it was in that Southern town that I first experienced a thrill of terror before graveyard statues that were reputed to stalk through the cemetery at midnight, and it was on that campus that I hustled, stiff-legged and with rounded eyes, past a darkened King House, where the eponymous portrait was reliably known to cast its baleful eyes upon children who ventured along at night. The three principal chapters of this book represent in a very special sense an homage to my boyhood, to my home town, and to many of the stories that I first read at that time and in that place. If these chapters have managed to retain and convey even a fraction of the childhood sense of wonder at magic images, then they have succeeded. Although the material is highly organized for the purposes of exposition, I hope that the historical narrative has at no point suffered for the sake of systematic rigor. This book is supposed to be fun.

The three central and substantive chapters provide the examples for the theoretical speculations of the introduction and conclusion, which have respectively a synchronic and a diachronic focus. The introduction, systematic in its organization, defines what I mean by "image" and examines three principal ways in which images can be used in literature. That discussion is intended to bring a bit of precision, at least for the purposes of this book, into the often fuzzy usage of four important critical terms: image, theme, motif, and symbol. The conclusion is historical in its orientation: it explores some of the factors that account for the phenomenon I define as "disenchantment" and suggests certain general implications of the material. For it is one of my principal aims to show that what I call "literary iconology" can go far beyond the limits of old-fashioned *Stoffgeschichte.* I believe that these "disenchanted images" demonstrate the essential literariness of literature: after all, magic mirrors and haunted portraits occur only in books or on the stage—not in "life." At the same time, their varying use by succeeding literary generations reflects and, to a certain extent, is affected by changes in the general cultural consciousness. Clearly, the image of walking statues means one thing to a romantic age that believes in mesmerism and delights in automata, and something quite different to an era informed by positivism and the psychological insights of William James.

Any such study as this is obviously the captive of its own examples. Yet I have not willfully chosen them: I took every single one that I could find—by systematic scholarly research, by serendipity, and by the help of friends and colleagues. For their suggestions and for the examples they provided I am indebted above all to my three most amused and amusing research assistants, Gretchi, Jan, and Eric Ziolkowski. I am grateful to all my friends in Montevallo for offering me the initial opportunity to formulate my thoughts on the disenchantment of images and for providing me with such a gratifying audience for the early version of these chapters—especially my cousins Irene Butkiewicz and Olga Kochanska. My colleague Earl Miner was kind enough to read the completed manuscript and to give me the benefit of his advice and encouragement. I would like to take this opportunity to express my thanks to the many associates at Princeton University Press with whom I have worked closely over the years and from whom I have learned much: Herb Bailey, Miriam Brokaw, Margot Cutter, Joanna Hitchcock, and Carol Orr. In particular, Jerry Sherwood showed her friendship by devoting her considerable literary sensibility and editorial acuity to this book. The dedication represents an inadequate expression of gratitude to my wife for twenty-five years of shared experience that has been constantly magic and never disenchanted.

Theodore Ziolkowski

Princeton, New Jersey
March 26, 1976

Contents

DISENCHANTED IMAGES

CHAPTER ONE

Introduction

> "When *I* use a word," Humpty Dumpty said, in rather a scornful tone, "it means just what I choose it to mean—neither more nor less."
>
> —*Through the Looking Glass*

Jean Cocteau's remarkable film, *The Blood of a Poet*, begins with a series of startling sequences.[1] The poet—naked to the waist and wearing a Louis XV wig—is standing at an easel, drawing what appears to be a self-portrait. Hearing a knock at the door, he glances away for a moment. When he turns back to his drawing, he is astonished to see that its mouth now displays a set of solid teeth. After a frantic attempt to wipe away the living mouth, he opens the door to a friend. But when he holds out his hand, his friend stares at it in horror and rushes away in such a fright that he tumbles down the stairs. Shrugging his shoulders in uncomprehending amusement, the poet goes to wash his hands. Presently he notices the sound of bubbling in the basin. A close-up reveals that the bubbles are coming out of a mouth in the palm of his right hand, "like a wound and the lips of a wound." In an access of disgust the poet tries to shake the mouth from his hand. When the mouth cries for air, he smashes a window pane and thrusts his arm out into the open. Finally, dashing to the door and locking it, he raises the mouth to his own lips in a passionate kiss. The camera follows the dexterous mouth as it moves down the young man's neck, caresses his shoul-

[1] *Le Sang d'un poète* (Monaco: Editions du Rocher, 1957); English translation by Carol Martin-Sperry in Jean Cocteau, *Two Screenplays* (New York: Orion, 1968). Both editions include the text of Cocteau's talk following the première at the Théâtre du Vieux-Colombier on January 30, 1932, as well as the brief Preface of 1946.

der, and slides toward his breast, leaving moist traces as it glides along the contours of his body. During the fade-out we see the poet convulsed in an autoerotic ecstasy.

When he wakes up the following morning, the mouth is still inside his hand, snoring gently and murmuring incoherently. Stealthily approaching a life-sized plaster statue of a woman now standing in the room, the poet claps his hand over its mouth and forces the living mouth onto its face. Thereupon the statue, opening its eyes, says to the poet: "Do you think it's that simple to get rid of a wound, to close the mouth of a wound?" The camera reveals that the room no longer has any doors or windows: a large mirror stands where formerly the door had been. The poet screams at the statue to open the door, but the statue replies that there is only one way out: through the mirror. When the poet objects that people cannot walk through glass, the statue reminds him ironically that he had once written that it was possible to enter mirrors. The poet moves around nervously for a few moments. Then, stepping onto a chair that has suddenly materialized beside the mirror, he touches the glass three times gingerly with his ring. Finally he climbs up onto the frame of the mirror and stares at his reflection. Exhorted by the statue, he hurls himself into the glass and disappears as though into a pool of water. It is unnecessary for our purposes to recapitulate the following scenes, which take place in the realm within or behind the mirror.

Since its première in 1932 Cocteau's epoch-making film has been widely and variously interpreted.[2] It has been suggested that the animated mouth represents the power of art to transcend the inanimate matter from which it is created and, coming to life, to express higher truths. The poet who has been blessed, or cursed, with this power discovers to his dismay that the voice of poetry marks him like a wound, and

[2] C. G. Wallis, "The Blood of a Poet: Cocteau's Art," *Kenyon Review*, 6 (1944), 24–42; and Frederick Brown, *The Impersonation of Angels: A Biography of Jean Cocteau* (New York: Viking, 1968), pp. 293–301.

he attempts to rid himself of the stigma by applying it to the art of antiquity (the statue). According to one view, the mirror stands allegorically for contemporary art, which reflects the poet's own world (his room). A different and more biographical interpretation regards the world behind the mirror as the poet's (Cocteau's) past, which he recaptures by entering the mirror, where he encounters scenes from his earlier works.

Cocteau refused to endorse any interpretation of his film, reasoning that any exegesis he might offer would inevitably be wrong since it would amount to "a text written after the images."[3] It was the images, he stressed, that had priority as he created his film—images and not a conceptualized scheme accessible to intellectual articulation. Even if we are willing to concede that the images defy interpretation, however, it is perfectly legitimate to ask where Cocteau got such images as an animated portrait, a talking statue, and a magic mirror. In his talk at the Théâtre du Vieux-Colombier following the première Cocteau observed that he was trying to film poetry the way deep-sea photographers film the bottom of the sea. "It meant letting down within me a diving bell like the one that they let down into the sea, to great depths." Years later, in his Preface to the scenario, he used a similar analogy, saying that the images rose from "the great darkness of the human body" ("la grande nuit du corps humain").

This view of the profound depths of the collective unconscious, from which the poet recovers images like Jungian archetypes, itself constitutes a striking and poetic metaphor that appealed to many of Cocteau's contemporaries. But is it accurate? The Russian Formalists held a radically different theory of images. In his influential essay "Art as Technique" (1917) Victor Shklovsky maintained that images change very little from century to century, from nation to nation, from poet to poet. "The more you understand an age, the more convinced you become that the images a given poet

[3] *Le Sang d'un poète*, p. 113: "un texte écrit après coup sur les images."

used and which you thought his own were taken almost unchanged from another poet. . . . Poets are much more concerned with arranging images than with creating them. Images are given to poets; the ability to remember them is far more important than the ability to create them."[4]

Who is right about the origin of images—the French poet with his romantic faith in his direct personal access to the image-making collective unconscious or the Russian critic with his sober theory concerning the conscious literary transmission of traditional images? In one sense the present study amounts simply to an attempt to answer that fundamental question of poetics. This endeavor will require us to examine the history of these three images in considerable detail. What is their cultural source? Where and when do they enter literary history? What associations do they bear? What contexts do they prefer? What generic affinities do they display? But before we attempt to deal with the large issues, let us come to grips more modestly with a few simple questions implicit in Cocteau's examples. First of all, what exactly do we mean by "image"? Second, what functions do images perform in the literary work? Finally, what unifies these three images and sets them apart from all other possible images?

The word "image" is one of the most common and, at the same time, most troublesome terms in literary criticism.[5] Let us therefore follow the advice of Humpty Dumpty, himself no mean semanticist, and define as lucidly as possible the meaning of the key terms we shall be employing. From the examples supplied by Cocteau's film it should be obvious that the word "image" is being invoked here in a very specific and limited sense. Most dictionaries—I have re-

[4] *Russian Formalist Criticism*, trans. and with an Introduction by Lee T. Lemon and Marion J. Reis (Lincoln: Univ. of Nebraska Press, 1965), p. 7.

[5] We shall be concerned here only with the English term. There are similar confusions in German and French, but in those languages the terms have a different history and different associations.

ferred to the *Oxford English Dictionary*, Webster's Third *New International Dictionary*, and the Random House *Dictionary of the English Language*—cite as the primary meaning of "image" an imitation, representation, reproduction, or likeness of the external form of any object, especially of a person, either in solid or surface form—that is, as an icon, a statue, or a painting. This basic meaning betrays the etymology of the word, which is related to Latin *imitari*, "to imitate." The second principal meaning in all three dictionaries refers to the optical counterpart of an object, as in a mirror reflection. The magic mirrors, animated portraits, and walking statues to be discussed in the following chapters represent images in these two primary senses of the word, and not in the various more recent and transferred senses.[6]

Taken in these two primary senses, the word "image" is at home in a variety of contexts, ranging from the history of religion to the art of photography, where it poses no problem of understanding. But as soon as the word shows up in a literary context, we encounter possibilities of confusion, for "image" is widely employed to designate at least three separate phenomena.[7] First, it is sometimes used in a sense quite close to its primary meaning to specify an object that actually figures in the literary work—an object that is more than the incidental objects of furniture or landscape required by the narrative and, at the same time, less conspicuously a

[6] I would explicitly exclude the currently fashionable understanding of the term as an artificially constructed "pseudo-ideal," which Daniel J. Boorstin has analyzed in *The Image, or What Happened to the American Dream* (New York: Atheneum, 1962). The point needs to be stressed because our thinking is affected more than we often care to admit by the language that we hear every day. This trivialized use of the term "image" confronts and affronts us constantly in the various media.

[7] Ray Frazer, "The Origin of the Term 'Image,'" *ELH*, 27 (1960), 149–61; Norman Friedman, "Imagery," *Encyclopedia of Poetry and Poetics*, ed. Alex Preminger (Princeton, N.J.: Princeton Univ. Press, 1965), pp. 363–70; and P. N. Furbank, *Reflections on the Word 'Image'* (London: Secker & Warburg, 1970), pp. 1–24.

bearer of meaning than what we commonly and popularly call a "symbol." As William York Tindall defines it, the image is "a definite object, or at least the semblance of an object, which, though nothing much in itself, has received import from experience and memory."[8] Tindall cites as an example the signboard representing Dr. Eckleburg's eyes in F. Scott Fitzgerald's *The Great Gatsby*, but we might equally well speak of the torture machine in Kafka's *The Penal Colony*, the madeleine in Proust's *The Remembrance of Time Past*, or the golden bowl in Henry James's novel of that title. In each case we are dealing with an object that has an unquestioned physical presence in the fictional world: it exists and fulfills a real function. This is the sense implicit in Shakespeare's lines about the poet in *A Midsummer Night's Dream*:

> And as imagination bodies forth
> The forms of things unknown, the poet's pen
> Turns them to shapes and gives to airy nothing
> A local habitation and a name.
> Such tricks hath strong imagination,
> That, if it would but apprehend some joy,
> It comprehends some bringer of that joy;
> Or in the night, imagining some fear,
> How easy is a bush supposed a bear!
>
> (Act V, Scene 1)

Here it is clearly the function of imagination, still conceived in a literal sense as the image-making faculty, to produce concrete images that embody insubstantial thoughts and feelings: images are "shapes" that have "a local habitation and a name." These images are *things* with a tangible reality in the context of the literary work: not the abstract sensation of fear, but the fear-inspiring bear itself. This basic meaning of "image," which still survives today, was for several centuries the only sense of the word in literary discussions.

[8] William York Tindall, *The Literary Symbol* (1955; rpt. Bloomington: Indiana Univ. Press, 1962), p. 9.

Wordsworth still believed that images are "sensible objects really existing, and felt to exist"; and as such "they may form the materials of a descriptive poem, where objects are delineated as they are."[9]

In the course of the later seventeenth and eighteenth centuries the word "image" and its collective form "imagery," which originally possessed the concrete and specific meanings implicit in etymology and in Renaissance vocabulary, gradually assumed two new and wholly unrelated meanings. First, for many critics the term became virtually synonymous with "figure of speech"—originally metaphor, but also simile and other forms of trope. In his study of "The Origin of the Term 'Image'" Roy Frazer has outlined the paradoxical process whereby the concrete notion of "image" gradually came to designate the very figurative devices for which it was originally invoked as a substitute. Second, another group of critics has found it useful to classify the "mental images" that occur in literary works. This concept, borrowed from psychology and deriving originally from Hobbes, refers to "the reproduction in the mind of a sensation produced by a physical perception": notably visual, auditory, olfactory, gustatory, tactile, organic, and kinesthetic.[10] As a result, since the eighteenth century the term "image" in criticism has lost much of its original sharpness to the extent that it has been expanded to incorporate new meanings from the fields of rhetoric and psychology. To put it most simply: if we see a study of Homer's imagery, we have no way of knowing at first glance whether it deals with his rhetorical figures and tropes, with his proclivity for certain classes of mental images, or with the objects that play an iconic role in his poetry.

Because of such potential confusions some critics have proposed that the word "image" should be discarded altogether as a critical tool. P. N. Furbank argues with con-

[9] Christopher Wordsworth, *Memoirs of William Wordsworth* (Boston: Ticknor, Reed, and Fields, 1851), II, 477.

[10] Friedman, "Imagery," p. 363.

siderable plausibility that the term should at least be divested of its associations with figures of speech.[11] "Image" is hardly a sensible synonym for "metaphor" because a picture is not a comparison, an icon is not an analogy. Furbank is by no means alone in making this objection. In his magisterial study of metaphoric forms Hermann Pongs suggests that there is an ontological difference between metaphor, which he calls a Greek mode, and image (*Bild*), which he regards as Germanic.[12] Even if we reject Pongs's psychosocial theory of history, we can still agree with his conclusion that metaphor attempts to illuminate the essence of things by exposing previously unrecognized analogies, whereas the image aims at rendering things visible iconically.

The association of image with "mental image" is equally tenuous. From a psychological standpoint, of course, it is possible to gain interesting and valid insights into the author's mind by determining his preference for mental images of various kinds. Yet mental imagery helps us very little in our understanding of the literary work because the reader must inevitably supply the response, the impression, that is already in his own mind. What strikes one reader as a tactile image may seem primarily visual to another (e.g., rain or ice or glowing metal). As Furbank puts it, "mental images are what you tell yourself that they are."[13] Moreover, Norman Friedman points out that "in focusing upon the sensory qualities of images themselves, it diverts attention from the *function* of these images in the poetic context."

No doubt the terminological ambiguity will persist, for all three of these critical definitions—image as icon, as mental image, and as figure of speech—enjoy the sanction of usage.[14]

[11] *Reflections on the Word 'Image,'* p. 1.

[12] *Das Bild in der Dichtung*. Vol. 1: *Versuch einer Morphologie der metaphorischen Formen* (Marburg: N. G. Elwert, 1927), esp. pp. 1–24.

[13] *Reflections*, p. 15.

[14] Not to mention such specialized and idiosyncratic definitions as, for instance, Yeats's mystical conception of the image as a great reconciling force.

With no desire to enter the theoretical debate, this book attempts to use the term "image" as consistently and precisely as possible. First, it restricts itself to images in the primary sense as representations of the appearance of a person in the form of statues, paintings, or optical reflections. Second, in every case these *literal* images also happen to be *literary* images in the primary critical sense of the word—that is, the iconic representation of concrete objects that are depicted as having physical presence in the work itself. As in Cocteau's film, the mirrors, statues, and paintings exist in the reality of their fictional world and function in its action; they are not adduced indirectly by way of metaphor, and they are not implied through sensory associations aroused by mental imagery.

Now that we have delimited our subject matter, our next task is to determine how such iconic images function in their literary contexts. Any literary image can be used in a variety of ways. It can *be* something; it can *do* something; or it can *mean* something. To stay with the examples provided by Cocteau's film, the statue exists there as a figure that plays a role in the action; the animated portrait, in contrast, exists only as a function since it does nothing but produce the mouth that attaches itself to the poet's hand; the mirror, finally, exists as a gateway to the poet's past. For the sake of convenience let us classify these three chief functions as theme, motif, and symbol.

Like the word "image," the terms "theme," "motif," and "symbol" are used by literary scholars and critics in a confusing variety of ways and with no notable consistency. For the purposes of this study, however, the terms will be employed in specific senses accepted widely in international usage. Increasingly, and especially in recent studies seeking to rehabilitate the area of comparative literature that the Germans call *Stoffgeschichte* and that is known as "thematics" in English and *thématologie* in France, the term "theme" is used to designate the specific literary shaping of an exemplary or archetypal life familiar from myth or, sometimes, history.[15] As Harry Levin observes, "Normally the assumption seems to be that a theme is identifiable by, if not completely interchangeable with, some particular hero."[16] This tendency is evident in the titles of several recent studies. Louise Vinge has traced *The Narcissus Theme in Western European Literature*,[17] and W. B. Stanford has outlined *The Ulysses Theme: A Study in the Adaptability of a Traditional Hero*.[18] Charles Dédéyan has devoted six volumes to *Le Thème de Faust dans la littérature européenne*[19] while Raymond Trousson, one of the foremost advocates of *thématologie*, has advanced many of his arguments in his study, *Le Thème de Prométhée dans la littérature européenne*.[20] In German the usage is not so consistent: Elisabeth Frenzel's

[15] Elisabeth Frenzel, *Stoff-, Motiv- und Symbolforschung* (Stuttgart: Metzler, 1963); Raymond Trousson, "Plaidoyer pour la Stoffgeschichte," *Revue de Littérature Comparée*, 38 (1964), 101–14; Raymond Trousson, *Un Problème de littérature comparée: les études de thèmes* (Paris: Minard, 1965); Harry Levin, "Thematics and Criticism," *The Disciplines of Criticism: Essays in Literary Theory, Interpretation and History*, ed. Peter Demetz, Thomas Greene, and Lowry Nelson, Jr. (New Haven: Yale Univ. Press, 1968), pp. 125–45; Ulrich Weisstein, *Einführung in die Vergleichende Literaturwissenschaft* (Stuttgart: Kohlhammer, 1968), pp. 163–83 ("Stoff- und Motivgeschichte"); Manfred Beller, "Von der Stoffgeschichte zur Thematologie: Ein Beitrag zur komparatistischen Methodenlehre," *Arcadia*, 5 (1970), 1–38; Adam John Bisanz, "Zwischen Stoffgeschichte und Thematologie: Betrachtungen zu einem literaturtheoretischen Dilemma," *Deutsche Vierteljahrsschrift*, 47 (1973), 148–66; S. S. Prawer, "Themes and Prefigurations," in *Comparative Literary Studies: An Introduction* (London: Duckworth, 1973), pp. 99–113; François Jost, "Grundbegriffe der Thematologie," *Theorie und Kritik: Zur vergleichenden und neueren deutschen Literatur*, ed. Stefan Grunwald and Bruce A. Beatie (Bern and Munich: Francke, 1974), pp. 15–46; and A. J. Bisanz, "Stoff, Thema, Motiv: Zur Problematik des Transfers von Begriffsbestimmungen zwischen der englischen und deutschen Literaturwissenschaft," *Neophilologus*, 59 (1975), 317–23.

[16] "Thematics and Criticism," p. 133.

[17] Lund: Gleerups, 1967.

[18] Oxford: Blackwell, 1954.

[19] Paris: Lettres Modernes, 1954–67.

[20] Geneva: Droz, 1964.

valuable thematological lexicon is called *Stoffe der Weltliteratur*.[21] But several scholars have recently urged that the traditional word *Stoff* be replaced by the internationally acknowledged term *Thema*.[22] In any case, contemporary critical consensus in German, French, and English tends increasingly to prefer the word "theme" to identify mythic or historical figures defined by their unmistakable character traits (e.g., Faust and Don Juan) or by archetypal situations that are inevitably associated with them (e.g., Oedipus and Antigone).

The term "motif," in contrast, designates the elements from which traditional narrative literature is constructed, a sense observed most rigorously by folklorists. In a representative passage Stith Thompson defines motifs as "those details out of which full-fledged narratives are composed."[23] A similar usage is becoming more widespread among literary scholars. According to Elisabeth Frenzel, the motif is "the smaller unit of a thematic construct."[24] Thus the motif of resurrection supplies a constitutive element in the radically different themes of Osiris, Adonis, Proserpina, and Jesus. In a somewhat more general sense, Manfred Beller defines the motif as "the general situation" (*die allgemeine Grundsituation*) underlying the specific literary shaping that we call theme.[25] In this sense one would speak, for instance, of the

[21] *Stoffe der Weltliteratur: Ein Lexikon dichtungsgeschichtlicher Längsschnitte*, 2nd rev. ed. (Stuttgart: Kröner, 1963).

[22] Weisstein, *Einführung*, p. 173; Joachim Schulze, "Geschichte oder Systematik: Zu einem Problem der Themen- und Motivgeschichte," *Arcadia*, 10 (1975), 76–82. In this connection it should be noted that Hellmuth Petriconi, one of the leading German scholars of literary "themes," used the term in a broader sense, in which "theme" is virtually identical with the Jungian archetype. See Margot Kruse, "Literaturgeschichte als Themengeschichte," in: H. Petriconi, *Metamorphosen der Träume: Fünf Beispiele zu einer Literaturgeschichte als Themengeschichte* (Frankfurt am Main: Athenäum, 1971), pp. 195–208.

[23] *Motif-Index of Folk-Literature*, rev. ed. (Bloomington: Indiana Univ. Press, 1955), I, 10.

[24] *Stoff-, Motiv- und Symbolforschung*, p. 6; see also pp. 26–33.

[25] Beller, "Von der Stoffgeschichte," p. 5.

quester-motif; but to the extent that the motif is embodied in a specific figure a precise speaker would allude to the Parzival theme or the Odysseus theme. Summing up the views of Frenzel, Trousson, and others, Ulrich Weisstein concludes that "themes are rendered concrete through characters, while conversely motifs are derived from situations."[26]

The term "symbol," finally, can be used to indicate a variety of "analogical embodiments" ranging from concrete objects to actions, structures, or entire literary works.[27] According to fairly broad understanding, the image becomes a symbol when a concrete object appearing within the literary work assumes a meaning that points beyond the immediate associations accruing to it from experience and memory. Wellek and Warren define the symbol as an image that "persistently recurs, both as presentation and representation."[28] Frenzel observes that the image (*Bild*) is not necessarily a symbol but that it often functions as such when it becomes the "crystallization point" for the conceptual intentions of a literary work.[29] Northrop Frye remarks that "the central emblematic image" in a literary work is known as a symbol.[30] And W. Y. Tindall says that an image becomes a "constituent symbol" when it is a verbal embodiment of thought and feeling.[31]

An iconic image in literature, then, can function as theme, motif, or symbol depending upon the circumstances. To the extent that the image is tied to a specific figure whose story it constitutively defines, the image functions as theme. To the extent that the image supplies merely one element of a larger action or situation, it functions as motif. And to the extent that the image signifies something other than itself, it func-

[26] Weisstein, *Einführung*, p. 174.

[27] Tindall, *The Literary Symbol*, pp. 12–13.

[28] René Wellek and Austin Warren, *Theory of Literature* (1949; rpt. New York: Harcourt, Brace-Harvest Book, 1956), p. 178.

[29] *Stoff-, Motiv- und Symbolforschung*, p. 37 and p. 74.

[30] *Anatomy of Criticism* (1957; rpt. New York: Atheneum, 1966), p. 92.

[31] *The Literary Symbol*, p. 105.

tions as symbol. Obviously, these various functions sometimes overlap. An image that enters the work as a motif can grow into a symbol. It would be pointless to force images into rigid categories simply for the sake of conceptual tidiness. The categories are useful only to the extent that they enable us to organize the material of this book provisionally and to speak with a certain degree of precision about our topic.

Yet the three images that we shall be discussing tend in fact to display a principal function and, therefore, to fall generally into certain categories. The image of the animated statue is widespread in folklore and literature. Usually it functions as a motif: in the legend of Don Juan, for instance, the stone guest is associated with just one of the many seductions the hero undertakes; it is simply the most important in a series of motifs. In the tale of Venus and the Ring, in contrast, the central event that dominates all the other action is that the statue of Venus comes to life: the animated statue is not a motif in somebody else's theme; the other figures are defined by their association with the statue. It is characteristic that in this case the image has given its name to the entire theme. To take the second example: in Oscar Wilde's *The Picture of Dorian Gray* the image of the portrait, which recurs persistently throughout the novel, has a function that becomes clearly symbolic: it represents the hero's soul. But in most works the haunted portrait shows up simply as a passing motif within a larger plot: e.g., as a standard furnishing of the castle in Gothic romances. Finally, the magic mirror often occurs simply as a motif—in fairy tales, for instance, where the wicked queen consults her magic mirror for information. But this image displays a definite proclivity to assume symbolic dimensions: the reflected image signifies the viewer's soul, or the mirror itself represents a realm of art or death that lies beyond the looking glass.

It will be obvious to many readers that the approach outlined above is familiar in art history as iconography, which Panofsky has defined as "a description and classification of images much as ethnography is a description and classification of human races."[32] I have rehearsed the terminology in such detail because literary history and criticism have not yet come so far as art history in agreeing on procedures for talking about something as fundamental as images. However, it would be shortsighted to stop at iconographic analysis, which "collects and classifies the evidence but does not consider itself obliged or entitled to investigate the genesis and significance of this evidence." Any thorough study should go on to an iconology of our images, which Panofsky calls "a method of interpretation which arises from synthesis rather than analysis" and which takes into account the influence of theological, philosophical, and political ideas upon the images as well as the purposes and inclinations of the individual artists.

This brings us to the third question suggested by the three images at the beginning of Cocteau's film: are they random or do they constitute a meaningful set? The common denominator linking them, whether they appear as theme, motif, or symbol, is the fact that they originated in a magico-religious context. This should hardly be surprising since virtually all images in the primary sense of the word betray a profound relationship to magic in the prehistory of mankind.[33] To take a familiar example, the drawings of food animals found in caves all over the world represent the efforts of primitive man to gain power over his environment by means of image magic. To move closer to the specific set of images at issue here, anthropologists and historians of religion have long been aware of the intimate associations between images of the human body and the soul. "Everything that reproduces the human silhouette—whether a shadow, a

[32] "Iconography and Iconology: An Introduction to the Study of Renaissance Art," in Erwin Panofsky, *Meaning in the Visual Arts* (Garden City, N.Y.: Doubleday-Anchor, 1955), p. 31.

[33] See Goblet d'Alviella, "General and Primitive Images," in *Encyclopedia of Religion and Ethics*, ed. James Hastings, vol. VII (New York: Scribner, 1915), pp. 110–16.

reflection, a drawing, or a sculpted image—is considered among the majority of peoples as being not only a simple combination of lines or an innocuous figure, completely independent of the living individual. It is believed, rather, that there exists an intimate connection, both physical and psychological, between the image and the person that it calls to mind, between the figured representation and the real being."[34] In short, we are dealing here not merely with literal and literary images in the senses defined above, but also specifically with images that entered the European cultural consciousness bearing distinctly magical and religious associations. It is this affinity with the human soul that sets these three images apart from all other images that might occur in a literary work. The iconological question that I hope to answer is this: how did these images make their way out of magic into literature and, long after the disappearance of the faith that originally justified their supernatural powers, survive in such modern works as Cocteau's film? It is this process of secularization that I propose to call "disenchantment" in order to suggest the magical associations that originally adhered to the three images under consideration here.

The following chapters, then, are unified in at least three ways. First, they have a common subject matter: magic images representing the human body and, by extension, the human soul. Second, they share a methodology: the iconographic analysis of those images in an effort to classify their various literary functions. Finally, they move toward the same goal: the iconological apprehension of the process whereby these magic images become "disenchanted." In the light of the various definitions and distinctions offered above, we are now prepared to delimit with reasonable precision the topic of this study: a literary iconology of magic images and the stages of their disenchantment.

[34] M. Weynants-Ronday, *Les Statues vivantes: Introduction à l'étude des statues égyptiennes* (Bruxelles: Fondation Égyptologique Reine Élisabeth, 1926), p. 96.

CHAPTER TWO

Image as Theme: Venus and the Ring

In his twelfth-century *Chronicle of the Kings of England* William of Malmesbury tells the story of a wealthy young nobleman of Rome who has just been married.[1] After the wedding feast the youth and his friends go out to "promote digestion" by playing ball. During the game the young man places his wedding ring for safe-keeping on the outstretched finger of a bronze statue standing nearby. When he goes back later, the statue's finger is clenched fast so that he is unable to remove the ring. Saying nothing to his companions, he returns that evening with some servants, only to discover that the finger is again extended and the ring gone. Concealing all this from his bride, he has just climbed into bed that night when he becomes aware of something between them—something dense and cloudlike that prevents their embraces (*quiddam nebulosum et densum . . . quod posset sentiri, nec posset videri*). Then he hears a voice whispering: "Embrace me, since you wedded me today. I am Venus, on whose finger you put the ring, and I shall not give it back." Some days pass, during which the young man is inhibited by Venus from any intimacy with his wife. Finally, moved by his wife's complaints, he discloses the matter to her parents. They, in turn, take the problem to a certain Palumbus, a "suburban priest" (*presbyter suburbanus*) skilled in black

[1] The story occurs in Book II, Chap. 13, Paragraph 205. I have consulted the text in *Willelmi Malmesbiriensis monachi Gesta regum Anglorum atque Historia novella*, ed. Thomas Duffus Hardy (London, 1840), I, 354–57; and William of Malmesbury, *Chronicle of the Kings of England*, ed. J. A. Giles (London, 1847), pp. 232–34.

magic and conjuration. Promised a substantial reward if he can bring the lovers together, Palumbus gives the young man a letter and instructs him to take it at a certain hour of the night to a certain crossroads, where he will see a wondrous procession of figures of both sexes, of every age and condition, on foot and on horseback, both joyful and sad. He is to stand in silence until the company has passed and then hand the letter to a person, taller and more corpulent than the others, who will follow in a chariot. Doing as he is told, the youth witnesses the marvelous procession, including Venus "in meretricious garb," riding on a mule and making "wonderfully indecent gestures" (*gestus impudicos*). When the chief approaches and addresses him sternly, the young man delivers the letter. The demon, not daring to ignore the priest's familiar seal, reads the epistle and, raising his hands to the heavens, exclaims: "Almighty God, how long wilt thou endure the iniquities of the priest Palumbus?" Then he sends his followers to take the ring from Venus, who reluctantly surrenders it. The young man is promptly restored, with no further misty obstacles, to the impatient embraces of his wife. But Palumbus, when he hears how the demon complained of him to God, knows that the end of his days is near. Making atonement by cutting off all his limbs, he confesses unheard-of crimes to the pope in the presence of the entire populace of Rome.

The story of Venus and the Ring, of which William of Malmesbury has left us the earliest known version (c. 1125), was one of the most popular tales of the Middle Ages.[2] The story was held to be true by William of Malmesbury, who places its occurrence roughly a hundred years earlier (A.D. 1037). If we can believe Robert Burton, who retells the story in *The Anatomy of Melancholy* to illustrate the power of love, it was still considered credible at the beginning of the seventeenth century. "One more I will relate out of

[2] For a full discussion of the medieval variants see Paull Franklin Baum, "The Young Man Betrothed to a Statue," *PMLA*, 34 (1919), 523–79.

Florilegus, *ad annum* 1058, an honest historian of our nation, because he telleth it so confidently, as a thing in those days talked of all over Europe." Burton concludes his account by assuring us that "Many such stories I find in several authors to confirm this which I have said. . . ."[3]

Viewed within a larger context, the legend of Venus and the Ring belongs, as a specific thematic embodiment, to the general category of stories dealing with the motif of animated statues, which can be documented in folklore and literature from India to Iceland.[4] The two walking statues most familiar in Western culture are no doubt those in the stories of Pygmalion and Don Juan. But Ovid's tale in the *Metamorphoses* (Bk. x) of the young sculptor who, shocked at the licentious behavior of the women of Cyprus, carved a beautiful and chaste ivory image that Venus brought to life for him, is merely one of many such legends known to classical antiquity. In the *Odyssey* (Bk. vii) Homer reports that Hephaestus fashioned animated mastiffs of gold and silver to guard the portals of Alcinous' palace on the island of Phaeacia. According to Diodorus Siculus' *Library of History* (iv.76) Daedalus contrived statues so lifelike that they could both see and walk. The Greeks also knew various stories of avenging statues. In the *Poetics* (Ch. 9) Aristotle cites the statue of Mitys at Argos, which fell upon his murderer and killed him. There are other famous cases, such

[3] *The Anatomy of Melancholy* (New York: Dutton-Everyman, 1964), iii, 47–48.

[4] For examples see Baum, pp. 533–36 and 540–44; Stith Thompson, *Motif-Index of Folk-Literature*, rev. ed. (Bloomington: Indiana Univ. Press, 1955–58), vi, 746 ("statue"); John Austen, *The Story of Don Juan: A Study of the Legend and the Hero* (London: Martin Secker, 1939), pp. 132–43 ("Miraculous Statues"); Dorothy Epplen MacKay, *The Double Invitation in the Legend of Don Juan* (Stanford, Cal.: Stanford Univ. Press, 1943), pp. 11–40; and Derek de Solla Price, "Automata and the Origins of Mechanism and Mechanistic Philosophy," in *Science Since Babylon*, enlarged edition (New Haven: Yale Univ. Press, 1975), pp. 49–70.

as that of the statue of the athlete Nicon, which smashed a rival who had presumed to taunt it.

Similarly, the statue of the deceased *commendatore*, which accepts Don Juan's scornful invitation to dinner and then drags the blasphemous don down to hell, is representative of various avenging statues known to late medieval Spain. The ballad of "The Cid and the Jew," for instance, relates how the statue of the great hero comes to life when a Jew pulls its beard, whereupon the terrified non-believer is promptly converted.[5] More recently, Gustavo Adolfo Bécquer revived the legend in his story "The Kiss" ("El Beso," 1863), in which the statue of a devoted husband, outraged when a drunken officer kisses the statue of his wife, comes to life long enough to crush the offender. These tales are not restricted to exotic places and remote times, of course. At the Library Company in Philadelphia a statue of Benjamin Franklin was reputed by local legend in the nineteenth century to come down from its pedestal each night when it heard the clock strike midnight.

The belief in animated images occurs most frequently in religious contexts. Many ancient peoples—the Egyptians, Sumerians, Jews, Babylonians, Indians—believed that the statues of their deities were animated by the incorporation of the god in the image.[6] For this reason these peoples liked to steal the divine statues of their enemies in order to benefit from the virtue inherent in them. Numerous stories from other cultures attest to the religious belief that statues come to life. Thus we hear of a Burmese statue of the Buddha that grew a mustache. In Japan, statues of Jizo walked about at night in disguise. In Scandinavia, a statue of Thor talked and even wrestled with warriors. The Spartans chained down

[5] Austen, *The Story of Don Juan*, p. 139.

[6] The details in this paragraph are based on M. Weynants-Ronday, *Les Statues vivantes: Introduction à l'étude des statues égyptiennes* (Bruxelles: Fondation Égyptologique Reine Élisabeth, 1926), pp. 114–19.

their statue of Ares, just as the Thyrians shackled their image of Baal, lest the deities desert the city.

Catholic legendry is filled with tales of statues, images, and icons (of Jesus, Mary, and the various saints) that wink, beckon, sweat, bleed, cry, sing, speak, and perform various other wonders. Often, of course, such beliefs are encouraged by the subtlety of a clergy anxious to preserve the faith of its congregations. We know from archaeology that Egyptian priests sometimes employed tricks of lighting as well as various mechanical devices to produce the illusion of movement in statues.[7] The Louvre preserves a painted wooden head of the Egyptian jackal god of the dead, which "talked" by means of a speaking trumpet concealed in hollows leading down from the mouth. The Museum of the History of Religion and Atheism in Leningrad displays the means by which an icon of the Virgin Mary can be caused to weep "real" tears. The wave of iconoclasm during the Reformation often exposed the mechanisms by which magic images performed their "miracles." At the Abbey of Boxley, in Kent, a certain image had been venerated for its ability to move its head, scowl, and acknowledge prayers. When pulled down, it was revealed that the miraculous animation was produced by the manipulation of "certain engines of old wire."[8] In his early story, "A Fragment of Stained Glass" (1911), D. H. Lawrence tells of a wonder-working statue from two points of view in order to show how legends arise. The pious monks inside the church see the statue fight off the devil, who is attempting to break into the sacred precincts; the ignorant peasant boy outside dislodges the statue while climbing up to obtain a bit of stained glass for his sweetheart.[9] Yet faith overcomes all obstacles of mere reason.

[7] Austen, *The Story of Don Juan*, p. 133.

[8] Cited by Frances Yates in a review of John Phillips, *The Reformation of Images: Destruction of Art in England, 1535–1660*, in *The New York Review of Books*, 30 May 1974, p. 24.

[9] From the collection *The Prussian Officer* (1914); rpt. *The Complete Short Stories*, I (New York: Viking-Compass, 1961), 187–96.

One of the most recent "miracles" of this sort took place on July 17, 1972, in Room 315 of the Ramada Inn in New Orleans, where a cedarwood statue of the Virgin Mary is alleged to have shed real tears in the presence of reliable witnesses.[10]

The belief in animated statues is related to a widespread version of the creation-myth, according to which the first men were images of clay—that is, statuettes—brought to life by the local deity. This myth is known all over the world, from the Blackfeet Indians of Montana to the Black Tatars of Siberia.[11] In the Babylonian Gilgamesh Epic the goddess of creation fashions the hero's companion, Enkidu, of clay and water. According to Greek mythology Prometheus created the first man and woman of clay and animated them by means of the fire he had stolen from the gods. In the version of the creation that Ovid recounts at the beginning of his *Metamorphoses*, the celestial force models men out of living clay and running water. In the Judaeo-Christian world the legend is most familiar from the book of Genesis: "And the Lord God formed man of the dust of the ground, and breathed into his nostrils the breath of life; and man became a living soul" (Genesis 2:7). This act of creation is repeated typologically by the child Jesus of the apocryphal gospels, who shapes sparrows of clay, which he brings to life.[12]

From these myths of creation it is an easy step to the animistic belief that images of the human body can be similarly inspirited under certain circumstances by creators who are less than demiurges.[13] In ancient Egyptian funeral rites

[10] James K. Glassman, "Miracle at The Ramada Inn," New Orleans *Figaro*, 29 July 1972, p. 5.

[11] Joseph Campbell, *The Hero with a Thousand Faces*, 2nd ed. (Princeton, N.J.: Princeton Univ. Press, 1968), pp. 289–95 ("Folk Stories of Creation"); also Stith Thompson, *Motif-Index*, I, 206 ("Man made from mineral substance").

[12] E.g., the "Infancy Gospel of Thomas," Chap. 2.

[13] On the magical significance of primitive art see E. H. Gombrich, *The Story of Art*, 4th rev. ed. (New York: Phaidon, 1951), pp. 20–28; and Edwyn Bevan, *Holy Images: An Inquiry into Idolatry and*

the soul of the deceased was supposed to enter a statue representing his body, and the moment of transition from body to statue was celebrated by a special animation ceremony.[14] One Egyptian word for "sculptor" means literally "he who keeps alive." The portrait-busts of the Romans also had magico-religious significance. Above all, the ability to animate the inanimate is a power associated in the popular imagination so closely with divinity that every self-respecting thaumaturge claimed to have that power.[15] Simon Magus boasted that he could make statues laugh and dance. During the Middle Ages such feats were attributed almost routinely to any man so wise that he was assumed to have been a magician. The *Gesta Romanorum*, the most popular storybook of the Middle Ages, tells us that magic statues of bronze were fashioned by Virgil, who was widely considered to have been a sorcerer (Tale LVII). Albertus Magnus is reputed by legend to have created an android, which was subsequently destroyed by none other than Thomas Aquinas. The most familiar tale concerning Roger Bacon deals with the talking Brazen Head that he was said to have animated through sorcery.

But the magic also runs in the other direction: not just from the person to the image, but also from the image back to the person. This belief provides the theoretical basis for image-charms, a form of magic that goes back to paleolithic times.[16] Normally an image is fashioned of stone, clay, or wax; then an action is performed upon the image in order to produce a sympathetic effect upon the person represented—usually for the purposes of love, harm, or healing. Such

---

Image-Worship in Ancient Paganism and in Christianity (London: George Allen and Unwin, 1940), esp. pp. 13–45.

[14] Weynants-Ronday, *Les Statues vivantes*, p. 112.

[15] E. M. Butler, *The Myth of the Magus* (Cambridge, England: Cambridge Univ. Press, 1948), p. 80 and pp. 156–57.

[16] See the article "Bildzauber," *Handwörterbuch des deutschen Aberglaubens*, ed. Hanns Bächtold-Stäubli (Berlin and Leipzig: De Gruyter, 1927), vol. I, cols. 1282–98.

charms, evident in the earliest stone carvings of primitive man, have been used through the ages—down to the witchcraft of the seventeenth century and the voodoo rites still performed today in various parts of the world. Every time an irate group of citizens burns a political figure in effigy, they are re-enacting a ritual of sympathetic image-magic so prevalent in the Middle Ages that it was formalized in law.[17] Ancient beliefs do not always disappear when people stop accepting them: they transform themselves. One of the favorite retreats for secularized rituals is children's literature: the stories of Pinocchio, Raggedy Ann, Winnie the Pooh, and the Gingerbread Boy are all vestiges of the animistic belief in the vivification of inanimate images.

The widespread association of magic with statues in ancient times—both as the animation of statues and as image-charms—helps to account for, and is reflected in, the general prohibition of graven images in the monotheistic religions that gradually arose in the Middle East.[18] When Moses went up Mount Sinai, one of the first things the Lord told him was: "Thou shalt not make unto thee any graven image, or any likeness of anything that is in heaven above, or that is in the earth beneath, or that is in the water under the earth" (Exodus 20:4). In Deuteronomy the prohibition is spelled out in even greater detail to include "the similitude of any figure, the likeness of male or female, The likeness of any beast that is on the earth, the likeness of any winged fowl that flieth in the air, The likeness of any thing that creepeth on the ground, the likeness of any fish that is in the waters beneath the earth" (4: 16–18). The explicitness of these injunctions suggests that the jealous God of the Old Testament knew exactly what sort of people he was dealing with: a

[17] Wolfgang Brückner, *Bildnis und Brauch: Studien zur Bildfunktion der Effigies* (Berlin: Erich Schmidt, 1966): *Executio in effigie* played a role in European legal practice down to the time of the Spanish Inquisition, which burned effigies of indicted heretics who had already died or fled.

[18] Bevan, *Holy Images*, pp. 46–83.

superstitious tribe prepared to hurl itself on its knees before such impressive idols as the golden calf. The animistic practices of idolatry are much easier for the primitive mind to comprehend than the abstract notion of a non-anthropomorphic spiritual deity like Jehovah. The Pentateuch is a vivid record of this significant anthropological development.

Both the Koran and the early Christian Church retained the opposition to graven images as relics of paganism. St. Paul's address to the Athenians on the Areopagus (Acts 17: 22–31) is typical of early Christian diatribes against images "graven by art and man's device." In Moslem lands this prohibition affected the development of the visual arts, which had to get along without the human body as a motif. Bernard Berenson has suggested that the Jews, otherwise so distinguished in the arts and sciences, produced relatively few great painters and sculptors, at least until the twentieth century, specifically because of this injunction.[19]

However that may be, the Jews and Moslems adhered to the ancient biblical prohibitions much more faithfully than did the Christians. In fact, the rapidity with which graven images became an accepted part of ecclesiastical decoration in the West attests the tenaciousness of animistic attitudes. In part, of course, the graven images fulfilled educational needs. To inform a predominantly illiterate congregation about the life of Jesus as well as the deeds of a steadily growing number of saints, it was useful to depict them visually in the places of worship. This pedagogical impulse produced the sculptural glories that surround and inhabit the principal medieval cathedrals. Yet the feeling that there is something inherently idolatrous and pagan about this practice of setting up statues in places of worship showed up from time to time in the waves of iconoclasm that wrecked the churches—notably under the iconoclast emperors of the later Roman Empire and during the Reformation. In the eighth century, Emperor Leo III was incited to his riot of image-smashing

[19] *Aesthetics and History* (1948; rpt. Garden City, N. Y.: Doubleday-Anchor, 1954), pp. 178–86 ("The Jews and Visual Art").

specifically by the taunts of the Jews and Moslems, who accused Christianity of reverting to pagan practices.

Now many of these associations with evil, sorcery, iconolatry, and the pagan past reverberate in the legend of Venus and the Ring. To be sure, from a modern Freudian point of view the legend can be interpreted quite nicely as an almost classic example of the rationalization of sexual impotence. How convenient for the new husband to be able to blame the goddess Venus for his failure to perform satisfactorily during the first nights of his marriage! Yet the implications obviously go much further. Of all the pagan deities, Venus managed to sustain herself most vividly in the medieval imagination, for she represented the seductive passion to which an ascetic Christianity was austerely opposed. However, this figure underwent the process of demonization that transformed all the classical deities during the twelfth and thirteenth centuries. Rather than ignoring or denying the existence of the classical gods, the Church found it more expedient to declare that they were nothing but devils. Venus is no longer a symbol of the classical joy of life: she has become the devil incarnate, or at least his principal agent of temptation.[20] This transformation is evident if we examine our story in critical detail.

The theme as we know it from its earliest recorded version in William of Malmesbury consists of three distinct motifs: the motif of the young man who gives a ring to a statue, which then comes to life; the motif of the necromancer who

[20] Friedrich von Bezold, *Das Fortleben der antiken Götter im mittelalterlichen Humanismus* (Bonn and Leipzig: Kurt Schroeder, 1922), esp. pp. 60–71. Walter Pabst, *Venus und die mißverstandene Dido: Literarische Ursprünge des Sibyllen- und des Venusberges*, Hamburger Romanistische Studien, Reihe A, Bd. 40 (Hamburg: Cram, 1955), pp. 114–15, points out that violence and cruelty are combined with love in the character of Venus from the very beginning: e.g., the stories of Adonis, Psyche, Paris, and others. See also Robert Schilling, *La Religion romaine de Vénus depuis les origines jusqu'au temps d'Auguste* (Paris: Boccard, 1954).

has the power to conjure up the devil; and the motif of the Wild Hunt. If we examine the first motif, which is the characteristic one for this theme, we find nothing to suggest a Christian setting—no mention of God, Church, or clergy. In fact, the only evidence for placing the story in medieval times rather than in classical antiquity is the fact that Venus is regarded no longer as a sublime goddess but as a somewhat malevolent demoness. It is commonly assumed for this reason that in its earliest form the theme of Venus and the Ring embodied the struggle between the forces of an emergent Christianity and the energies of a still vital paganism for the soul of the young man. It is no accident, of course, that this theme is situated in Italy, the principal battleground in the contest between classical paganism and the Church.[21]

By the time of William of Malmesbury the situation has changed: by combining the original story of Venus and the Ring with the other two motifs the author has made it more explicitly Christian. The chief of the medieval Wild Hunt—a Germanic legend—is conventionally Satan himself. The moment Venus is portrayed as being a member of his retinue, she is no longer simply a pagan demoness but specifically an accomplice of the devil. The struggle is therefore no longer one between paganism and Christianity but, within Christianity, a struggle between good and evil or God and the devil. Appropriately, the mediator in this struggle is the strange and ambivalent figure of Father Palumbus, the "suburban priest" from an intermediate realm, who has the power to address compelling letters to the archenemy. Although the basic story of Venus and the Ring remains the same, the meaning of the image itself changes along with the context: the originally pagan demon has become a satanic devil.

[21] Baum, "The Young Man Betrothed to a Statue," pp. 543–48, summarizes the controversy surrounding the place of origin. Many scholars agree that the legend originated in Italy; but others (e.g., Pabst, *Venus und die mißverstandene Dido*, p. 118) argue that Malmesbury had no Italian source for his account, which represents the projection of the northern imagination upon Italy.

It was no doubt inevitable that a legend as popular as that of Venus and the Ring should produce variants, of which two deserve mention. No more than twenty years after William of Malmesbury the first important variant showed up in the mid-twelfth-century German collection of tales and legends known as the *Kaiserchronik*.[22] According to the three hundred lines of rimed couplets devoted to this legend (ll. 13102–13392) the incident occurred in Rome during the reign of one of the emperors Theodosius. One day two noble brothers, who still pay homage to the pagan deities, are playing ball with their friends. One of the brothers—here named Astrolabius—accidentally throws the ball into the walled-in ruins of a dilapidated temple, which has been declared off-limits by royal authority. (The closed temple suggests that we are dealing with a period of active struggle between emergent Christianity and surviving paganism.) Clambering over the wall to recover his ball, Astrolabius catches sight of a statue of incredible beauty. As he moves toward it, the statue motions to him. Seeing that it is a statue of Venus, Astrolabius declares his undying love for her and pledges himself to her by giving her his ring. His brother and friends eventually get him out of the temple, but during the following days and weeks Astrolabius begins to waste away with his fervor for the unattainable Venus. Finally the youth, who in his desperation to relieve his passion says that he would even be willing to become a Christian, appeals to the priest Eusebius, who formerly practiced black magic. Conjuring up the devil, the priest forces the adversary to accompany him to hell, where he recovers the ring for Astrolabius. By order of the pope the statue of Venus is removed from the enchanted garden to the Castel Sant-Angelo, where it is ritually exorcised and consecrated to the memory of the

[22] For a discussion of the German version of the legend see Ernst Friedrich Ohly, *Sage und Legende in der Kaiserchronik* (1940; rpt. Darmstadt: Wissenschaftliche Buchgesellschaft, 1968), pp. 203–210; and Christian Gellinek, *Die deutsche Kaiserchronik: Erzähltechnik und Kritik* (Frankfurt am Main: Athenäum, 1971), pp. 82–91.

archangel Michael. Astrolabius and his friends, out of gratitude and reverence, have themselves baptized as Christians.

The differences between the two versions are conspicuous. First, the story has been wholly demonized: the spirit that animates the statue is no longer the pagan Venus but the devil himself. Second, the element of erotic attraction, wholly absent in William of Malmesbury, has been added: Astrolabius gives his ring to the statue not by accident but because he is inflamed with love and lust for Venus. It is this erotic enchantment, rather than any legal bond, that plays the key role in the plot. Third, the motif of the wedding and wedding-night is missing; Astrolabius merely pines away in love-sickness; there is no indignant bride. Finally, it is the priest Eusebius who approaches the devil in order to recover the ring, and he suffers no tragic fate.

Whereas the German *Kaiserchronik* adapted the pagan legend into a morality tale of Christian conversion, in France the story of Venus and the Ring was assimilated even more radically. Through the familiar process of iconotropy—whereby the medieval Church almost indiscriminately translated classical and secular material of every sort into Christian terms—the story was transmogrified into one of the miracles of the Virgin. According to this version, which was recorded in many Old French prose and verse forms after it came into existence around 1200, the statue on whose finger the young man places his ring is an image of the Virgin Mary, not Venus.[23] In this case the statue wins the soul of the young man. When he tries to embrace his bride, the Holy Mother chastely interposes herself to remind him that he has promised himself to her. Forsaking his earthly bride,

[23] See the exhaustive discussion of the French versions by Baum, "The Young Man Betrothed to a Statue," pp. 548–74. A representative example is Gautier de Coinsi's "Du Varlet qui se maria à Nostre-Dame, dont ne volt qu'il habitast à autre," in *Fabliaux et Contes des Poètes François des XI, XII, XIII, XIV et XVe Siècles*, ed. Etienne Barbazan. New rev. ed. Dominique Martin Méon (Paris: Warée, 1808), II, 421–27.

the youth becomes a monk and dedicates his life to the service of Our Lady.

For various reasons these two major variants soon died out. The German version weakens the plot by doing away with the wedding motif and by transferring the action of the second half to the priest Eusebius. The French variant deprives the legend of the powerful mythic element—the struggle between paganism and Christianity—by reducing it to another miracle of the Virgin.[24] But for several centuries the original and dramatically more effective version, stemming from William of Malmesbury, remained one of the most popular legends in late medieval and early Renaissance Europe. On the basis of an engraving by Albrecht Dürer—"The Dream of the Doctor" (1497–98)—Erwin Panofsky infers that the theme was still familiar to every well-educated German as late as 1500.[25] In Dürer's engraving the elderly scholar's temptation is symbolized by a figure of Venus wearing a ring on her left hand and with a ball lying at her feet—the iconographic motifs that unmistakably characterize this theme.

The legend of Venus and the Ring was not originally a narrowly "literary" topic. It was adduced as an edifying *exemplum* in such works as Vincent of Beauvais' *Speculum Historiale*, John de Cella's *Flores Historiarum*, John of Hovedon's *Speculum Laicorum*. St. Antonius of Florence's *Chronica sive opus historiarum*, and various other chronicles down through the fifteenth century. During the next two centuries the legend continued to be frequently cited, but it moved out of the popular culture represented by the medieval chronicles into the more scholarly medium of the baroque

[24] It is worth noting that Alfred Döblin includes among the various stories encapsulated in his last novel, *Hamlet, oder die lange Nacht nimmt ein Ende* (1956), a slightly modified version of the French variant under the title: "Erzählung vom Knappen, der seinen Ring verlor."

[25] *The Life and Art of Albrecht Dürer*, 4th ed. (Princeton, N.J.: Princeton Univ. Press, 1955), pp. 71–72.

encyclopedic compendia. We have already had occasion to mention Burton's *The Anatomy of Melancholy*. In addition, three or four other works of the period served as important sources for the nineteenth- and twentieth-century writers who eventually rediscovered the theme. One of these was Martin Del Rio's handbook of magic entitled *Disquisitionum magicarum libri sex* (1599–1600). Del Rio, a professor at Belgian and Austrian universities and one of the most fanatical witchhunters of his day, fervently believed all the magical and supernatural lore that he compiled in his preposterous volume, which was widely reprinted for almost two hundred years. The same legend was also cited in more critical studies of magic, such as Joannes Christianus Frommann's *Tractatus de fascinatione* (1675). It was recounted at length in such influential reference works as Heinrich Kornmann's compilation of pagan and modern views of Venus, *Mons Veneris / Fraw Veneris Berg* (1614) as well as E. G. Happel's often cited volume of "memorable occurrences," *Größte Denkwürdigkeiten der Welt oder so genandte Relationes Curiosae* (1687).[26]

Predictably, the Enlightenment had little interest in animated statues. Among the "extravagant prodigies" of the Don Juan theme that Voltaire enumerates in his biography of Molière (*Vie de Molière*, 1739), he singles out with particular distaste "une statue qui marche et qui parle." But the romantic revival of interest in matters medieval and mysterious rescued the legend of Venus and the Ring from the handbooks and encyclopedias to which it had been consigned since the Renaissance. Although it is probably impossible to pinpoint the causes underlying the revival of any specific cultural theme, it is easy enough to account for the general climate of opinion that made the public of the early nineteenth century receptive to stories about animated statues.

[26] Pabst, *Venus und die mißverstandene Dido*, pp. 14–15, stressing the importance of Kornmann as a sourcebook for future generations, calls it "ein Buch von europäischer Wirkung."

First, the second half of the eighteenth century witnessed a remarkable resurgence of interest in the art of sculpture, a logical corollary of the new awareness of Greek classicism that emerged during the same period in Germany. Beginning in 1755 with Winckelmann's *Thoughts on the Imitation of the Greek Works of Painting and Sculpture* and proceeding by way of Lessing's *Laokoon* (1766), Herder's essay *On Plastic Art* (1778), and Goethe's *Italian Journey* (1786–88; published 1816) down to such romantic aestheticians as Friedrich and August Wilhelm Schlegel, Greek sculpture came to represent for the cultivated European mind classical art at its highest level[27]—in contrast to painting, which was principally a post-medieval and Christian mode. Although the late eighteenth century was essentially a period of sterile academicism in the plastic arts, sculpture was clearly displacing painting in the conventional hierarchy of aesthetic forms.[28] The revival of classicism not only forced painters to accommodate their figures to so-called classical ideals (e.g., the monumental canvases of David); it also brought classical sculpture very much into the public eye through statues and bas-reliefs that were commissioned to decorate public buildings and squares.

Second, two other legends of animated statues, revived around this time, emerged as representative works of the period. The success of Mozart's *Don Giovanni* (1787) rescued from the popular theater and puppet stage the story of the arrogant don who was dragged down to hell by the avenging statue of the murdered *commendatore*. And two decades later the idealizing interpretations of E.T.A. Hoff-

[27] See Henry Hatfield, *Aesthetic Paganism in German Literature: From Winckelmann to the Death of Goethe* (Cambridge, Mass.: Harvard Univ. Press, 1964); and Stephen A. Larrabee, *English Bards and Grecian Marbles: The Relationship between Sculpture and Poetry especially in the Romantic Period* (New York: Columbia Univ. Press, 1943).

[28] Germain Bazin, *The History of World Sculpture*, trans. Madeline Jay (Greenwich, Conn.: New York Graphic Society, 1968), p. 84.

mann and his contemporaries transformed the bullying seducer of the traditional legend (e.g., Tirso de Molina's *El Burlador de Sevilla y convidado de piedra*) into an archetypal romantic hero in quest of the eternal. At the same time, the theme of Pygmalion was taken up by various pre-romantic thinkers—notably Rousseau, Herder, and Hamann—as an embodiment of the power of the titanic artist to enliven through his genius the dead materials of reality.[29]

Rousseau's monodrama, *Pygmalion* (written 1763; performed 1770), generated a singular new theatrical fashion that lasted for about forty years: the "attitudes."[30] These attitudes—the "mimoplastic art" of representing works of art by mimic means, especially gestures and draperies—were essentially the creation of one woman, Emma Hart, the subsequent Lady Hamilton. (The art was practiced by two other well-known *artistes* before its disappearance as a form, the Danish dancer Ida Brun and the German actress Henriette Hendel-Schütz.) But as a result of intense publicity by influential people, this curious practice of imitating famous statues became quite fashionable for several decades among European intellectuals. Lady Hamilton's attitudes were captured in various paintings by George Romney and in a series of widely distributed drawings by Friedrich Rehberg. Goethe saw Lady Hamilton perform several times during his Italian journey (cf. the entry for March 16, 1787) and recorded his enthusiasm for his friends in Weimar. (Two decades later he described the art in his novel *Elective Affinities.*) Horace Walpole wrote to Mary Berry (August 17, 1791) that Lady Hamilton "acts all the antique statues in an Indian shawl." This bizarre conceit of representing "living statues" is simply

[29] Hermann Schlüter, *Das Pygmalion-Symbol bei Rousseau, Hamann, Schiller* (Zürich: Juris, 1968); Emil Staiger, "Der neue Geist in Herders Frühwerk," *Stilwandel: Studien zur Vorgeschichte der Goethezeit* (Zürich: Atlantis, 1963), pp. 121–73; and Hans Sckommodau, *Pygmalion bei Franzosen und Deutschen im 18. Jahrhundert* (Wiesbaden: Franz Steiner, 1970).

[30] Kirsten Gram Holmström, *Monodrama, Attitudes, Tableaux Vivants: Studies on some trends of theatrical fashion 1770–1815* (Stockholm: Almquist and Wiksell, 1967), pp. 110–208.

another example of the late eighteenth-century obsession with statues: with statues *per se*, with statues that come to life, with people who turn into statues, and with the ambiguous relationship between people and statues. During the 1780's, for instance, it was a vogue in Italy to visit the galleries at night in order to view the statues by torchlight, which produced the illusion that the statues were alive and moving.

The preoccupation with animated statues was paralleled around the turn of the century by the curious fascination with the phenomenon of automata.[31] The various automata that could walk, talk, play cards, and perform a variety of other feats included such famous examples as Vaucanson's automatic flute-player and trumpet-player as well as other musical automata by Johann Nepomuk Maelzel, the inventor of the metronome. No doubt the most renowned automaton of the age was Wolfgang von Kempelen's Turkish chessplayer, which fascinated Edgar Allan Poe when it was brought to the United States.[32] The stories of E.T.A. Hoffmann are peopled with automata so lifelike that the hero falls in love with them, as in his tale "The Sandman" (best known, perhaps, as the Olimpia-episode in Offenbach's *The Tales of Hoffmann*). In these cases the fascination is almost always related to the fear produced by the confusion of reality and illusion, a typically romantic phobia.

Romanticism was based on the philosophical belief that mind and matter are fundamentally identical, a belief that received its classic formulation in the words of Schelling that "nature aspires to be visible spirit while spirit aspires to be invisible nature."[33] This philosophical tenet led to the conviction among many scientists—notably the practition-

[31] Paul Sucher, *Les Sources du merveilleux chez E.T.A. Hoffmann* (Paris: Félix Alcan, 1912), pp. 104–08 ("Les Automates").

[32] Ambrose Bierce wrote a tale about a mechanical chessplayer that becomes so infuriated at being checkmated that it strangles its creator. See "Moxton's Master," in *The Collected Works of Ambrose Bierce* (New York: Neale, 1910), III, 88–105.

[33] "Die Natur soll der sichtbare Geist, der Geist die unsichtbare Natur seyn." This famous statement occurs at the end of Schelling's *Ideen zu einer Philosophie der Natur* (1797).

ers of *Naturphilosophie*—that inanimate matter could be brought to life since it is separated from the animate only by degree, not by any inherent qualities. Such discoveries of the age as galvanism, mesmerism, and animal magnetism seemed to provide scientific evidence of this phenomenon.[34] These speculations provided, in turn, the scientific basis for such literary works as Mary Shelley's *Frankenstein* (1818), which—far from being wild fictional invention—explicitly invoked theories of Erasmus Darwin and the adherents of *Naturphilosophie.* In his preface to his wife's novel, Shelley wrote that "The event on which this fiction is founded has been supposed, by Dr. Darwin, and some of the physiological writers of Germany, as not of impossible occurrence."[35] I am not suggesting, of course, that sophisticated people in the early nineteenth century expected statues to come to life. But the intellectual climate was such that the animation of a statue not only was theoretically possible; it also provided the public imagination with an ideal image for its central belief in the unity of all matter. At the same time, it titillated the romantic sensibility by appealing to its sense of terror. These facts help to account for the remarkable literary revival of the legend of Venus and the Ring during the first decades of the nineteenth century.[36]

[34] On romantic *Naturphilosophie* and its implications see Alexander Gode von Aesch, *Natural Science in German Romanticism* (New York: Columbia Univ. Press, 1941); and Walter D. Wetzels, "Aspects of Natural Science in German Romanticism," *Studies in Romanticism*, 10 (1971), 44–59.

[35] Mary Wollstonecraft Shelley, *Frankenstein or The Modern Prometheus*, ed. James Rieger (Indianapolis: Bobbs-Merrill, 1974), p. 6.

[36] The theme of Venus and the Ring was of course not the only legend of animated statues. In Russia, for instance, Pushkin was obsessed with the notion of statues that come to life and dealt with it in several of his works, notably the narrative poem "The Bronze Horseman" (1833). Roman Jakobson's study, "La Statue dans la symbolique de Pouchkine" (1937; rpt. in Jakobson's *Questions de poétique* [Paris: Seuil, 1973], pp. 152–89), is vitiated in part by his neglect of the European sources of the theme and the important

ONE of the earliest revivals can be found in *Little's Poems* (1802) by Tom Moore.[37] Moore's verse-tale "The Ring" displays a few superficial changes: the scene has been shifted from Italy to Saxony; the hero and heroine are called Rupert and Isabel; the game is tennis rather than handball. In the sixty-two quatrains the "female fiend" is never identified specifically as Venus; she is simply "a heathen goddess, or / Perhaps a heathen queen." The exorciser is named Father Austin, "whom all the country round believed / A devil or a saint!" and he writes his message to the devil in blood. In general, however, "the horrid, horrid tale" alters none of the essential motifs that Moore found in Frommann's *Tractatus de fascinatione*. All the traditional miracles are taken for granted: the statue's crooked finger, the "strange disorder'd crowd" at the crossroads, the devil's curse on the priest. The principal difference that betrays the period of composition is evident in the mood. The phantom that incommodes the young couple on their wedding night resembles a Gothic ghoul more than the classical *Venus rediviva*:

> Soon Rupert 'twixt his bride and him,
> A death-cold carcase found;
> He saw it not, but thought he felt
> Its arms embrace him round.
>
> . . . .
>
> And when he bent, the earthy lips
> A kiss of horror gave;
> 'T was like the smell from charnel vaults,
> Or from the mouldering grave!

The sheer frequency of occurrences suggests that the

French and German parallels. In Pushkin's works, curiously, the animated statue is always the instrument of a malevolent power but never, as Jakobson stresses, the incarnation of a woman.

[37] *The Poetical Works of Thomas Moore* (Boston: Phillips, Sampson, 1856), pp. 45–48. In a note to "Little's" manuscript Moore specifically cites "Fromman *upon Fascination*" as his source.

theme enjoyed a particular popularity in Germany. At the same time, for all the variety in treatment, a few basic similarities alert us to common impulses motivating the revival. August Apel's novella, "The Wedding Ring" (1812), which appeared in a widely read journal, shows that the author was familiar with the original source at first hand.[38] The story begins when the narrator buys an old edition of William of Malmesbury at an auction. He relates the tale of Venus and the Ring in precise detail, expanding modestly in places in such a way as to emphasize the inherent eroticism of the theme: for instance, the traditional cloud of mist becomes a veil, which Venus opens to expose her nude beauty. However, the legend serves merely as the catalyst for a tale of Gothic horror that bears only a faint resemblance to our theme—a tale that the narrator learns by pursuing a notation in the margin of the old volume. A young German nobleman traveling in Italy falls in love with a beautiful girl, who is rumored to have dealings with the devil. When she suddenly dies, he places a ring on her finger. Brought back to life magically by a necromancer, she lives for a time with the young German, who eventually deserts her when he realizes that she is an apparition of the devil. On his wedding day she shows up in Germany and promises to give back his ring in return for a kiss; but in his arms she turns into a moldering corpse, and the young man dies of horror.

Many other writers of the period were familiar with the theme from various sources, but they were less interested in simply retelling the legend than in exploiting its individual motifs. According to the paralipomena to his *Romances of the Rosary* (written from 1803 to 1812), Clemens Brentano planned to adapt the legend, which he got from Kornmann's *Mons Veneris*, for the exposition of his

[38] "Der Brautring, Novelle," *Die Musen. Eine norddeutsche Zeitschrift*, ed. Friedrich de la Motte Fouqué and Wilhelm Neumann (Berlin, 1812), III, 110–53.

poetic cycle.[39] Kosme, a virtuous young painter and the son of Tannhäuser, has inherited a ring handed down over the centuries from the Virgin Mary. While playing ball he puts his ring on the finger of a Venus-statue and is later unable to recover it. That night, for the first time in his life, he has a lustful dream, and when he wakes up the next morning he finds a different ring on his finger. From this point on there is no further similarity between our legend and Brentano's poem: the magic ring of Venus enables Kosme to seduce a nun, and their three daughters become the principal heroines of the romances. But once again we note the explicit eroticism that characterizes most German treatments of the theme.

On March 3, 1810, Joseph von Eichendorff noted in his diary that Brentano had spent two excited hours outlining for him the plan of his *Romances*.[40] It was presumably through Brentano that Eichendorff and his brother Wilhelm became acquainted with the theme that captivated them both. In his poem "Venus the Enchantress" (1816) Wilhelm makes use of the ring-motif, but he blurs the sharp profile of the traditional theme for the sake of romantic dreaminess.[41] After the wedding festivities the bridegroom wanders

[39] *Romanzen vom Rosenkranz*, in Clemens Brentano, *Werke*, ed. Wolfgang Frühwald, Bernhard Gajek and Friedhelm Kemp, I (Munich: Hanser, 1968), 996.

[40] Joseph Freiherr von Eichendorff, *Werke und Schriften*, ed. Gerhart Baumann, III (Stuttgart: Cotta, 1958), 245. See Robert Mühlher, "Der Venusring: Zur Geschichte eines romantischen Motivs," *Aurora: Eichendorff Almanach*, 17 (1957), 50–62. Mühlher, who discusses German romantic examples, focuses on the single motif of the ring rather than on the theme as a whole. As a result, he includes several versions that have little in common with our theme. In general, Mühlher sees the ring as a magic instrument whereby the demonic powers of nature are awakened, Venus as the sinister aspect of art, and the marriage to Venus as the fatal descent of the romantic artist into the destructive realm of nature.

[41] "Die zauberische Venus," in *Joseph und Wilhelm von Eichendorffs Jugendgedichte*, ed. R. Pissin (Berlin: Frensdorff, [n.d.]), pp. 145–48.

out into the garden to contemplate his bliss in solitude. (Note that Germanic introspection has replaced the original Mediterranean gregariousness.) When he decides to go boating on the lake, he places his ring on the finger of the marble Venus standing conveniently on the shore. Returning later to see the statue close its fingers over the ring, he falls down in a faint. On awaking it appears to him as though the statue were stirring, and he feels the pangs of passion. Embracing the statue in the hope of animating it through his warmth, he forgets his bride and his wedding vows. He builds himself a tiny hermit's cell on the lakeshore and spends the remainder of his days beside the bewitching statue.

The more famous Eichendorff brother was also fascinated by the image of *Venus rediviva*, which he used in one of his finest stories, "The Marble Statue" ("Das Marmorbild," 1818), to embody the dangerous lure of nature and pagan antiquity. "The Marble Statue," however, contains absolutely none of the motifs associated with the theme of Venus and the Ring. But in Eichendorff's romance, *Julian* (1852), the young Apostate places his ring on the finger of a Venus-statue as a token of his allegiance to the pagan gods, but flees in fright when he imagines that the statue's eyes move.[42] Later the statue, still wearing his ring on its finger, appears to him in a dream to announce that Constantius is dead and that he, Julian, is now the emperor. Shortly thereafter his army is strengthened by the arrival of Faustine, an exiled princess who wishes to win back her kingdom by allying herself with Julian and who fights in battle with superhuman powers. To Julian's consternation, it turns out that Faustine not only looks like the statue of Venus; she also wears Julian's ring. From this point on, however, the romance bears little resemblance to our theme. When Julian, ultimately betrayed by Faustine, has been killed, the poem ends with a typically Eichendorffian warning against succumbing to the demonic powers that constantly seek to control us:

[42] "Julian," in *Werke und Schriften*, I (1957), 409–48.

Du aber hüt' den Dämon, der in der Brust dir
gleißt,
Daß er nicht plötzlich ausbricht und wild dich
selbst zerreißt.

In 1828 Willibald Alexis (a pseudonym for Wilhelm Häring) published his novella "Venus in Rome" in the fashionable *Taschenbuch für Damen*.[43] Although Goethe is of course not mentioned in this tale set in early sixteenth-century Rome, the story seems at times almost like an inversion of Goethe's *Roman Elegies* (1795) and the love of classical Rome that the cycle embodied. There are many parallels—names, places, situations, etc.—between Goethe's elegies and Alexis' story. Above all, however, Alexis' hero, Hubert von Stein, arrives in Rome behaving like a man who has gone slightly mad from reading the *Roman Elegies* too often. The worst example of a pedantic young German on his *Bildungsreise*, he wanders through the streets of Rome declaiming Latin and tediously preferring everything ancient to anything modern: sculpture to painting, classical to Renaissance architecture, pagan to Christian philosophy and literature, and so forth. Through the sorcery of the surly priest Palumbus, who—a true "suburban" priest—lives in the ruined Baths of Nero outside Rome, Hubert is bewitched by the young Roman beauty, Faustine. (Palumbus casts a spell over Hubert's image in his magic mirror; as a result, when he first sees Faustine he is magically attracted to her.) For several years he lives with her—they even have a child together. Finally Hubert's wife, Mathilde, arrives from Germany and, with the aid of her servant Eckard (another name familiar from the Venus legends), rescues Hubert and takes him home again, cured once and for all of his excessive infatuation with pagan antiquity, which has been exposed in all its darkness and evil.

The story of Venus and the Ring is encapsulated as a

[43] "Venus in Rom," in *Gesammelte Novellen*, by Willibald Alexis (Berlin, 1831), III, 1–162.

subplot into this historical romance, in which such figures as Martin Luther, Pope Leo X, and the painter Raphael appear. Hubert has come to Rome to visit a former comrade-at-arms, Theodor Savelli. When he inquires at Savelli's palace, the servants snicker and Savelli's wife acts evasive. When Hubert finally runs into Savelli one night in the Colosseum, he learns that his friend has suffered the traditional misfortune: on the day of his wedding to a Venetian beauty, he placed his ring on the finger of a Venus-statue for safekeeping while playing ball. Unable to remove the ring later, he hacked off the statue's hand with his sword but lost the ring. When he went in to his bride that night, "an invisible hand passed over my eyes," and he fell asleep. The next morning his scornful wife drove him from her house and bed, telling him not to come back until he has recovered his wedding ring and, by implication, his potency. Savelli has wandered through Rome and the surrounding countryside for several years, a figure of ridicule and contempt, while his wife, aided by the sinister Cardinal Chrysogono, has consoled herself for her husband's insufficiencies with a succession of lovers. At the end of the story the half-crazed Savelli attempts to recover his ring from a figure on horseback that he takes to be Venus, during a midnight procession through the city. It turns out to be Cardinal Chrysogono, one of the leaders of an unsuccessful conspiracy against the pope, who is now fleeing the city; but Savelli, in his madness and hatred, cuts off the cardinal's hand and recovers "his" ring. Suddenly sobered by events, he returns to his wife and forces her to take her own life in order to atone for all the years of shame and humiliation during which she deceived him. As Hubert and his wife go back to a rejuvenated Germany, they leave behind a despondent Savelli, symbol of an exhausted Rome.

In "Frau Venus" (1838) Franz von Gaudy transposes the tale from eleventh-century Rome to fourteenth-century Verona, complicating the plot slightly by adding the Montague-Capulet motif: the young nobleman, Ottaviano Sagramosa, and his beloved, Vergogna Castellani, belong to families that have feuded for generations.[44] When Ottaviano, thanks to the interference of the goddess, seems to have scorned Vergogna on their wedding night, her hot-tempered brother wants to take instant revenge. He is dissuaded until the unhappy young husband has had a chance to find a solution to his dilemma. There are various insignificant changes: the brother, Filippino, is the adversary whom Ottaviano defeats in the ball game; the statue on whose finger he places the ring is one he has known and admired since childhood. In general, however, Gaudy is true to the traditional plot-line. (The additional length of the story results principally from Gaudy's Biedermeier delight in the meticulous description of such occasions as the wedding feast and the ball-game.) The miracles are related with no attempt to rationalize them. When the two lovers get into bed, "a hazy, milkwhite mist spread out between him and his bride, became thicker and thicker, assumed the shape of the statue of Venus, embraced the young man with cold arms, and whispered gently: 'Vergogna is not your bride. You have betrothed yourself to me.' " Everyone concerned takes the supernatural occurrences for granted. Since the story is located within a totally Christian context, it is assumed that Ottaviano, in full innocence, has fallen into a trap set by the devil. The role of Palumbus is assigned to a Moorish doctor who dabbles in black magic. After Ottaviano recovers his ring in the traditional manner, the statue of Venus falls down and shatters, the Moorish Palumbo disappears, and the young couple lives happily ever after.

If we now glance for one last time at these six representative treatments, we can detect several underlying similarities that characterize them as a set. In the first place, they all remain quite traditional in two respects. Without exception the writers of the romantic generation continue to accept the supernatural: in many cases the statue actually comes to life.

[44] "Frau Venus," in *Venetianische Novellen*, by Franz von Gaudy (Bunzlau, 1838), I, 189–234.

In addition, in every case the image retains its customary negative valence: Venus embodies the dark forces of nature and the corrupting powers of pagan antiquity that threaten the Christian soul. However, two further underlying similarities mark these works as, respectively, German and romantic. First, they share the pronounced eroticism that has characterized German treatments of the theme since the *Kaiserchronik*: the young man is bound to Venus by lust and not by any mere legalistic bond. Second, the original struggle between Christianity and paganism has here been nationalized: we find German innocence pitted against Italian wiles. All in all, then, the popularity of the theme—in which the devout German youth rejects Venus with her associations of pagan culture and Mediterranean *joie de vivre* —amounts to a disavowal by a new generation of the principal ideals of Weimar classicism.

THE next major turning-point in the history of the theme was reached in 1837 in Paris. In that year two of the foremost ironists of the age—a German journalist writing in exile and a French Inspector of Historical Monuments, who were casually asquainted as fellow contributors to the *Revue des Deux Mondes*—almost simultaneously published works that crucially modified the theme of Venus and the Ring. Heinrich Heine's essay on folklore entitled *Elemental Spirits* (1837) provided the first radically new interpretation of the legend, while Prosper Mérimée's tale, "The Venus of Ille" (1837), gave the theme its finest fictional reshaping since William of Malmesbury.

It is more than likely that both writers, the professional inspector of monuments as well as the cultural journalist, were inspired at least in part by one of the major archaeological events of the period: the discovery of the Venus de Milo, which was brought to Paris with great éclat in 1820. The widely celebrated occasion touched off a veritable cult of Venus that lasted for several decades. Artists vied in their proposals for restoring the armless beauty to her original state: e.g., holding a mirror, holding a dove, holding up her gown, or gesturing in various ways.[45] Yet Heine's revaluation of the theme required no external stimulation since it represents the fusing of two motifs that fascinated him during his entire life: the theory of the "gods in exile" and an almost perverted obsession with classical marble statuary.

In many of his works, culminating in the late essay "The Gods in Exile" (1853), Heine elaborated an idea that he got from Gibbon's *The Decline and Fall of the Roman Empire*, among other places: the idea that after the triumph of Christianity the ancient deities did not simply vanish; instead, they went into exile (an idea that appealed to Heine, the political exile), assuming the shape of animals (e.g., in Egypt) or retreating into the statues that represent them. The statues therefore represent a state of sleep, not a stony death. There the gods await the day when they can once again emerge to stand before men in all their splendor. These classical deities embody the "Hellene" virtues of life, light, sun, passion, that will be prized again when the cool, rational, ascetic qualities of "Nazarene" culture have had their day.

Heine's version of what has been called the "clashing myths" of nineteenth-century German culture[46] helps to account for his obsession with marble statues, which he finds perfect in their beauty yet cold and remote in their detachment from the world of men.[47] His works, from the very beginning, teem with references to statues. Almost to the point of predictability he compares lovely women, in their radiance and inviolability, to statues. E. M. Butler points out that in Italy "hardly a woman whom he came across but put him in

[45] Dolf Sternberger, *Heinrich Heine und die Abschaffung der Sünde* (Hamburg: Claassen, 1972), p. 204 and pp. 400–401.

[46] Henry Hatfield, *Clashing Myths in German Literature from Heine to Rilke* (Cambridge, Mass.: Harvard Univ. Press, 1974), esp. pp. 12–52 ("Heine and the Gods").

[47] On Heine's ambivalent attitude toward statues see E. M. Butler, *The Tyranny of Greece over Germany* (1935; rpt. Boston: Beacon Press, 1954), pp. 241–300; and Dolf Sternberger, *Heinrich Heine und die Abschaffung der Sünde*, pp. 181–205 ("Marmorbilder").

mind of some statue."[48] Not only does Heine attribute to women statuesque characteristics; he treats statues as though they were women. The narrator of *Florentine Nights* (1836) recalls a beautiful statue lying in the grass in the park of his mother's estate.[49] Smitten by its beauty, he creeps out one night to embrace the stone deity: ". . . finally I kissed the lovely goddess with a passion, a tenderness, a desperation, as I have never again kissed in all my life." Never, he confesses, has he been able to forget the sensation that penetrated his soul when "the enrapturing frigidity" of the marble lips touched his mouth. "Ever since that day a marvelous passion for marble statues has grown in my soul." Twenty years later, shortly before his death, Heine remarked to a friend that he had really never loved anything but dead women and statues.[50]

Now it is particularly in the figure of Venus that Heine's two obsessions come most naturally together: his belief in the "gods in exile" and his weird attachment to marble statues. As he remarks in his book *On the History of Religion and Philosophy in Germany* (1834) "the gloomy madness of the monks afflicted poor Venus most cruelly; she in particular was regarded as a daughter of Beelzebub, and the good kind Tannhäuser even says to her face:

> O, Venus, schöne Fraue mein,
> Ihr seid eine Teufelinne![51]
> (O, Venus, lovely lady mine,
> You're nothing but a devil-ine.)

Heine first alludes to his love affair with Venus in his early narrative, *The Journey through the Harz Mountains* (1824).

[48] *The Tyranny of Greece over Germany*, p. 260.

[49] *Florentinische Nächte*, in Heinrich Heine, *Sämtliche Werke*, ed. Ernst Elster (Leipzig and Vienna: Bibliographisches Institut, [n.d.]), IV, 326–27.

[50] Cited in E. M. Butler, *The Tyranny of Greece over Germany*, p. 277.

[51] Heine, *Sämtliche Werke*, IV, 174.

In a nightmare he witnesses a strange assembly in the Göttingen university library, of lawyers and legal scholars from past and present, who loudly debate niceties of law before the goddess Themis. Fleeing this tumult, Heine reaches the adjoining room, where "the sacred images of the Apollo Belvedere and the Medicean Venus stand side by side: I fell at the feet of the goddess of beauty, in her gaze I forgot all the dissolute activity that I had escaped, my eyes drank in voluptuously the proportion and the eternal charm of her blessed body. . . ."[52] Almost thirty years later, in the postscript to his finest volume of poems, *Romanzero* (1851), Heine recounts the (somewhat fictionalized) story of his last excursion before he became bedridden for the rest of his life—appropriately enough, with the ravages of the disease of Venus, syphilis. "With the greatest difficulty I dragged myself to the Louvre, and I almost collapsed when I entered the sublime hall where the blessed goddess of beauty, Our dear Lady of Milo, stands on her pedestal. I lay at her feet for a long time and wept so fervently that even a stone would have been moved to pity. Indeed, the goddess gazed down upon me sympathetically, but at the same time as disconsolately as though she wanted to say: Don't you see that I can't help you? I have no arms!"[53]

This background enables us to appreciate Heine's recapitulation of the story of Venus and the Ring in *Elemental Spirits*, a compilation of legends and speculations on myth and folklore. He stays quite close to the original version that he found, as he informs us, in Kornmann's *Mons Veneris* and Del Rio's *Magical Disquisitions.* But the context in which Heine relates the tale makes his version more meaningful than any of the versions produced in Germany during the preceding decades. Heine is explicitly intent upon elucidating the profound meaning underlying the familiar fables that he discusses. Referring to the victory of Christianity

[52] *Die Harzreise*, in *Sämtliche Werke*, III, 22–23.

[53] "Nachwort zum *Romanzero*," in *Sämtliche Werke*, I, 487.

over paganism, he argues that the iconoclasm of the early Christians is easy to comprehend. "They could not and would not spare the old temples and statues, for in them there still lived that ancient Greek serenity, that *joie de vivre*, which appeared to the Christian to be the work of the devil. In these statues and temples the Christian saw not only the objects of an alien cult, a futile heresy lacking all reality: he regarded these temples as the strongholds of real demons, and to the gods that these statues represented he attributed an uncontested existence; they were nothing but devils."[54] All that classical joy has now been lost, says Heine. The Greek deities still reside in their ancient temples, but as a result of Christ's victory they have lost all their power. They are no more than poor devils who must hide, by day, among the owls and toads in the ruins of their former splendor. At night they rise up in enticing shapes in the hope of seducing some innocent wanderer or bold fellow.

Although Heine goes on to retell the medieval legend with seemingly negligible changes, the context restores to the theme an inherent significance and seriousness that it had lost: it is once again clearly a struggle between the forces of paganism and Christianity. But in this contest between Hellene and Nazarene it is no secret where Heine's sympathies lie (at least, at this point in his life): with the handsome gods of antiquity, who have been stripped of their dignity and authority in order to enrich a single pallid deity, the Christian Jesus. This transformation in attitude justifies the changes that Heine has made in his retelling of the story of Venus and the Ring.[55] In general, he shifts the emphasis subtly in such a way as to enhance Venus. According to the medieval tradition, the demoness in the wondrous procession is dressed like a whore and makes indecent gestures. Here, in contrast, the serene and lovely goddess, riding in a chariot rather than on a mule, is resplendently clad in royal purple

54 *Elementargeister*, in *Sämtliche Werke*, IV, 422.
55 *Sämtliche Werke*, IV, 425–28.

and garlanded with roses. (It is no accident that Heine refers to Venus, in both his early and late works, in terms normally reserved for the Virgin Mary.) In the medieval legend Venus is a demon in the service of the devil; in Heine's version the letter of conjuration is handed over directly to the goddess. (This is a clear and pronounced alteration that has no precedent in Kornmann or Del Rio.) To the extent that the goddess has become once again the representative of pagan antiquity and the tragic heroine of the tale, Christianity is the adversary and the exorciser Palumbus is reduced simply to a representative of the Church. When the goddess utters the traditional exclamation against Palumbus, it is no longer a fiendish curse but rather a lament coupled with a prediction that respect for classical beauty and values will one day be restored. "Cruel priest Palumnus! [*sic*] You are still not content with the harm that you have done unto us! But an end will soon be put to your persecutions." Heine's changes, seemingly so insignificant in comparison with the alterations of other authors, turn out to be quite radical. Rather than inventing variations on the plot, he has restored and intensified the original significance of the theme. Here, for the first time in the history of the theme, the author takes the side of Venus, of pagan antiquity, against Christianity and "Nazarene" civilization.

ALTHOUGH the popularity of the theme was greatest in Germany, at least one variant achieved a certain currency in contemporary France: Louis Hérold's opéra-comique *Zampa* (1831).[56] In this play, which is set in seventeenth-century Sicily, we find the statue of Alice de Manfredi, a local patron saint, who has died twelve years previously following her seduction by the pirate, Zampa. As the action begins, Zampa has returned to marry a girl named Camille, although she is betrothed to his brother, Alphonse. Driving Alphonse

[56] Pierre Jourda, "Zampa et La Vénus d'Ille," *Le Divan*, 30 (1945–46), 67–72.

away, Zampa defies the statue of the woman he violated by putting the ring upon its finger. The statue clenches its fist and makes a menacing gesture. But Zampa persists and goes through with the wedding even though the statue strides about making threats during the entire ceremony. When the defiant corsair finally carries his bride to bed, the waiting statue drags him off to hell in a fiery ending reminiscent of *Don Giovanni.*

Apart from its representative value as evidence for the continuing popularity of animated statues, Hérold's *Zampa* would hardly be worth mentioning were it not one of the probable sources for the undisputed fictional masterpiece based on our theme, Mérimée's "The Venus of Ille" (1837). Mérimée was fond of playing games of mystification concerning his sources: the two sources that he mentioned for "The Venus of Ille"—"Pontanus" and "Freher"—are completely spurious.[57] Yet the tale itself proves beyond a doubt that he was familiar with the ancient theme, and the discussion up to this point should have made it evident that many sources were readily available by 1837 to a learned archivist like Mérimée.

Unlike any of the other versions so far discussed, Mérimée's story is set squarely in his own contemporary society—the France of Louis Philippe—and it is recounted by a first-person narrator who contributes to the credibility by claiming to have witnessed the events that he narrates.[58] The (unnamed) narrator, who shares many of Mérimée's interests and characteristics, is touring the province of Roussillon in the French Pyrenees—an area long notorious for its witchcraft—to inspect the classical and medieval monuments of

[57] Maurice Parturier, "Sur les sources de 'La Vénus d'Ille' " *Le Divan*, 30 (1945–46), 73–81. See also Parturier's introduction to "La Vénus d'Ille" in Prosper Mérimée, *Romans et Nouvelles*, ed. Maurice Parturier, II (Paris: Garnier, 1967), pp. 79–85. It is useless for our purposes to engage in the furious and continuing debate on Mérimée's specific source since it is clear that he knew at least one of the major sources.

[58] *Romans et Nouvelles*, II, 87–118.

the region. (Both the framework and the principal characters of the story reflect Mérimée's own trip to the Pyrenees in 1834.) At Ille he has been recommended to M. de Peyrehorade, a local gentleman knowledgeable in the history and antiquities of Catalan. As he approaches the town, he learns from his guide that a perfectly preserved bronze statue was unearthed in Peyrehorade's garden only two weeks earlier. Upon his arrival in Ille, the narrator is informed that M. de Peyrehorade's son, Alphonse, is to be married two days later on Friday—a good day for a wedding, his host assures him, because it is the day of Venus (Fr. *vendredi* = Latin *Veneris dies*). On the morning of the wedding day, while the narrator is seated before the statue, trying to sketch it, a game of pelota begins nearby between the local players and a group of Spanish muleteers passing through the village. Alphonse, the village champion, is already dressed for his wedding. But seeing that his team is being sorely beaten by the visiting players, he tears off his coat and begins to take part. When he misses the first ball, Alphonse complains that the unaccustomed wedding ring is interfering with his prowess. Taking it off, he places it on the extended finger of the newly unearthed statue. No one pays the least attention, for in the renewed game Alphonse plays so brilliantly that the Spaniards are soundly beaten. Afterwards he taunts the champion of the opposing team by offering to give him a handicap in the return match.

The wedding party has already reached the bride's house before Alphonse remembers that he neglected to retrieve his ring, but he mentions it to no one lest his friends tease him by calling him the statue's husband. Fortunately, he has an extra ring handy, and the wedding takes place as scheduled. That evening, when the party returns to Ille for the wedding feast, the narrator notices that the bridegroom disappears for a moment before taking his place at the table and then returns looking pale and serious. Much later, and after much drinking, Alphonse calls the narrator aside and tells him that he was unable to remove the ring because the statue had closed its finger over it. Although the narrator feels a momentary chill of terror, he assumes that the young man is simply drunk. He promises to go out and look for himself; but since it has begun to rain he decides to wait until the following day. Some time after retiring he hears heavy footsteps going past his room, and again at dawn he hears the creaking of the staircase as the steps go back down.

The household is awakened shortly thereafter by bells, slamming doors, and screams. In the bridal chamber the half-dressed young husband is stretched out, dead, across the bed while the bride sobs convulsively in a corner. The young man looks as though his death was violent and his agony terrible. The wedding ring is found on the carpet beside the bed. The bride tells a completely incoherent story. As she lay in bed waiting for her husband to arrive, her face turned modestly to the wall, a heavy weight plumped onto the bed and she felt "something as cold as ice" touch her skin. Soon the door opened a second time and her husband greeted her. Then she heard a cry. Looking around, she saw her husband on his knees beside the bed in the embrace of a giant figure that was strangling him. Although she lost consciousness at the terrible sight, she swears repeatedly that she recognized the bronze Venus from M. de Peyrehorade's garden. Upon reviving she saw the phantom once again with her husband in its arms. Then a cock crowed. The statue dropped the body and departed.[59]

Since such mad ravings can obviously not be believed, suspicion is turned upon the Aragonese pelota player, who was heard muttering threats after his humiliating defeat. But the man has a good alibi and, moreover, maintains proudly

[59] One source that has not, to my knowledge, been taken into account is Mary Shelley's *Frankenstein*. The scene describing Alphonse's death displays a remarkable similarity to the paragraph in which the monster appears on the eve of Frankenstein's wedding and strangles his bride, leaving her body flung across the nuptial bed. Mérimée met the beautiful young widow of the English poet when she came to Paris in 1828 and fell passionately in love with her.

that if he had wanted revenge he would have sought it on the spot with his knife—not stealthily in the dark of night. The case is not solved. The narrator departs shortly after the funeral. M. de Peyrehorade dies a few months later. His wife has the statue melted down and cast into a church bell.

Now, although the familiar outline of the plot is clearly recognizable, Mérimée has made notable changes in the meaning of the image and the treatment of the supernatural. First of all, there is no longer any trace of the original conflict between Christianity and paganism, as there is in the contemporary German versions. Not only has Mérimée omitted the motifs of the necromancer's letter to the devil and the Wild Hunt, reducing the legend to its original element; the Church has virtually disappeared along with Father Palumbus. To be sure, the statue is melted down to be made into a church bell. But otherwise there is no mention of Church or clergy, and the narrative is wholly secular. The conflict here, as almost always in Mérimée's stories (e.g., *Carmen* and *Colomba*), takes place between primitive passion and the sterility of modern civilization. Venus exemplifies the power of pure passion that is indignant at the bourgeois commercialization of love in nineteenth-century France. One of the first things the narrator learns is that M. de Peyrehorade is rich and that he is marrying his son into an even wealthier family: the bride, despite her remarkable beauty, was chosen for reasons of money, not love. Alphonse, a strong and athletic young man with a handsome but stupid face, also cares about little but money. The narrator notes that, on the first evening, Alphonse speaks to him only once—to inquire where he had purchased his watch chain. The following day Alphonse entertains the guest by showing him the carriage he has bought for his bride and the expensive stable of horses, whose prizes he proudly enumerates. As for his marriage, the best part of it is that his bride is very rich, since her aunt left her a fortune. "I'm going to be very happy," he assures the narrator. Thereupon he displays the ring he has acquired for the wedding: a lovely antique band into which a cluster of diamonds has been tastelessly set.

It is into this complacent and money-minded bourgeois world, which has buried all true human emotion, that the statue of Venus is brought—out of the earth where it has lain buried for centuries. Her contempt for this world is evident in the mixture of disdain, irony, cruelty, and beauty that the narrator observes in her face. The "diabolical" expression of her inlaid eyes causes him to feel ill at ease in her presence, and the simple village folk lower their eyes before her baleful gaze. No one in the entire community is capable of appreciating the statue and the ancient values that it embodies. The villagers fear it as being a pagan "idol"; Mme de Peyrehorade wants to melt it down for a church bell; Alphonse in his stupidity is totally unaware of it; and even M. de Peyrehorade sees in this chef d'oeuvre from the finest period of Roman sculpture little more than an opportunity to win a name for himself in the world of archaeology. Venus, in turn, avenges herself on this effete civilization so totally lacking in comprehension. One of the workers who help to uncover the statue has his leg broken when the statue falls on him. When a villager throws a stone at the statue, the stone rebounds and strikes him in the head. After the statue is melted down and cast into a church bell, the grapevines in the local vineyards freeze for two years. In short, the statue is no longer a religious image, but a cultural one; the goddess of love and passion takes her revenge on a modern world that has forgotten how to treasure true human emotion. She bears out the warning inscribed on her pedestal —*Cave amantem*—which the narrator translates to mean: "Take care if *she* should fall in love with you!"

All this mystery is set into a story that is calculatedly ambiguous regarding the supernatural. Here for the first time the miracles are not taken for granted. To be sure, an air of malevolence is built up from the start by the series of accidents associated with the statue and by the malicious expression on her face. In addition, the repeated references to the bride's marked resemblance to the statue suggest that Venus has come to Ille, on this occasion, specifically to prevent an ill-matched and mercenary alliance. Yet the story is related in such a way that there is a natural explanation for everything that happens. This is in part the function of the first-person narrator, through whose consciousness all the information is filtered. In the earlier versions of the legends, both medieval and romantic, the narrator reported the incidents as objectively true. Here, in contrast, no one but Alphonse actually claims to have seen the statue close its finger over the ring; and he is drunk and excited when he does so. Similarly, there is a perfectly rational explanation for the various evil deeds the statue is alleged to have committed—from breaking the worker's leg to throwing the stone back at the superstitious villager. Finally, despite his alibi it is perfectly possible that the murder was committed by the Spanish pelota player, who is described as being both "a giant" and as dark-skinned as the bronze statue. The fact that the terrified bride claims to have seen the statue is explained by the investigating magistrate as a result of the public obsession with the statue during the two weeks since its discovery.

At every turn, in short, Mérimée leaves open the possibility of a rational explanation; the legend no longer *must* be accepted as magical, even by romantic convention. A rational or a supernatural explanation is possible depending upon the individual point of view.[60] This ambiguity is intentional and, in large measure, the real point of Mérimée's story. According to an often-cited anecdote, when a young reader once asked Mérimée if the statue really killed Alphonse, the author replied: "Goodness, child, I have no idea." For all his rationalism, Mérimée was keenly aware of mysteries that

[60] A. W. Raitt, *Prosper Mérimée* (London: Eyre and Spottiswoode, 1970), pp. 182–88; and Ivan Nagel, "Gespenster und Wirklichkeiten: Prosper Mérimées Novelle *La Vénus d'Ille*," *Die Neue Rundschau*, 68 (1957), 419–27. Nagel points out that Mérimée was one of the last writers to unify realism and the fantastic, which subsequently separated into two streams in France: those of Zola and Lautréamont.

elude rational explanation, and he wanted to infect his readers with the same degree of doubt concerning the limits of human reason. In his personal life Mérimée held certain superstitions: for instance, he regarded the ancient stones and cameos that he collected as magical talismans,[61] a belief not far removed from the notion that ancient statues might be magically animated. Like many agnostics, Mérimée was profoundly interested in religion, mythology, and superstition.[62] The "myth" that enabled him to communicate both his contempt for a world rendered progressively more effete by civilization and his ambivalent attitude toward the supernatural was the theme of Venus and the Ring.

"THE Venus of Ille," which Mérimée regarded as his finest tale, gave classic form to the theme that had obsessed a generation of romantic writers. Thanks to his brilliant use of intentional ambiguity, Mérimée was able to exploit all the conventional associations of the animated statue and, at the same time, not offend the new sense of rationalism emerging toward the middle of the nineteenth century.[63] In view of his success, it is small wonder that the theme challenged no major writer for an entire generation.[64] When it was taken

[61] Raitt, *Prosper Mérimée*, p. 217.

[62] Raitt, *Prosper Mérimée*, p. 133 and p. 183; Frank Paul Bowman, "Narrator and Myth in Mérimée's *Vénus d'Ille*," *French Review*, 33 (1960), 475–82.

[63] A modern version of the same motif—in this case a series of disasters on an isolated farm in the Sologne caused by the statue of a malevolent Melusine unearthed in the marshes—has been written by Claude Seignolle: *La Malvenue* (1952); rpt. in *Les Malédictions* (Paris: G. P. Maisonneuve et Larose, 1963), pp. 15–172. The analogies, though not overwhelming, are conspicuous enough to suggest that Seignolle, also the editor of volumes on the devil in folklore, had in mind Mérimée's classic model.

[64] There were minor writers, of course, of whom Richard Monckton Milnes was typical. See his essay "The Goddess Venus in the Middle Ages," in *Poems, Legendary and Historical*, New Ed. (London, 1846), pp. 18–49. The essay, which deals principally with the Tannhäuser legend, tells the story of Venus and the Ring in a foot-

up again, in the 1870's, the options were wholly different.[65]

Occasional writers, for purely antiquarian reasons, retold the old story exactly as they found it in the medieval sources. "The Ring Given to Venus" is one of twenty-four ancient and medieval legends that William Morris relates in *The Earthly Paradise* (Part IV; 1870).[66] The scene has been shifted to the English coast, and the names have been changed accordingly. (The hero is now called Laurence.) As a result of Morris' delight in descriptive passages—notably the wedding at the beginning and the Wild Hunt at the end—the text has grown from the fewer than one hundred lines in William of Malmesbury's chronicle to over thirteen hundred lines of rimed couplets. Basically, however, Morris has not gone a step beyond Malmesbury and the other medieval versions. The plot is intact, and the miracles are related with no attempt at rationalization. By the same token, the image of the Venus-statue still represents nothing but the medieval struggle between good and evil. At the beginning of his poem Morris tells us of the city

> That rife was wicked sorcery there:
> And why I know not: if it were
> Wrought by a lingering memory

---

note to Milnes's own poem entitled "The Northern Knight in Italy." Milnes's essay is of interest mainly as an indication of the widespread romantic view of the theme: ". . . in the early Christian imagination, the goddess Venus stood out as the very queen of devildom. . . . No wonder, then, that Venus is the great bond between Pagan and Christian tradition" (p. 20).

[65] Post-romantic treatments of the theme have been mentioned recently by Barbara Fass, *La Belle Dame sans Merci and the Aesthetics of Romanticism* (Detroit: Wayne State Univ. Press, 1974), pp. 134–48; and Patricia Merivale, "The Raven and the Bust of Pallas: Classical Artifacts and the Gothic Tale," *PMLA*, 89 (1974), 960–66. Fass interprets the theme essentially as an attack on the institution of marriage; Merivale sees the figure of Venus as "a chief repository for Dionysian aspects of classical artifacts for most of the century."

[66] *The Collected Works*. With an Introduction by his daughter May Morris (London: Longmans, Green, 1911), VI, 136–74.

Of how that land was wont to be
A dwelling-place, a great stronghold
Unto the cozening Gods of old.

Again, at the end, when the Master of the procession curses "Dan Palumbus," he refers to him in the traditional manner as an ambivalent cross between priest and necromancer:

"And must such double men abide?
Not mine, not mine, nor on thy side?
For as thou cursest them I curse:—
Make thy souls better, Lord, or worse!"

Morris expects his audience, for the duration of the poem, to suspend disbelief and to accept the magic as a convention. As a result, he is able to incorporate all the traditional elements into his poem. Authors who wished to adapt the legend for more modern purposes, however, could not use the full version. As we have seen, in order to make his story plausible to an earlier nineteenth-century audience Mérimée had to do away with both Father Palumbus and the Wild Hunt; but he managed to retain a degree of uncertainty about the animation of the statue itself. By 1870 this kind of ambiguity was no longer acceptable. If a writer was still to use the theme of Venus and the Ring, the mystery had to be shifted from the external world into the mind of the viewer himself: magic yields to psychology. The 1870's provide us with two fascinating, though totally different, examples of this development.

It is perhaps predictable that the man who lent his name to the phenomenon of masochism should have been fascinated by the legend of Venus and her fatal effect upon men. The theme plays a minor yet fundamental role in Leopold von Sacher-Masoch's most famous novella, *Venus in Furs* (1870).[67] The story is ostensibly the first-person narrative

[67] *Venus im Pelz* (Leipzig: Wigand, 1904). The story, without the "editor's" introduction, has been reprinted in Reinhard Federmann, *Sacher-Masoch oder die Selbstvernichtung* (Graz and Vienna:

of a young Carpathian nobleman, Severin von Kusiemski, who spends an evening telling a friend about his affair with Wanda von Dunajew. The plot is simple. Kusiemski is so totally bewitched by Wanda that he signs a pact to be her slave and to accompany her in that capacity to Italy. Sacher-Masoch permits his narrator to describe his perverted raptures at great length: he craves to be whipped by Wanda, especially when she is wearing her great fur coat. (It goes without saying that the furs with which this Venus is often clad emphasize her basic animality.) In Florence she deserts Severin and takes up with a cruel and handsome Greek, telling Severin that she truly loved him but that she could never give herself wholly to such a submissive man. This experience cures Severin and makes a man of him: the Severin who tells the story has developed into a healthy sadist who prefers to beat women rather than a sickly masochist who wants to be whipped by them.

It is not immediately apparent from the plot what this story has to do with the Venus theme. However, the ideas of the book as well as its images make it clear that Sacher-Masoch was influenced by Heine's interpretation of the theme and by his obsession with marble statues. As a child, Severin had been oppressed by churches and by images of the saints; he worshipped, instead, the plaster cast of a statue of Venus that his father kept in his study. (His rejection of the "pale thin virgin" for his "antique Venus" reminds us of Heine's juxtaposition of Nazarene and Hellene.) On one occasion, visiting the statue at night and overcome by an insuperable desire, he embraced the beautiful body and kissed the ice-cold lips—like the narrator of Heine's *Florentine Nights*. The goddess, who appears to him in a dream and raises her arm in a threatening gesture, provides a clear

---

Stiasny, 1961), pp. 50–158; an English translation (from the French!) is available in Gilles Deleuze, *Masochism: An Interpretation of Coldness and Cruelty*, trans. Jean McNeil (1967; rpt. New York: Braziller, 1971), pp. 117–229.

analogy to the animated statue who claims the youth who has betrothed her.

In the garden of the resort where the Venus-ridden Severin first meets Wanda there stands a statue of Venus, a copy of a statue in Florence. In true Heinesque fashion, Severin initially mistakes Wanda for the statue and vice-versa. The main part of the story deals with Severin's attempt to shape Wanda into a living copy of the statue—an attempt that succeeds beyond his expectations inasmuch as Wanda takes on not simply the appearance but also the mentality of a cruel Venus. On the level of language this effort reveals itself in Severin's tendency to use such words as "marble" or "stony" or "cold" to describe the eyes, shoulders, breasts, and hands of the living woman. He paints a portrait of Wanda in her furs, in which the real woman is depicted as identical with the statue of Venus; and he writes a poem apostrophizing her as Venus, "the devilishly charming myth-woman." In Florence, shortly before their break, a young German artist paints Wanda as "Venus in Furs" with whip in hand and her foot implanted on Severin's chest. (It is this portrait that gives the novella its title and that, when seen at the beginning of the book, incites Severin to relate the story of his disastrous love for Wanda.)

If we now look once again at the meaning of the image and the treatment of the supernatural, we can differentiate this story from earlier versions. As an image, Sacher-Masoch's Venus has not advanced beyond the Venus of Heine and Mérimée: the statue represents pure pagan passion that can dominate and even destroy men weakened by civilization and Christianity. The difference emerges principally in the treatment of the supernatural; for here the statue is no longer magical at all, not even in the ambiguous sense of "The Venus of Ille." Instead, in a psychologically plausible manner Sacher-Masoch has transferred the significance of the image onto the living woman, describing her in terms of stone and marble and attributing to her the malevolent characteristics of the pagan Venus. Wanda herself is the *Venus rediviva.* The magic now takes place in the minds of the observers: Severin's dream of the avenging statue and the narrator's dream that opens the book. Here the narrator is talking to Venus, who suggests that modern men "nurse a secret longing for a life of sheer paganism." Yet Christianity has made devils of the ancient gods, turning Venus into a creature of evil. (Again we hear clear echoes of Heine.) Stay in your northern mists, she warns him. Do not dig up the pagan world. Modern man cannot endure the gods—and they, in turn, would freeze to death in the harsh northern climate. Severin's account of his Venus in furs bears out this admonition.

A similar internalization of the magic permits us to establish an otherwise unlikely parallel between the two contemporaries, Sacher-Masoch and Henry James. In James's early story, "The Last of the Valerii" (1874),[68] there is no ring, and the statue is not even a Venus but a marble Juno. Yet even though James was not working directly with the medieval or Renaissance sources, we know that his story was inspired by Mérimée's "The Venus of Ille," which James had translated in the late eighteen-sixties.[69] Though unsuccessful in his efforts to place the translation in an American magazine, James regarded Mérimée's tale as "a masterpiece of art" and attempted to adapt it in his own story.

James transposes his tale to Rome of the Risorgimento, where a rich young American girl, in a typically Jamesian alliance, has married an Italian nobleman of distinguished but impoverished lineage. Over her husband's objections, Martha engages an archaeologist to excavate the gardens of the Valerio family villa in search of buried treasure. (The story is set in a time of frenzied archaeological activity in Rome, which James had witnessed.) When the workmen unearth a statue of Juno, the Signor Conte is strangely fas-

[68] *The Complete Tales of Henry James*, ed. Leon Edel (London: Rupert Hart-Davis, 1962), III, 89–122.

[69] P. R. Grover, "Mérimée's Influence on Henry James," *Modern Language Review*, 63 (1968), 810–17.

cinated by the masterpiece from the finest period of Greek sculpture. Moving the statue to a deserted garden house, the count jealously shuts it off from public view. During the following months he transfers much of his ardor from his wife, whom he increasingly neglects, to the statue. Finally the *contessa* liberates her husband from the statue's unnatural charm by having it buried once again in the ancient soil from which it was unwisely removed.

The parallels between James's story and "The Venus of Ille" are numerous and instantly apparent. First, it is not a retelling of the medieval legend, but a transposition into contemporary terms. Second, like Mérimée, James has done away with two of the original three motifs—the necromancer's letter and the Wild Hunt—in order to focus on the statue's effect on the young man and his marriage. Third, the story is recounted as the first-person narrative by an unnamed outside observer—in this case, Martha's godfather, a self-styled "unscrupulous old *genre* painter." Fourth, the fascinating statue, "an embodiment of celestial supremacy and repose," is unearthed in the family garden. Finally, James uses the statue to embody essentially the same (non-Christian) conflict between paganism and civilization as the one that obsessed Mérimée. Yet James has inverted these motifs in such a way as to make of them a characteristically Jamesian narrative with wholly new implications.[70]

In the first place, although James hints at the mercenary motives that played a major part in Mérimée's indictment of civilization, he makes very little of them. Camillo, to be sure, is pleased with the "pretty fortune" that Martha brings as her dowry; yet he is honestly devoted to her with the "intensity of feeling" that is characteristic of his rather slow mind. Martha, in turn, is very much in love with her *conte* although her own mother shrewdly remarks that she is really infatu-

[70] For a discussion of the story see Leon Edel's introduction to *The Ghostly Tales of Henry James* (New Brunswick, N.J.: Rutgers Univ. Press, 1948), pp. v–xxxii; and Leon Edel, *Henry James: The Conquest of London (1870–1881)* (Philadelphia: Lippincott, 1962), pp. 102–05.

ated with his villa and his "patrimonial marbles"—those symbols of European culture that will cleanse her tainted American dollars and give them a noble purpose. It is well-meaning Martha who precipitates the action by engaging men to explore the garden for buried antiquities. As an image, in other words, James's statue is no longer an avenging goddess of love returned from the past to punish a crass modern civilization that puts financial gain ahead of love. The statue, to be sure, represents the pagan past, but it is the past as culture, not as eroticism. Hence the statue represents Juno rather than Venus. In the words of the antiquarian excavator, "There's a pagan element in all of us . . . and the old gods have still their worshippers." Unlike Mérimée, however, James believes that the past constitutes a serious threat to the values of civilization and should best be left buried in the ancient earth.[71] To this extent, his story exemplifies his basic theme of innocence versus corruption. For it is Martha, that representative of Puritan innocence, who finally rescues her husband from the chaotic dangers of the buried European past that she has unthinkingly conjured up.

James's treatment of the supernatural varies as greatly as his transvaluation of the image, for here the image has been completely disenchanted—a process that reveals James as the contemporary of Sacher-Masoch. Not even the calculated ambiguity of Mérimée remains, for James has shifted the magic entirely into the consciousness of the afflicted hero, Count Valerio. The story does not deal with the intrusion of the supernatural into reality, like the early versions; it does not tantalize the reader with the ambiguous nature of the supernatural. Rather, we have what the narrator calls "a precious psychological study" focusing on the mind of Valerio (a family name that James borrowed from a tomb beneath the basilica of San Stefano along the Appian way).

[71] In James's tale "Adina" (1874) Sam Scrope throws back into the Tiber—"the moldering underworld of the Roman past"—the imperial topaz of Tibernius, dug up in the Campagna, that has brought such unhappiness to him and his fiancée, Adina.

From the first mention of Camillo his "pagan" nature is stressed. His head, strong and handsome, as the painter-godfather readily concedes, resembles a famous bust of the emperor Caracalla and his speech has inherited the "massive sonority" of the age of Augustus. His confessor once told him that he was "a good boy but a *pagan*," and the narrator finds that Camillo's purely sensuous nature makes him the perfect model of "the natural man." Oppressed by the "heavy atmosphere" of St. Peter's, the *conte* feels most at home in the Pantheon, where the overlay of Christian altars has not succeeded in masking the pagan origins of the temple. This superstitious man, unable to look statues in the face, calls them "ghosts" of the "poor disinherited gods." Accordingly, he opposes the excavations and he urges his wife, whose Puritan mentality is unencumbered by such reflections, to let the statues lie buried in the past where they belong. A "natural" man who has lost his faith in the old gods of his ancestors and yet is unable to accept Christianity, Camillo reverts to the faith of his forefathers when he is confronted with the overpowering beauty of the "majestic marble image." Setting her up in a deserted garden house, he begins by offering libations of wine to the goddess and ends up by making blood sacrifices.

Although there is no traditional exchange of rings in this story, James has invented an incident that takes its place. When the workmen disinter the statue, the count is awakened from his siesta by a dream that a Juno has been found and that "she rose and came and laid her marble hand on mine." This marble hand has the same metaphorical role as the traditional ring: in the concluding paragraph we learn that years later the count still kept the hand of the reburied statue locked away in his cabinet. Although the goddess does not interpose herself physically between the count and his young wife, the effect is very much the same, for Camillo neglects Martha so conspicuously that she has reason to suspect that he may be having an affair with another woman. At length she realizes that in her husband's consciousness the statue has become reality and that she, his wife, has been reduced to a mere fiction. The count's infatuation with the statue becomes so compelling that the narrator finally urges him to consult either a priest or a physician. But since the count rejects this suggestion, no Father Palumbus appears in the story. The count is not freed from his consuming passion until his wife, taking matters into her own hands, has the statue buried again in the earth from which it was removed.

"The Last of the Valerii" is still clearly though indirectly indebted for its entire conception to the legend of Venus and the Ring. Yet in order to make the story acceptable by modern standards of plausibility James had to strip down the legend so radically that the distinctive profile of the medieval original is virtually effaced. Whereas Mérimée, through his intentional ambiguity, was able to retain the motif of the ring and leave suggestively open (for a generation of readers just emerging from romanticism) the question of the animation of the statue, James has completely internalized the enchantment. But as Thomas Mann pointed out to Karl Kerényi, psychology is the means whereby myth is dedemonized and " 'transmuted' for humane ends."[72] The image of the Venus-statue has been wholly disenchanted in the treatments by James and Sacher-Masoch. Once a form has reached this point, it must either disappear from the canon of literary materials or be restored to the point of recognizability. But how, on the eve of the twentieth century, can an image with clearly magical associations—that is, an animated statue—be restored to this point? At least three possibilities have suggested themselves: pure fantasy, horror fiction, and travesty.

THE first possibility—pure poetic fantasy—is well represented by Gabriele D'Annunzio's comedy *La Pisanelle ou le*

[72] Letter of February 18, 1941; in *Mythology and Humanism: The Correspondence of Thomas Mann and Karl Kerényi*, trans. Alexander Gelley (Ithaca, N.Y.: Cornell Univ. Press, 1975), p. 100.

Jeu de la Rose et de la Mort (1913).[73] The play takes place in thirteenth-century Cyprus (the legendary home of Venus) during the reign of the Princes of Lusignan and at the time of the struggle between the Eastern and Western Churches. The story of Venus and the Ring is told in the Prologue by the prince of Tyr, the king's uncle, in order to stir up his nephew against the sorcery of the Greek bishops. The hero in this version is a young man named Rinier Lanfrance, the son of a Pisan merchant. The first part of the tale—wedding, ball game, ring—is largely traditional. That night, when Venus climbs into bed, she orders Rinier to get rid of his "concubine" and assures him that he need not be afraid of her great weight, for each night she will be transformed by his ardor into human flesh:

> Chaque nuit je viendrai
> comme dure statue;
> mais dans tes bras, soudain,
> de chair serai vêtue.[74]

The bride dies of shock at the sight of this monstrosity, and Rinier, though he survives, is doomed since the Church is unable to save him from the clutches of the archenemy. Here, despite the alterations, we still have the medieval legend in a recognizable form. But it is made acceptable to the modern audience in at least three ways. First, we are dealing with a poetic drama in which magic is accepted as a convention. Second, the action is set in a superstitious age. Third, the story is related for propagandistic purposes and not shown on the stage.

The fact that D'Annunzio avoided any direct representation of the animated statue suggests his awareness of the danger that the image might all too easily degenerate into the grotesqueness of the horror story or the ridiculousness of the burlesque. At least two English horror stories of the nine-

[73] *Tragedie, Sogni e Misteri*, ed. Renato Simoni, 6th ed. (Verona: Mondadori, 1960–68), II, 591–841.

[74] Ibid., p. 615.

ties seem to have been inspired by motifs from the theme of Venus. Although Arthur Machen's "Novel of the Iron Maid" (1890)[75] hints at Burton's *The Anatomy of Melancholy* as its source, the action suggests a familiarity with Mérimée. The narrator (named Burton) visits a certain Mr. Mathias, who as a hobby collects instruments of torture. His prize possession is "a large statue of a naked woman, fashioned in green bronze, the arms were stretched out, and there was a smile on the lips; it might well have been intended for a Venus, and yet there was about the thing an evil and deadly look." As Mr. Mathias displays his bronze Venus to the narrator, he inadvertently activates a hidden mechanism between her breasts, and the statue strangles him to death as Burton helplessly looks on. "I have never forgotten the hideous agony on Mathias's face as those relentless arms tightened about his neck. . . . The head had slowly bent down, and the green lips were on the lips of Mathias." Although we have here, as in Mérimée's story, the bronze statue of a cruel Venus who crushes a man to death, Machen does not elaborate the incident into a real story: it is narrated purely for its horror value.

Another set of motifs is exploited by Vernon Lee (pseud. for Violet Paget) in her story "Dionea" (1890).[76] In this epistolary narrative an elderly doctor writes to a wealthy patroness in Rome, who provides money for the education of the foundling Dionea. His first letters report various mysterious circumstances of Dionea's life involving the evil eye, love philtres, and so forth. When she reaches maturity, a young sculptor named Waldemer takes her as the model for a statue of Venus. But he gradually becomes so infatuated with the Venus-like Dionea that he sacrifices his own wife to her and then hurls himself from a cliff. Dionea disappears at the same time, and rumor has it that she was in fact a

[75] *The Three Imposters, or The Transmutations* (London: John Lane, 1895), pp. 186–96.

[76] *The Snake Lady and Other Stories by Vernon Lee*, ed. Horace Gregory (New York: Grove, 1954), pp. 126–54.

reincarnation of Venus, born of the sea and now returned to the sea. Vernon Lee refers specifically to Heine in her text, and certainly the notion of the return of the gods from exile as well as the confusion of statue and person are Heinesque. Yet the plot, in which a man sacrifices his wife for a statuesque Dionea (or a Dionea-like statue?) reminds us of Henry James's hapless Camillo and his infatuation. But here, in the Gothic counterpart to James's cool novella, the human sacrifice actually takes place.

The potential for travesty has been implicit in the theme at least since Heine, who manages to retain a degree of ironic detachment even when he is talking about his own obsession with marble statues. It is hardly by chance that we detect a clearly Heinesque flavor in the popular *Legends of Florence* (1895–1896) by Charles Godfrey Leland since the author, who published a twenty-volume translation of Heine's complete works, was well-acquainted with the relevant passages. Leland, who made his American reputation with a series of ballads in German-American dialect about Hans Breitmann, subsequently left his native Philadelphia and spent most of his life in Europe, where he devoted himself to gypsy lore, sorcery, and the occult. It is consistent with this interest in the supernatural that Leland related several tales of animated statues.[77] In "A Legend of the Speaking Statues of the Via Cerretani" a magician causes statues to speak in order to prove that they were created by the brilliant young sculptor Florio and not by his master, Fabiano. In another story ("The Sculptor and the Goddess Venus: The Origin of the Venus di Medicis") a young sculptor falls in love with a statue in the temple of Venus. He steals the beloved image and, when it comes to life, marries it. Venus then appears and reproaches him for his deed. He promises to atone by sculpting a statue of the goddess. This statue turns out to be the famous Venus di Medicis, and the youth be-

[77] *Legends of Florence: Collected from the People and Re-told*, Second Series (New York: Macmillan, 1896), pp. 53–56, pp. 57–60, and pp. 242–47.

comes Italy's greatest sculptor. Leland also retells the legend of "Venus and the Ring"; although he mentions Heine and Southey, his version is the translation of an Italian ballad that he reproduces in his text. Two points are of interest in our connection. First, the only respect in which Leland's version differs from the traditional legend is the fact that the young man hands the letter directly to Venus, as in Heine's recapitulation. Second, the straightforward poetic retelling of the legend is qualified by a clearly parodistic prefatory poem:

> There was a Spanish Bonifacius
> Who wrote of mortals loving statues;
> But an Italian changed the plan,
> And made a statue love a man,
> And come between him and his bride
> Till he was nearly petrified
> With fear. But soon a brave magician
> Did rescue him from this position,
> Where he in grief was wallowing,
> As you may read i' the following.

We reach the level of full-fledged travesty with *The Tinted Venus* (1885), a "farcical romance" by F. Anstey (pseud. for Thomas Anstey Guthrie), a staff-writer for *Punch* from 1887 to 1930.[78] Specific allusions in the text to Morris' *The Earthly Paradise* suggest that the author had in mind a specific butt for his parody. Anstey sets his novel among lower-middle-class Englishmen of his own time, but unlike Mérimée and Henry James he does not attempt to rationalize or internalize the magical elements: the goddess Venus actually animates a statue in late nineteenth-century London, and most of the humorous effects stem from the incongruity of that fact and the total lack of comprehension among the other characters, who have never heard of Aphrodite.

The basic plot is the familiar one. The hero, Leander Tweddle, is "a gentleman in the haircutting persuasion,"

[78] *The Tinted Venus: A Farcical Romance* (New York: Appleton, 1886).

who through a series of accidents happens to place the wedding ring intended for his fiancée on the finger of a statue in an amusement park. When he gets home that night, the statue shows up in his apartment and makes the traditional claim upon his affections. First he tries to dissuade her reasonably. "I don't mean it as any reproach to you, but you can't deny you're an Eathen, and, worse than that, an Eathen goddess. Now all my family have been brought up as chapel folk, Primitive Methodists, and I've been trained to have a horror of superstition and idolatries, and see the folly of it. So you can see for yourself that we shouldn't be likely to get on together." Since the goddess remains insistent, Leander tries another tack: he puts her in his barber shop so that she can see that he is not worthy of her divine affections. But this fails too: the goddess, profoundly impressed by his powers, considers Leander great amongst the sons of men. "Do you not compel them to furnish sport for you? Have I not seen them come in, talking boldly and loud, and yet seat themselves submissively at a sign from you? And do you not swathe them in the garb of humiliation, and daub their countenances with whiteness, and threaten their bared throats with the gleaming knife, and grind their heads under the resistless wheel? Then, having in disdain granted them their worthless lives, you set them free; and they propitiate you with a gift, and depart trembling."

The familiar plot is complicated and expanded by two additions. First, Leander tries to conceal everything from his fiancée and his friends. To this end he disguises the statue with a wig and make-up—hence the "tinted Venus"—so that no one will notice that a statue is pursuing him around the city. Second, there is a subplot involving criminals and a detective from Scotland Yard. It turns out that the statue animated by the goddess Venus is not a cheap plaster sculpture but a valuable Greek marble stolen by a gang of thieves and merely hidden for a time among the statues in the amusement park. In the end, Leander frees himself from the goddess by going to a modern necromancer, a chemist, under the pretence of having the gold in the wedding ring tested. As soon as Venus removes the ring, the statue again becomes inanimate. The relieved Leander deposits it secretly at Scotland Yard, returns to his patient bride, and with the reward money establishes a prosperous and fashionable hair-cutting salon in one of the leading West End thoroughfares.

Anstey's comic novel requires little comment. It is a clever adaptation of the medieval legend to modern circumstances purely in a spirit of fun. There are passing references to the implicit conflict between religions, as when the goddess is unable to call down the thunderbolt of Zeus upon the offending Leander and his bride. " 'You see, mum,' " he tells her, " 'You musn't expect to have everything your own way down here. We're in the nineteenth century nowadays, mum, and there's another religion come in since you were in fashion!' " But not a touch of seriousness is left to the image of the Venus-statue, which has become nothing but a vehicle for comedy in a farce in which the supernatural is taken completely for granted. Yet it is important to keep in mind one general principle: parody, if it is to be effective, requires among the audience a widespread familiarity with the subject being parodied; otherwise the parody is meaningless and ponderous. The very fact that the theme of Venus and the Ring is parodied in 1885, then, indicates that the subject is generally familiar to the anticipated audience.

Apparently with no knowledge of Anstey's work or his other literary predecessors, Anthony Burgess went directly to Burton's *The Anatomy of Melancholy* as the source for his comic novella, *The Eve of Saint Venus* (written 1950), which is set among the rural gentry of present-day England.[79] Basing his cast of characters on the comedies performed at the Aldwych Theater in London, Burgess set out to write, as he tells us in the Foreword to the American Edition (1970), "a novella constructed rather like one of the old Aldwych farces, with classical unity of time and setting, an ageless

[79] *The Eve of Saint Venus* (New York: Norton, 1970).

'county' atmosphere, a cast of stock characters"—set in the framework of the ancient story of Venus and the Ring.

In Burgess' novel the statue is neither a Roman bronze nor a Grecian marble, but a cheap clay figure fashioned by a Sicilian stonemason after the model of his pregnant daughter, for a pleasure garden in Syracuse. Along with others of the same sort it has come into the possession of Sir Benjamin Drayton, whose daughter Diana is to be married the following day to a young structural engineer—the embodiment of modern rationalism—named Ambrose Rutterkin. Again the plot is complicated by a subplot: at the last minute Diana, abetted by her friend Julia Webb, a lesbian journalist, refuses to go through with the wedding and sets out with Julia for the continent to pursue a career in art. Basically, however, the plot is the traditional one. Wandering in the garden with his friend and best man, Crowther-Mason, Ambrose practices for the wedding by putting the ring on a finger of the Venus and, as both young men declare, the finger closes over the ring. Frightened by this incident and shaken by the news that Diana is going away with Miss Webb, Ambrose returns to his hotel, where he gets drunk and goes to bed. Soon he is disturbed by a naked woman speaking Greek, who climbs into bed with him. When Ambrose later tells this story to the others, Sir Benjamin has a ready explanation: it must have been a Greek prostitute driven out of Soho by the new vice laws. But the vicar, a man who thinks about sin "with a kind of wistful nostalgia" and who hopes that Ambrose is really possessed by the devil, decides that an exorcism would be in order. He fetches books and equipment for it, and, as the ritual proceeds, the four men get drunker and drunker. Meanwhile, a frightful storm builds up outside, accompanied by what they take to be the sea-fragrance of Venus. (It turns out to be ozone.) After an hour a terrific bolt of lightning strikes a tree, which falls and shatters Sir Benjamin's sculptures, including the plaster Venus. Meanwhile, Diana returns, having decided that she wishes more masculine security and company than Miss Webb can provide. The farce ends happily as the wedding day dawns. At the last minute a pigeon flies up to the window with the lost wedding ring tied around its neck with a strand of hair.

Although the author leaves open the question of the supernatural, he provides a number of clues suggesting that the whole affair is an elaborate hoax engineered by Crowther-Mason, who has been fond of playing jokes on Ambrose ever since they were in school together. He was the only witness when the inebriated Ambrose was unable to remove the ring from the statue's finger. He could have bribed the Greek whore into Ambrose's bed. He is always prepared with comments and suggestions that stimulate the others: for instance, it is he who incites the vicar to perform the exorcism. However, it really does not matter very much since rationalization is not the point in a farce of this sort—any more than it was in *The Tinted Venus*. Here everything depends on drunkenness, the weather, and the madness of the zany Englishmen of the silly rural society at which Burgess is poking fun.

However, two points deserve to be mentioned. First, the vicar is a real caricature of Father Palumbus, half priest and half necromancer, who has been missing from treatments of the legend since early romanticism. This author of a monograph on *Sin and the Good Life* feels sorry for himself because there is no longer any good old-fashioned sin for him to deal with—only "the same old round of joyless fornications, mechanical slanders, malice clothed as self-righteousness." So the vicar is eager to believe in the presence of the evil spirit. Indeed, as he intones the exorcistic formulas of the *Rituale Romanum*, he keeps slipping unintentionally into the language of the pagan *Pervigilium Veneris* (thereby creating the syncretic Saint Venus of the title).

It is the vicar who suggests, while speculating on the origin of devils, that "the ancient gods never died. They joined the opposition when the new administration took over"—an updated statement of the venerable view concerning the demonization of the classical deities. Thereby the vicar brings into Burgess' farce the conflict between paganism and Christianity that has been inherent in the theme of Venus and the Ring since its inception. Burgess, however, gives the theme a twist reminiscent of Sacher-Masoch. In the Foreword he remarks that the deeper theme of his *jeu d'esprit* concerns the importance of physical love. That, more than paganism in any cultural sense, is what his Venus signifies. This idea is stated quite early in the novel. "People are scared of nakedness," Lady Drayton tells Sir Benjamin. " 'They'll be scared of those statues of yours. The English take their pleasures sadly.' " Much later Crowther-Mason—that *advocatus diaboli* or, in this case, *Veneris*—suggests in a spirit quite contrary to that of Henry James that the past is never discarded. " 'The past is made richer by the unfolding present. The gods are still alive . . . there's nothing malicious about this visitation. Why can't a goddess of love be a tangible aspect of the terrible, unknowable deity?' " The novel ends with a hymn to sensual love, in which all the figures join as in the concluding chorus of an opera. Ambrose and Diana, who had been on the point of entering rather mechanically into a *mariage de convenance* arranged in their childhood, are now suddenly awakened by the events of the "Eve of Saint Venus" (which constitutes a canonization of the pagan deity) to the pleasures of the senses. It is almost as though Mérimée had written a happy ending to "The Venus of Ille."[80]

[80] Burgess' farce and the entire theme of Venus and the Ring finds its homosexual parallel in E. M. Forster's story, "The Classical Annex" (written 1930–31), recently published in: E. M. Forster, *The Life to Come and Other Stories*, ed. Oliver Stallybrass (London: Edward Arnold, 1972), pp. 146–50. In Forster's story the curator of a municipal museum in the provinces discovers one afternoon that the statues in the classical annex have come to life. In particular, a poor Late Roman statue of an athlete or gladiator has developed an erection so prominent that his fig-leaf has been knocked off. Only by making the sign of the cross can the curator get the statues under control. On his way home, the curator considers the steps that must

IF WE now look back over eight centuries of the theme of Venus and the Ring, we see that the function of the image has in one sense remained remarkably constant: in every case the statue of Venus represents a subcurrent of pagan antiquity that has survived into, or been unearthed by, modern Christian civilization. The value of the image varies, of course, according to the context in which it occurs. In medieval times and down to German romanticism, the image occurred principally in a religious context, representing either pagan deities or satanic demons in opposition to Christianity; accordingly, the image carried a strong negative valence. Since romanticism the image can be found less frequently in a narrowly religious and more often in a generally cultural context: the statue of Venus embodies the power of primitive passion in contrast to the sterility of civilization. The image is viewed either positively or negatively depending on the standpoint of the writer. For Henry James and, less seriously, for F. Anstey, the statue represents a dangerous intrusion into the order of nineteenth-century society, a threat to order and civilization. For Heine, Mérimée, Sacher-Masoch, and Burgess, in contrast, the image of Venus represents a vigorous and welcome challenge to a bland and effete society. Needless to say, the physical appearance of the statue—whether seductive white marble, sinister dark bronze, or cheap plaster; whether standing in a dilapidated temple, buried in the earth, or decorating a pleasure garden—reflects in each case the attitude toward classical antiquity held by the society being portrayed (but not necessarily by the author, of course).

---

be taken to exorcise the "impish powers of darkness" that have taken over the statues. At home he learns that his football-playing son has gone to the museum to meet him—with a duplicate set of keys. Hastening back to the museum, the curator is dismayed to hear grunts and giggles coming from the classical annex. Making the sign of the cross, he flicks on the lights and discovers that his son, *in flagrante delicto*, has been frozen into a new work henceforth advertised as "a Hellenistic group called The Wrestling Lesson."

Even though the function of the image—always an antipode to the prevailing society, whether medieval or modern—has remained fairly constant, we have noted at least four pronounced stages in the process of its disenchantment. In the Middle Ages and down through the chronicles and handbooks of the Renaissance and Baroque the image is accepted quite matter-of-factly as magical. From William of Malmesbury to Robert Burton it is taken for granted that a statue might become animated in just such a manner as that described in the popular legend. This belief in the vivification of the statue for evil or pagan or satanic purposes is nothing but the mirror opposite of the widely accepted miracles of the Christian saints. During the late eighteenth and early nineteenth centuries this attitude changed. On the one hand, rationalism and common sense argued that statues do not come to life. On the other hand, romantic *Naturphilosophie* provided a theoretical justification for the animation of inanimate matter. Many writers of the period, content to accept magic as a useful literary convention, employed the theme of Venus and the Ring as a convenient metaphor to express the basic romantic belief in the unity of all being and the threat of the unconscious. Toward the end of the romantic period the balance between reason and convention begins to shift: Mérimée feels impelled to provide the means of rationalization, but he does not yet explicitly deny the possibility of the supernatural. With Sacher-Masoch and Henry James we reach a third stage of disenchantment: all the magic is internalized and transferred from the image into the mind of the observer. The statue no longer comes to life, even ambiguously: it is only in the wishful dreams of Severin and Camillo that the goddess seems to live. At this point, as we noted, the theme has been stripped of so many of its characteristic motifs—first the Wild Hunt, then the necromancer, and finally the ring itself—that it threatened to become unrecognizable. Although individual motifs make their way into horror fiction, it is only in parody or poetic fantasy that the full form of the theme can be resurrected. These four stages

—from acceptance of magic (either literally or conventionally) through rationalization and psychological internalization to parody and fantasy—provide a basic model for the disenchantment of images, which we can now test on the examples of the haunted portrait and the magic mirror.

CHAPTER THREE

Image as Motif: The Haunted Portrait

Horace Walpole's *The Castle of Otranto* (1764) opens with a succession of prodigies that would presumably have been regarded as stupendous even in the fanciful twelfth-century Italy that provides the setting for the novel.[1] Manfred, the prince of Otranto, is about to marry off his young and sickly son, Conrad, to Isabella, daughter of the marquis of Vicenza. The wedding party has already assembled in the chapel when a terrified servant rushes in to announce that a calamity has befallen the bridegroom. Hurrying out to the courtyard, Manfred finds "the bleeding mangled remains of the young prince" crushed beneath a colossal helmet. (This helmet is the first of a group of dismembered parts from which the gigantic specter of Alphonse the Good, the former ruler of the principality, reconstitutes itself at the end of the story.) Callously spurning the consolations of his wife and daughter, Manfred withdraws for a few hours of stormy meditation and then summons the bereft bride. Explaining that his fate depends on having sons and heirs, he announces his determination to divorce his barren wife, Hippolita, in order to marry Isabella himself. Isabella, appalled, warns him that "Heaven itself declares against your impious intentions!" But Manfred, seizing the princess, raves, "Heaven nor hell shall impede my designs!"

By this point the catalogue of abominations has reached

[1] *The Castle of Otranto*, rpt. in *Three Gothic Novels*, ed. E. F. Bleiler (New York: Dover, 1966), pp. 27–106. The quotations here are taken from Chap. 1.

such a pitch that "the portrait of his grandfather, which hung over the bench where they had been sitting, uttered a deep sigh, and heaved its breast." Startled by the sound, Isabella takes the opportunity to make her escape from the ranting prince. "Manfred, distracted between the flight of Isabella, who had now reached the stairs, and yet unable to keep his eyes from the picture, which began to move, had, however, advanced some steps after her, still looking backwards on the portrait, when he saw it quit its panel, and descend on the floor, with a grave and melancholy air." Uncertain whether he is dreaming or whether devils are in league against him, Manfred demands an explanation from the ancestral portrait; the apparition, sighing, simply signals to his descendant to follow. "The spectre marched sedately, but dejected, to the end of the gallery, and turned into a chamber on the right hand. Manfred accompanied him at a little distance, full of anxiety and horror, but resolved. As he would have entered the chamber, the door was clapped to with violence by an invisible hand."

It is not my aim to recapitulate further the twists of plot that, first threatening the innocent and then frustrating Manfred's sinister machinations, eventually unite fair Isabella with Theodore, the rightful heir to the Castle of Otranto. Nor do I intend to enumerate the visions, ghosts, bleeding statues, and other supernatural horrors that terrify the characters with rhythmic regularity. Instead, let us follow the portrait of Manfred's grandfather after it vanishes behind the heavy door. For although it disappears from the Castle of Otranto, never to reappear there, it stalks directly into the literature of the nineteenth century, where in a variety of guises the haunted portrait plays a significant role.

Like most of the preternatural trappings Walpole introduced into the Gothic romance, a genre that he created virtually single-handedly, the haunted portrait was not an original invention. Among many primitive peoples, drawings of the human figure—along with mirror images and shadows—

have a common quality: they are regarded as projections of the human soul.[2] The savage mind does not regard these images as being *like* the soul or as being *symbols* of the soul: they *are* the soul. Hence the fear among many primitive peoples of being photographed: they are afraid that their spirits or souls will be caught in the reproductions and taken away by the photographer. This archaic belief underlies superstitions regarding haunted portraits. For if the portrait is the receptacle of the soul, then the soul or spirit of the deceased might well continue to animate the portrait long after the original body has died.

Portraits that allegedly become animated or even emerge from their frames constitute one of the most frequent forms of mass hallucination. "Miracles" of this type occur especially in excited crowds, whose expectations produce the hallucination while the hallucination, in turn, confirms the belief. As a result, such delusions often manifest themselves in clusters, like the sighting of flying saucers. In 1919, hundreds of people in the province of Santander, Spain—including educated professionals—signed statements averring that they had observed various paintings of saints move or step out of their panels.[3] Many other apparitions of this sort have been recorded—not just during so-called "dark" ages but in our own enlightened twentieth century. In May 1914, William Butler Yeats made a pilgrimage with friends to Mirabeau, near Poitiers, to witness a picture of Christ that had begun to bleed. Yeats wrote a long (unpublished) account of the miracle, which he took to be authentic.[4]

Because the phenomenon of the allegedly animated por-

[2] See M. Weynants-Ronday, *Les Statues vivantes*, pp. 66–96 ("L'Ame-portrait"); and Ernst Kris and Otto Kurz, *Die Legende vom Künstler: Ein geschichtlicher Versuch* (Vienna: Krystall, 1934), pp. 77–87 ("Abbild als Zauber").

[3] D. H. Rawcliffe, *Illusions and Delusions of the Supernatural and the Occult* (1952; rpt. New York: Dover, 1959), pp. 112–14.

[4] Richard Ellmann, *Yeats: The Man and the Masks* (1948; rpt. New York: Dutton, 1958), p. 194.

trait is so widespread, it has had a considerable effect on popular literature from India and Persia to the American Indians.[5] In one of the most familiar Chinese folk tales, known in various versions throughout China down to the beginning of the nineteenth century, a poor man obtains the picture of a beautiful young woman, of whom he becomes enamored.[6] One day when he comes home, he is astonished to find his meal already prepared, a wonder that repeats itself on the following days. The mystery is solved when, returning unexpectedly early, he surprises the girl who has emerged from the picture in order to go about her work. Seizing her before she can reenter the scroll, he marries her and they live happily together for many years. Eventually the woman must return to the picture-world from which she was permitted to escape for a limited period.

There is no shortage of Christian legends concerning portraits of saints that come to life for one reason or another. Robert Southey's "The Pious Painter" (1798) is typical of the category.[7] The poem concerns a virtuous artist who specializes in painting the devil. On one occasion the painter is working on a fresco that depicts the Virgin standing triumphantly astride the devil. Appearing to him in a dream, the devil warns the painter to make him appear more satanically handsome. But the next day the painter, profiting from this opportunity to observe the devil at first hand, retouches the painting to make the fiend look even more loathsome.

[5] See Stith Thompson, *Motif-Index of Folk-Literature*, II, 42, and VI, 582; and *Handwörterbuch des deutschen Märchens*, ed. Lutz Mackensen (Berlin and Leipzig: De Gruyter, 1930–1933), I, 253–55 ("Bild").

[6] Wolfram Eberhard, *Typen chinesischer Volksmärchen*, Folklore Fellows Communications, 120 (Helsinki, 1937), pp. 61–62 ("Die Frau aus dem Bild").

[7] *The Complete Poetical Works* (New York: Appleton, 1851), pp. 448–49. In "Christmas Eve" (from *Evenings on a Farm near Dikanka*, 1831–32) Gogol relates a similar story, based on the Russian legend "The Blacksmith and the Devil."

Suddenly the devil materializes behind him and, in a rage, stamps on the scaffolding until it breaks, whereupon the painter falls from the great height:

> "Help—help! Blessed Mary!" he cried in alarm,
> As the scaffold sunk under his feet.
> From the canvass the Virgin extended her arm;
> She caught the good Painter; she saved him from
> harm:
> There were hundreds who saw in the street.

At the sight of this wonder the devil flees, and the Pious Painter vows henceforth to paint him "more ugly than ever."[8]

No book of "true" hauntings would be complete without a few legends of haunted portraits; in this respect the ancient chateaux of Europe can claim no precedence over the less venerable mansions of the United States. Howard Lodge at Sykesville, Maryland, displays an ancestral portrait that according to various witnesses allegedly changes its expression. "When she disapproves of someone she shows it. And every once in a while, if you glance at her rapidly, she is not the woman you now see in the portrait, but somebody else."[9] At Shirley, an estate in Charles City County, Virginia, one of the "Carter women" became upset when her portrait was removed and put in the attic. She created such a commotion —for instance, by rocking her chair in empty rooms—that the family was eventually driven to replace the painting where it had originally hung.[10] Few old communities in this country are unable to boast of similar cases.

[8] Life has a notorious tendency to imitate art. *The New York Times* for 6 January 1973 reported that "a painter slipped and fell 35 feet from scaffolding inside St. Patrick's Cathedral, but landed on an 8-foot-high reproduction of Michelangelo's Pièta and escaped serious injury. The painter . . . told police he thought the statue of the Virgin Mary holding the body of Jesus might have saved his life."

[9] Hans Holzer, *The Ghosts That Walk in Washington* (Garden City, N.Y.: Doubleday, 1971), pp. 181–82.

[10] Marguerite Du Pont Lee, *Virginia Ghosts*, rev. ed. (Berryville: Virginia Book Co., 1966), pp. 111–12.

Walpole was counting on common associations of this sort to induce the reading public to accept the supernatural effects in *The Castle of Otranto.*[11] In his Preface to the first edition he concedes that "Miracles, visions, necromancy, dreams, and other preternatural events, are exploded now even from romances." But circumstances were different when the fictitious author—allegedly a thirteenth-century Italian—set down his account. "Belief in every kind of prodigy was so established in those dark ages, that an author would not be faithful to the manners of the times, who should omit all mention of them. He is not bound to believe them himself, but he must represent his actors as believing them." Walpole's instinct concerning the public mood and its readiness to accept miracles and the supernatural was accurate to the point of being inspired.

The various reasons for the success of the Gothic romance have often been analyzed.[12] Intellectually and aesthetically it anticipated the gradual movement from neoclassical ideals of order and reason to the new romantic belief in emotion and the imagination. Philosophically it exploited the new appreciation of terror that Burke had recommended as a means

[11] Walpole was even willing to risk the anachronism of a portrait in the twelfth century. Art history knows no portraits of this sort at such an early date; and Walpole himself, in his *Anecdotes of Painting in England* (1762–80), lists no painters before the reign of Henry III.

[12] Dorothy Scarborough, *The Supernatural in Modern English Fiction* (New York and London: G. P. Putnam, 1917); Jakob Brauchli, *Der englische Schauerroman um 1800 unter Berücksichtigung der unbekannten Bücher: Ein Beitrag zur Geschichte der Volksliteratur*, Diss. Zürich 1928 (Weida: Thomas und Hubert, 1928), esp. pp. 159–81; Montague Summers, *The Gothic Quest: A History of the Gothic Novel* (London: Fortune, [1938]), esp. pp. 17–59; Devendra P. Varma, *The Gothic Flame, Being a History of the Gothic Novel in England* (London: Arthur Barker, 1957), esp. pp. 206–31; Lowrie Nelson, Jr., "Night Thoughts on the Gothic Novel," *Yale Review*, 52 (1962–63), 236–57; Robert D. Hume, "Gothic versus Romantic: A Revaluation of the Gothic Novel," *PMLA*, 84 (1969), 282–90.

toward the experience of the sublime, and it constituted a literary counterpart to Kant's *Critique of Pure Reason* (1781), which argued that there are limits to human understanding. Morally it marked a shift from faith in a simple dualism to a fascination with the more complex interrelatedness of good and evil. Politically it embodied the new sense of freedom that characterized the revolutionary age. Psychologically it signaled a turn from the portrayal of manners in an integrated society to the analysis of lonely, guilt-ridden outsiders. In literature it exemplified a longing for adventure and excitement in explicit departure from the moralizing and essentially conservative tone of sentimental-domestic novels after the fashion of Richardson and Goldsmith. In short, the Gothic romance stands out as one of the earliest and most conspicuous symptoms of the incipient reaction against the Enlightenment.

Up to this point in the eighteenth century the supernatural had been restricted almost wholly to subliterary genres like the popular ballad or the folk tale, which had no place in the formalized hierarchy of genres. It was Walpole's contribution to introduce the supernatural into the novel, a form that had remained totally realistic during the first half of the century.[13] However, the image of a portrait-figure that actually climbs down from its frame to patrol the lonely corridors of desolate castles or monasteries turned out to be too drastic even for a generation that loved to be titillated by the supernatural and that was willing to accept the notion of animated statues. Walpole's first prominent imitator, Clara Reeve, makes this objection abundantly clear in her Preface to the second edition of *The Old English Baron: A Gothic Story* (1778).[14] Mrs. Reeve argues that in *The Castle of*

[13] Edith Birkhead, *The Tale of Terror: A Study of the Gothic Romance* (New York: Russell and Russell, 1963), p. 12.

[14] *The Old English Baron: A Gothic Story*, ed. James Trainer (London: Oxford Univ. Press, 1967). The novel was first published in 1777 under the title *The Championship of Virtue*. Clara Reeve anticipates by one hundred and fifty years an identical objection by

Otranto "the machinery is so violent, that it destroys the effect it is intended to excite." The appearance of a ghost is perfectly permissible, she asserts, as are enchanted swords and helmets. But she explicitly excludes the walking portrait from "certain limits of credibility" that must be respected. "When your expectation is wound up to the highest pitch, these circumstances take it down with a witness, destroy the work of imagination, and, instead of attention, excite laughter." The urge to avoid such less credible miracles sometimes produced curious rationalizations. In Charles Maturin's *Melmoth the Wanderer* (1820), the walking portrait that the young hero thinks he sees several times turns out to be nothing but his seventeenth-century ancestor who has been kept alive for a century and a half by his pact with "the enemy of souls." Reason prevails.

On the one hand, the age shared the new urge to be excited by such manifestations of the supernatural as haunted portraits. On the other hand, "reason" suggested that these magical phenomena were in the last analysis incredible. Accordingly, in many examples of the genre—e.g., the Gothic romances of Ann Radcliffe—every seemingly supernatural occurrence is explained rationally before the end of the novel. In its principle of *surnaturel expliqué* the Gothic romance is perhaps the most representative literary form of a schizophrenic century radically polarized into Reason and the Irrational, into Voltaire and Cagliostro. Walpole himself had provided a model in *The Castle of Otranto.* Throughout the novel people are terrified when they encounter what seems to be the walking portrait of Alphonse, an earlier prince of the castle; but it turns out eventually to be Theodore, his look-alike descendant and the rightful heir to the

---

another practitioner of the genre, Edith Wharton. In her essay "Telling a Short Story" (from *The Writing of Fiction*, 1925) Wharton writes: "Many a would-be tale of horror becomes innocuous through the very multiplication and variety of its horrors." Rpt. in *The Collected Short Stories of Edith Wharton*, ed. R.W.B. Lewis (New York: Scribner, 1968), p. xxxiii.

castle. Although Matthew Lewis, in *The Monk* (1796), does not hesitate to make use of other forms of the supernatural—e.g., the appearance of the devil—he stops short of pictures that become animated. However, a rationalized walking portrait is involved in an important episode of this Gothic classic. At the beginning the highly revered (but secretly vain and arrogant) abbot Ambrosio has been infatuated for two years with a painting of the Virgin, "the object of his increasing wonder and admiration." It turns out that the model for this lovely madonna was none other than the corrupt temptress Mathilda de Villanegas, who employed that device to inflame the once virtuous monk for her charms and to win his soul for the devil.

Virtually no Gothic romance is complete without a similar case of mistaken identity based upon an uncanny resemblance between a portrait and a living figure, whose appearance is first thought to be a walking portrait.[15] The anonymous thriller *The Wandering Spirit, or Memoirs of the House of Morno* (London, 1801) revolves entirely around a mysterious portrait and the subsequent confusions of identity. E.T.A. Hoffmann, Lewis' chief German emulator, used this device in several of his works, including his novel *The Devil's Elixirs* (1816), which was profoundly influenced by *The Monk.* In another of Hoffmann's tales, "Arthur's Court" (1815; the title refers to the name of the merchants' guildhall—and subsequently the stock exchange—in Danzig) the hero falls in love with the portrait of a young woman in medieval German dress.[16] He tries to track down the original, only to be told that the model was the artist's own daughter, who had died some time earlier. He is startled, therefore,

[15] William W. Watt, *Shilling Shockers of the Gothic School: A Study of Chapbook Gothic Romances* (Cambridge, Mass.: Harvard Univ. Press, 1932), p. 26, cites the animated portrait as "first by reason of seniority" among the requisites of the genre. "More often the 'animation' consists of an optical illusion caused by the troubled state of the heroine's mind."

[16] "Der Artushof," in Hoffmann's story-cycle *The Serapion Brethren* (1819–21).

when he encounters her face to face one day. The artist promptly flees with his daughter, and by the time the hero catches up with her again she has married the public prosecutor in a nearby town. The mystery of the walking portrait is resolved; but Hoffmann gives the motif a characteristically romantic twist. The hero realizes that, though he has lost the living model, his ideal continues to exist in the realm of art. Ideal beauty has nothing to do with the mortal woman who married the philistine Prosecutor Mathesius in Marienwerder.[17] Later in the century this preference for Art over Life, for the portrait over the original, turns out to have serious, indeed, often mortal, consequences.

The rationalization is not always limited to cases of mistaken identity. In one of the fantastic tales of Jan Potocki's modern Decameron, *Le Manuscrit trouvé à Saragosse* (1804–05), a Maltese knight kills another man in a duel.[18] When he returns the victim's sword to his ancestral estate in France, a portrait of an ancestor, the comte d'Angoulême, comes out of its frame and wounds the knight in a duel. Since there is no blood, the incident is explained as an illusion. But for the rest of his life the knight is unaccountably plagued by a recurrent nightmare on the same night of every week. In all these cases the characters within the fiction are confronted with what seems, at first glance, to be a walking portrait. But the seemingly supernatural occurrence is ration-

[17] Peter von Matt, *Die Augen der Automaten: E.T.A. Hoffmanns Imaginationslehre als Prinzip seiner Erzählkunst* (Tübingen: Niemeyer, 1971), p. 66, describes this as the typical sequence of Hoffmann's tales: the hero encounters a picture and succumbs to its magic; the picture comes to life in the form of a living girl whom he pursues and desires; at a crucial moment, however, he transforms her in his imagination back into an image—not of transitory human existence but of an ideal existing eternally in his imagination.

[18] *The Saragossa Manuscript: A Collection of Weird Tales*, ed. by Roger Caillois and trans. from the French by Elisabeth Abbott (New York: Orion, 1960), pp. 206–15. This tale was adapted and appreciably expanded by Washington Irving under the title "The Grand Prior of Minorca" (or "The Knight of Malta") in *Wolfert's Roost and Other Papers* (New York: G. P. Putnam, 1855), pp. 132–50.

alized away with the eventual realization that they are dealing with the original of the portrait, with a descendant who is identical in appearance, or with a vision. By means of rationalization the audience is able to eat their cake and have it too: their irrational needs are gratified by the chill of terror produced by a haunted portrait, yet their reason is consoled by the knowledge that, in the last analysis, everything happens according to the laws of nature.

THE Gothic romance reached its peak of popularity between 1795 and 1805, but the reaction set in during the same decade—a reaction that undermined the genre by the most effective of means, humor.[19] Jane Austen began writing her parody, *Northanger Abbey* (1818), as early as 1798. Within fifteen years the most famous of the parodies, Eaton Stannard Barrett's *The Heroine, or The Adventures of Cherubina* (1813), signaled the decline of the form. Inevitably, these parodies of the Gothic romance were soon enough turned against one of its most characteristic motifs: the haunted portrait. At the end of one of the anonymous "bluebooks" or "shilling shockers," in which the more literary Gothic romances were reduced to a style and length appropriate to the most unsophisticated audiences, there is a one-page fragment entitled "Mary."[20] The hero, Henry, is sitting in a chamber of his castle, gazing at the portrait of his dead love, Mary. Suddenly "the eyes of the portrait moved; the features, from an angelic smile, changed to a look of solemn sadness; a tear of sorrow stole down each cheek, and the bosom palpitated as with sighing." Then the clock strikes one—three times! Henry is horror-stricken when the figure of Mary appears in a shroud, beckoning to him and touching him with her icy hand. At that moment he wakes up to realize that he is—back in his master's kitchen, where the

[19] Varma, *The Gothic Flame*, pp. 173–205, discusses the decline of the genre around 1800 and the many parodies that were produced.

[20] "Mary, A Fragment," *Gothic Stories* (London, 1800), p. 48.

dog is nuzzling him with its cold nose. E.T.A. Hoffmann was also capable of using the walking portrait for humorous effects. In his "Fragment from the Life of a Fantast" (1820) the hero reports that his mother was tutored by the life-sized portrait of a beautiful woman, who emerged from her frame to teach his mother modern Greek and who, when she appeared at the tea-table, was regarded as being the French governess.

The first part of Washington Irving's *Tales of a Traveller* (1824) amounts to an elaborate parody of the Gothic romance in general and of haunted portraits in particular. The "Strange Stories by a Nervous Gentleman" that open the volume are recounted by a group of English gentlemen after a hunt-dinner given by a fox-hunting baronet in his ancient manor.[21] The events of the first tale—"The Adventures of My Uncle"—take place in a chateau in Normandy some years before the French Revolution. The uncle, spending the night in the tower room of the chateau, is awakened at midnight by the white-clad figure of a woman who enters his chamber, spends some time warming herself before the fire, and then—after "glassy looks" and supplications to heaven—glides slowly out again. The next morning in the picture gallery the uncle notices a full-length portrait of his nocturnal visitor. The host points out that the lady, the Duchess de Longueville, has been dead for more than a century. Prodded by the curious uncle, he begins to tell a remarkable story about the duchess, who played an important role in the wars of the Fronde. On one occasion, when she was occupying the apartment in which her apparition appeared, "a mysterious, inexplicable occurrence" is said to have taken place. At this point the host insists that they change the subject, hinting that there are circumstances connected with his family history that he does not like to relate. With this huge anticlimax, which clearly parodies the rationalizing Gothic romances, the story ends:

[21] *Works*, Hudson Edition (New York: Putnam, 1884), X, 19–139.

". . . and what did your uncle say then?"
"Nothing," replied the other.
"And what did the Marquis say farther?"
"Nothing."
"And is that all?"
"That is all," said the narrator, filling a glass of wine.

This story elicits from another member of the company "The Adventure of My Aunt," which also turns out to be a parody of the haunted portrait. Moreover, the entire collection of "Strange Stories by a Nervous Gentleman" is embraced by a framework involving a haunted portrait. The narrator, upon retiring that night, is so agitated by the various tales and so disturbed by the "baleful presence" of a mysterious picture in his room that he is unable to sleep. The next day the baronet tells the tale of "The Young Italian" in order to explain the effect of the picture. A painter murders his best friend, who has betrayed him in a love affair. Persecuted by the phantom of the slain man, he attempts to exorcise it by painting it, but he succeeds only in doubling his misery. Finally, after he has made atonement in the church, he surrenders himself to justice for the murder of his friend. On the surface this story seems to be a rather straightforward imitation of tales about haunted portraits with no attempt at parody: the portrait inspires the viewer with terror because the soul of the murdered man has somehow been ensnared in it. The baronet, moved by the pleas of his guests, consents to permit the others to view the mysterious portrait, one by one. "They all returned varying in their stories: some affected in one way, some in another; some more, some less; but all agreeing that there was a certain something about the painting that had a very odd effect upon the feelings." The narrator begins to speculate on the mysteries of human nature. "Who can account for so many persons of different characters being thus strangely affected by a mere painting." But the story ends with a parodistic twist. It turns out that the roguish host had instructed the housekeeper to show the guests an entirely innocuous portrait in a different room. In other words, stimulated by the collective hallucination, each guest responds not to the reality of the painting, but to the proddings of his own imagination and expectations. Thus Irving's Yankee humor disposes of the blatantly supernatural haunted portrait of legend and popular romance.

Although Washington Irving parodies the haunted portrait repeatedly and at notable length, he is merely one among many writers of the twenties and thirties who, in a reaction against the Gothic romance, refer jestingly to the phenomenon for purely comical effect. In "The Coffee-pot" (1831), one of his *Contes humoristiques*, Gautier invokes the same tradition.[22] The narrator of his tale, again in the course of a visit in Normandy, is witness one night when the oldest of the forefathers steps out of his portrait and unlocks the other frames in the picture gallery. All the ancestors come out, drink coffee, and dance to the music provided by the Italian orchestra woven in the tapestry. The narrator himself dances with one of the figures, who is called Angela. At dawn all the figures disappear back into their frames. The narrator learns that Angela was the sister of his host: she died two years earlier from a seizure following a dance of precisely the sort that the narrator had witnessed.

The same Mérimée who in "The Venus of Ille" used the theme of the animated statue for serious purposes was capable of exploiting the motif of haunted portraits for purely humorous effect in "The *Viccolo* of Madama Lucrezia" (1846).[23] The narrator, studying a portrait of Lucrezia Borgia by Leonardo, exclaims that the depiction is so verisimilar that the eyelids seem to move. Thereupon one of the ladies in the company, a German, begins to tremble and

[22] "La Cafetière," in Théophile Gautier, *Oeuvres* (Paris: Charpentier, 1883), XVI, 249–61.

[23] "Il Viccolo di Madama Lucrezia," in *Romans et Nouvelles*, ed. Maurice Parturier (Paris: Garnier, 1967), II, 521–45; here pp. 526–28.

relates the story of her sister-in-law, Wilhelmina. When Wilhelmina's fiancé went off to war in 1813, he presented her with his portrait, which she kept on a little table. One day, uttering a terrible cry, Wilhelmina fell over in a faint. Upon awaking she insisted that she had seen the portrait close its eyes; at the same moment she had felt a sharp pain as though a searing iron had pierced her heart. It turns out that Julius was killed that day, and the bullet that pierced his heart also shattered the portrait of Wilhelmina that he wore upon his chest. This anecdote of extrasensory perception can be matched by countless tales of a similar sort from the twentieth century, of course. But in this case the narrator's tone completely disqualifies any serious implications, suggesting that this sort of thing might happen in a semi-barbaric land like Germany but not in a civilized country like France. The tale begins with the narrator's apology that he is "very sorry to have to repeat so many barbarous names, but extraordinary stories happen only to people whose names are difficult to pronounce." At the end it turns out that Wilhelmina, far from languishing in tragic grief, is now happily married to a barrister. "If you went to Dessau, she would show you Julius's portrait."

Probably no American writer comes closer to Mérimée's curious ambivalence regarding the supernatural than his contemporary, Hawthorne, who makes frequent and profound use of haunted portraits in a number of his finest works. At the same time, he employs the motif at least once for an effect that is purely comical. The description of the study in "Dr. Heidegger's Experiment" (1837) sounds suspiciously like the scenario for a slapstick comedy:

> The greatest curiosity of the study remains to be mentioned; it was a ponderous folio volume, bound in black leather, with massive silver clasps. There were no letters on the back, and nobody could tell the title of the book. But it was well known to be a book of magic; and once, when a chambermaid had lifted it, merely to brush away

> the dust, the skeleton had rattled in its closet, the picture of the young lady had stepped one foot upon the floor, and several ghastly faces had peeped forth from the mirror; while the brazen head of Hippocrates frowned, and said—"Forbear!"[24]

Parodies of the Gothic romance continued down at least to Gilbert and Sullivan. In *Ruddigore, or The Witch's Curse* (1887) the descendants of Sir Rupert Murgatroyd have been cursed because of his ruthless persecution of witches.

> Each Lord of Ruddigore,
> Despite his best endeavour,
> Shall do one crime, or more,
> Once, every day, for ever![25]

When Sir Ruthven Murgatroyd tries to evade the family curse by assuming a disguise and a false name, all the portraits in the ancestral gallery come down from their frames to admonish him in a rousing chorus.

During the first third of the nineteenth century, in sum, the image of the haunted portrait was thoroughly disenchanted through the dual effects of rationalization and parody. But several points need to be made. First, parody always presupposes in its audience a widespread familiarity with the subject being parodied. The many parodies of haunted portraits that we have noted, therefore, can be taken as a symptom of continued interest in the image. Second, the phenomenon of rationalization must also be interpreted. If reason had been sufficiently offended, the simplest solution would have been

[24] From *Twice-Told Tales*; cited from *Twice-Told Tales and Other Short Stories*. With an Introduction by Quentin Anderson (New York: Washington Square Press, 1960), p. 167. In another tale from the second collection of *Twice-Told Tales* (1842), "Edward Randolph's Portrait," a "stifled whisper" goes about the town that the portrait says "Forbear!" to Lieutenant-Governor Hutchinson when he is on the point of ordering British troops to land in Boston (p. 204).

[25] *Plays and Poems of W. S. Gilbert*. With a Preface by Deems Taylor (New York: Random House, 1932), pp. 401–57; here p. 405.

to discard the image of the haunted portrait altogether. But this did not happen. The fact that the seemingly haunted portrait became one of the characteristic requisites of the rationalizing Gothic romances suggests the inherent appeal of the image.[26]

To be sure, the portrait in the later Gothic novels does not usually climb down from its frame and walk around; the sense of animation often resides in the painted eyes. Yet those eyes alone suffice to inspire terror, as in *Melmoth the Wanderer*, which is dominated by the portrait of an ancestor who died a century and a half earlier. "There was nothing remarkable in the costume, or in the countenance, but *the eyes*, John felt, were such as one feels they wish they had never seen, and feels they can never forget."[27] On a more sophisticated level we recognize here the archaic belief that the portrait becomes the asylum of the human spirit, and its "haunting" or "animation" is implied by the lifelike quality of the eyes. This phenomenon, as we shall see, obsesses many post-romantic writers; but the sensation is precisely the same universal one that still today can cause small boys to strike up a brave whistle as they hurry at night past a house in which such a portrait with "moving eyes" is known to hang.

Finally, despite all the rationalizations and parodies, the image of the haunted portrait remained so lively and pervasive that it did not disappear from later nineteenth-century literature.[28] In fact, the conspicuous resurgence of the image

[26] Eino Railo, *The Haunted Castle: A Study of the Elements of English Romanticism* (London and New York: Dutton, 1927), pp. 304–07: "From the very beginnings of terror-romanticism [the portrait] exercised a special fascination upon authors; it is to them not merely an inanimate object, but in some enigmatical way an animated being, like the picture in *The Castle of Otranto*" (p. 305).

[27] Charles Robert Maturin, *Melmoth the Wanderer*. Introduction by William F. Axton (Lincoln: Univ. of Nebraska Press, 1961), p. 13 (Chap. 1).

[28] In the form of the *tableau vivant* it even made its way into performing arts, especially after the publication of Goethe's novel *Elective Affinities* (1809), which describes the mechanics of the art in

in the 1830's suggests that the parodies were necessary to purify the image of its ridiculously exaggerated characteristics and to render it suitable for serious literary purposes. Since the haunted portrait—unlike Venus and the Ring—is a motif and not a theme, the image does not ordinarily dominate the entire work. It usually occurs, as in the examples already cited, as the leading motif in a single episode or chapter. Only occasionally is the motif allowed to expand into the dominant theme of the entire work. The fictions in which the motif occurs can of course vary immensely in theme, structure, and meaning. Above all, the treatment of the image varies according to the fictional mode in which it appears: romance, ghost story, psychological novel, humorous inversion, and so forth.

Depending on the aspect that is emphasized, we can provisionally distinguish three main categories of haunted portraits. To the extent that the portrait is tied to a specific place, we can speak of it as the *genius loci*. To the extent that a portrait painted in the past foreshadows present or future events, we can speak of it as *figura*. To the extent that a portrait painted in the fictional present stands in a magical relationship to its model, we can speak of it as *anima*. These categories are not always sharply distinct; but for the purposes of discussion it seems useful to take up our examples according to their principal aspect.

THE portrait as *genius loci* is the dominant category in the Gothic romance: we have already mentioned the ancestral portraits in *The Castle of Otranto* and *Melmoth the Wanderer*, the first and last major works of the genre. This portrait,

---

considerable detail and incorporates the performance of three such *tableaux*—after paintings by Van Dyck, Poussin, and Terborch—skillfully into the plot. Goethe comments specifically on the eerie sensation aroused in the spectators by the confusion of reality and illusion, precisely the attitude of ambivalence that underlies the obsession with haunted portraits. See Kirsten Gram Holmström, *Monodrama, Attitudes, Tableaux*, pp. 209–33.

representing the usually malevolent brooding presence of the house or family, made an easy transition from the Gothic romance to the classic ghost stories of the nineteenth century.

The appeal of such ghostly happenings is evident in the works of Sir Walter Scott, who discussed the leading Gothic romancers in his *Lives of Eminent Novelists and Dramatists* (1821–24). Scott began his career with the traditional Scottish respect for the supernatural, a respect only partly qualified by the ambivalent rationalism of his later *Letters on Demonology and Witchcraft* (1830).[29] In his novel *The Antiquary* (1816) the hero has a vision (Ch. x) in which the figures of a tapestry become animated; one of them even steps out of the tapestry and approaches the bed. Although Scott declares that he will not "impugn the doctrine" of any who suppose that the occurrence was "an impression conveyed rather by the eye than by the imagination," he nevertheless makes it clear that he understands the scene as a vision.[30] Only twelve years later, in "The Tapestried Chamber, or the Lady in the Sacque" (1828), he tells a stóry in which a walking portrait plays a role that is presented as frankly supernatural.[31] In the introduction of 1831 Scott apologizes, "There are hours and moods when most people are not displeased to listen to such things; and I have heard some of the greatest and wisest of my contemporaries take their share in telling them."

According to Scott's tale, which he had heard twenty years earlier from Miss Anna Seward, a certain General Browne had business in the western counties of England in the

[29] Coleman O. Parsons, *Witchcraft and Demonology in Scott's Fiction* (Edinburgh and London: Oliver & Boyd, 1964), pp. 7–15.

[30] In Poe's early tale, "Metzengerstein" (1832), there is also an animated tapestry. But Poe does not rationalize the supernatural as being a vision: the great steed actually emerges into reality, leaving a hole in the tapestry.

[31] *Castle Dangerous. Chronicles of the Canongate*, Standard Edition (Boston: Dana Estes, 1894), pp. 297–321. For a discussion of Scott's revisions see Parsons, *Witchcraft and Demonology*, pp. 129–31.

late eighteenth century. Finding himself in the neighborhood of Woodville Castle, the general decided to spend a few days with his old friend Lord Woodville, who was entertaining a group of hunting friends. (There are several noteworthy parallels between this story and Irving's "Strange Stories of a Nervous Gentleman.") He is put into a room called "the Tapestried Chamber," but the next morning he is so distraught that he announces his intention of departing immediately. At night, it seems, he sensed a strange presence in his room: a woman in an old-fashioned gown (a sacque) with a diabolical countenance that revealed "traces of the vilest and most hideous passions which had animated her while she lived." Lord Woodville confides that the general's experience confirms the rumor that the room is haunted, and he declares his intention of sealing it up. Before the general's departure they go for an inspection of the portrait gallery. Suddenly the general starts with fear when he recognizes the likeness of the lady who had appeared in his room the night before. His friend tells him that it is "a wretched ancestress . . . of whose crimes a black and fearful catalogue is recorded" and that "in yon fatal apartment incest and unnatural murder were committed." The complete absence of any real plot in the story suggests that Scott was content in this case merely to conjure up the horror of the supernatural by means of the walking portrait. At the same time, it is perfectly possible to assume that the general's vision was precipitated by an earlier glimpse of the striking portrait.

The Victorians were great fans and producers of ghost stories.[32] It is hardly surprising that the motif of the haunted portrait with the lifelike eyes should show up repeatedly in their tales of the supernatural. Not unexpectedly, the motif provides the focal point for one of the best-known stories by

[32] See Montague Summers' Introduction to his edition of *Victorian Ghost Stories* (London: Fortune, 1933), pp. ix–xlv; and H. P. Lovecraft, "Supernatural Horror in Literature" (1927); rpt. *Dagon and Other Macabre Tales*, ed. August Derleth (Sauk City, Wisc.: Arkham House, 1965), pp. 347–413.

the man who has been called "the Master of Horror and the Mysterious." In Le Fanu's "An Account of Some Strange Disturbances in Aungier Street" (1853) two medical students take up residence in a Dublin mansion that is rumored to be haunted by a "hanging judge," who committed suicide by hanging himself with a child's jump-rope over the bannisters of the house.[33] His ghost first appears to one of the young men in the form of repeated nightmares. Then it enters the house in the shape of a monstrous gray rat: "I felt it then, and know it now, the infernal gaze and the accursed countenance of my old friend in the portrait, transfused into the visage of the bloated vermin before me." Finally, the judge from the portrait actually appears before the second young man in a vision, holding a rope that is looped by one end around his neck and threatening to hang the young man with the other end. It is only after the young men flee the house in terror that they learn of the violent deaths suffered by previous tenants. The house itself is burned to the ground two years later.

Le Fanu's story presents an atmosphere rather than a plot. Sixty years later a second master of horror, the author of *Dracula*, adapted Le Fanu's elements in a much more intense tale of terror. In "The Judge's House" (1914) Bram Stoker reduces the number of heroes to one—here a mathematician rather than a medical student.[34] Otherwise, almost to the end, his story follows essentially the same line. Again we find the portrait of a notorious hanging judge, taken in the very room in which it now hangs; and the bell-rope suspended from the ceiling is the same gallows rope that served

[33] Joseph Sheridan Le Fanu, *Best Ghost Stories*, ed. E. F. Bleiler (New York: Dover, 1964), pp. 361–79. Le Fanu also used the motif of a house haunted by a hanging judge who committed suicide in "Mr. Justice Harbottle" (from *In a Glass Darkly*, 1872), but here there is no portrait as the *genius loci.*

[34] The story appeared originally in Stoker's *Dracula's Guest* (London: Routledge, 1914); it has been reprinted in *The Bram Stoker Bedside Companion*, ed. Charles Osborne (London: Victor Gollancz, 1973), pp. 56–75.

the judge on many occasions. The rat, which disturbs the hero by scurrying up and down the judge's rope, has its hole behind the judge's portrait. Becoming increasingly bold, the rat finally ventures into the room. "There, in the Judge's arm-chair, with the rope hanging behind, sat the rat with the Judge's baleful eyes, now intensified and with a fiendish leer." The rat can be driven away only when the student hurls his Bible at it. Finally the inevitable happens: the Judge himself steps down from his portrait frame and approaches the young man with the gallows rope dangling in his hand. But in Bram Stoker's version the hero does not escape. When the neighbors reach the house, alerted by the ringing of the alarm bell, "There at the end of the rope of the great alarm bell hung the body of the student, and on the face of the Judge in the picture was a malignant smile."

The same familiar pattern of the portrait as malevolent *genius loci*, characterized particularly by the light of animation in its eyes, shows up in Bulwer Lytton's story, *The Haunted and the Haunters; or, The House and the Brain* (1859).[35] Bulwer Lytton tried to rationalize his tale according to the principles of mesmerism and animal magnetism, which he used to such effect in his subsequent novel, *A Strange Story* (1862). Here the hero, with his servant and his dog, decides to investigate a house reputedly haunted by a dark shadow with "malignant, serpent eyes" whose presence is announced by chills of extreme frigidity. The servant is soon frightened away, and the dog dies of terror. But the narrator finally determines that the house is indeed haunted by the brain or consciousness of an eighteenth-century charlatan—someone like Cagliostro—who had set up in a hidden chamber various pieces of magical-electrical equipment that extended the impulses of his fiendish will. The wizard himself is represented in the secret room by his portrait. "It was a remarkable face—a most impressive face. If you could fancy some mighty serpent transformed into man, preserving

[35] *A Strange Story; and The Haunted and the Haunters* (Philadelphia: Lippincott, 1888).

in the human lineaments the old serpent type, you would have a better idea of that countenance than long descriptions can convey; the width and flatness of frontal—the tapering elegance of contour disguising the strength of the deadly jaw—the long, large, terrible eyes, glittering and green as the emerald—and withal a certain ruthless calm, as if from the consciousness of an immense power."

It is against this background of the Gothic romance and the contemporary horror story that we can best appreciate Hawthorne's achievement in *The House of the Seven Gables* (1851), where the motif of the haunted portrait as *genius loci* is sublimated into literary form. Hawthorne was an ardent fan of Lewis' *The Monk* and Maturin's *Melmoth the Wanderer.*[36] In his first novel, *Fanshawe,* one of the main characters is named Dr. Melmoth, and several quotations are borrowed from Maturin's romance. It is no surprise, then, to find that *The House of the Seven Gables* amounts to an adaptation of the Gothic romance to American circumstances. In addition, the second half of the nineteenth century witnessed in the United States a remarkable surge of interest in ghosts, mediums, spiritualism, and the occult. Hawthorne was the first important American writer to make serious literary use of this vogue.[37] Finally, although—or perhaps precisely because—his knowledge of painting was limited and parochial, he tended to regard the artist as "a worker of illicit black magic" and the work of art as a symbol of evil.[38] In the Gothic romance, whose trappings he revaluated for essentially moral purposes, Hawthorne found the image of an art-object, the haunted portrait, that lent itself perfectly to his intentions.

[36] Jane Lundblad, *Nathaniel Hawthorne and European Literary Tradition* (Cambridge, Mass.: Harvard Univ. Press, 1947), p. 87 and *passim.*

[37] Howard Kerr, *Mediums, and Spirit-Rappers, and Roaring Radicals: Spiritualism in American Literature, 1850–1900* (Urbana: Univ. of Illinois Press, 1972), esp. pp. 55–81.

[38] Millicent Bell, *Hawthorne's View of the Artist* (Albany: State Univ. of New York, 1962), p. 58.

In the Preface he explains that he called his work a romance rather than a novel in order to assume a certain fictional "latitude" that he would not have enjoyed otherwise.[39] "He will be wise, no doubt, to make a very moderate use of the privileges here stated, and, especially, to mingle the Marvellous rather as a slight, delicate, and evanescent flavor, than as any portion of the actual substance of the dish offered to the public." It is possible to draw detailed parallels between Hawthorne's romance and the genre upon which it is based: from the haunted castle that provides the model for the house with its history of usurpation (as in *The Castle of Otranto*) to Phoebe Pyncheon, the fair young heroine whose appearance catalyzes the action (as in Gothic romances from Ann Radcliffe to Victoria Holt). It is no accident that images of magic and witchcraft occur throughout the text. On one occasion we even find a conventional rationalization of the haunted portrait when Phoebe, seeing Judge Pyncheon for the first time, takes him to be the walking portrait of his ancestor.

But we shall limit our analysis to the function of the portrait as *genius loci*. The gabled house of the title was built around the middle of the seventeenth century by the original Colonel Pyncheon on land that he had usurped from Matthew Maule, a man rumored to be a wizard and executed for witchcraft. On the day of its "consecration," however, Colonel Pyncheon died at his desk—allegedly from Maule's dying curse. Ever since, Pyncheon's portrait has hung on the wall of the room in which he expired. "Those stern, immitigable features seemed to symbolize an evil influence, and so darkly to mingle the shadow of their presence with the sunshine of the passing hour, that no good thoughts or purposes could ever spring up and blossom there. To the thoughtful mind there will be no tinge of superstition in what we figuratively express, by affirming that the ghost of a dead progenitor

[39] *The Complete Novels and Selected Tales of Nathaniel Hawthorne*, ed. Norman Holmes Pearson (New York: Modern Library, 1965), p. 243.

—perhaps as a portion of his own punishment—is often doomed to become the Evil Genius of his family" (Ch. 1).

However that may be, the family goes into a steady decline. At the beginning of the novel the only inhabitants of the gloomy old house are the spinster Hepzibah Pyncheon, her half-mad brother Clifford, their country cousin Phoebe, and their tenant, the daguerreotypist Holgrave. Hepzibah feels "a reverence for the pictured visage, of which only a far-descended and time-stricken virgin could be susceptible" (Ch. 2). Whenever she looks at the portrait, she trembles under its baleful gaze. Her brother, with the delicate insight associated with introspection, is less tolerant of "that odious picture," which he identifies as "the evil genius of the house" (Ch. 7). In his tirade against property and real estate (Ch. 17) Clifford remarks with bitter irony that a man "lays his own dead corpse beneath the underpinning, as one may say, and hangs his frowning picture on the wall, and, after thus converting himself into an evil destiny, expects his remotest great-grandchildren to be happy there!" At the end of the novel it is revealed that the portrait did indeed have a hand in the twist of fortune that befell the family two centuries earlier. The Pyncheon fortune began to decline after Colonel Pyncheon's sudden death when the heirs were unable to locate a deed entitling them to a vast tract of land in the state of Maine. Clifford, haunted by the ancient portrait, vaguely recalls a vision from his childhood. "I could fancy that, when I was a child, or a youth, that portrait had spoken, and told me a rich secret, or had held forth its hand, with the written record of hidden opulence" (Ch. 21). Holgrave examines the frame and discovers a secret spring that reveals a recess in the wall, where they find a folded sheet of parchment, the legendary deed to the huge tract, which is now of course worthless. So Matthew Maule has finally exacted his revenge for Colonel Pyncheon's usurpation of his land. But the story ends happily rather than tragically in this inverted Gothic romance. It turns out that Holgrave is the descendant of Matthew Maule; he marries Phoebe, thus uniting finally the two hostile families.

In the main plot of *The House of the Seven Gables* the motif of the haunted portrait has been sublimated into an effect that is more poetic and ambivalent than the often crass rationalizations of the Gothic romances upon which it was based. To be sure, the active intercession of the portrait is justified on perfectly rational grounds. But Hawthorne has brilliantly heightened the effect by interpolating, within the novel, two episodes in which the portrait is actually said to come alive and walk. At one point (Ch. 13) Holgrave reads to Phoebe an account he has written of the early history of their two families. "The wild, chimney-corner legend" that Holgrave claims to follow attributes "some very strange behavior" to Colonel Pyncheon's portrait, which was reputed to be "so intimately connected with the fate of the house, and so magically built into its walls, that, if once it should be removed, that very instant the whole edifice would come thundering down in a heap of dusty ruin." (This turns out to be a figurative if not a literal anticipation of what actually happens since the family finally leaves the "ruinous" old house.) During an interview between Pyncheon's descendant and the descendant of that Matthew Maule from whom he had usurped the property, the legend records, "the portrait had been frowning, clenching its fist, and giving many such proofs of excessive discomposure. . . ." Finally, when it is proposed that the property should be restored to its rightful owner, "the ghostly portrait is averred to have lost all patience, and to have shown itself on the point of descending bodily from its frame."

A similar scene occurs in the famous passage (Ch. 18) describing Judge Pyncheon's death. The narrator apologizes for the ghost story that he is about to tell, maintaining that "these tales are too absurd to bristle even childhood's hair." Nevertheless he proceeds to record "the ridiculous legend, that, at midnight, all the dead Pyncheons are bound to assemble in this parlor . . . to see whether the portrait of their ancestor still keeps its place upon the wall, in compliance with his testamentary directions." The first spirit to appear is Colonel Pyncheon himself, clad just as in the portrait. "He looks up at the portrait; a thing of no substance, gazing at its own painted image!" Following this *danse macabre*, Hawthorne assures us that "the fantastic scene just hinted at must by no means be considered as forming an actual portion of our story." But we understand his intention full well. By including these two passages—the "wild, chimney-corner legend" and the "ridiculous legend"—he not only manages to smuggle the image of the haunted portrait into an otherwise perfectly rational romance; he also contrives to add a significant aura of the supernatural to the function of the portrait in the main plot. Here we see the sublimation of the Gothic romance at its finest. By means of his own irony Hawthorne keeps his aesthetic balance on the line between parody and the horror story.

IF WE TURN from the portrait as *genius loci*, which is always tied magically to the room or the building that it inhabits as its brooding spirit, to the portrait as *figura*, we can begin with an example that takes its magic as wholly for granted as does *The Castle of Otranto*: that textbook of German romanticism, Novalis' fragmentary novel, *Heinrich von Ofterdingen* (1802).[40] In the course of a journey from Eisenach to Augsburg during the idealized Middle Ages of the novel, Heinrich and his companions stop in a mountain village, where they meet a Bohemian miner. Entranced by his tales about the riches beneath the surface of the earth, the group accompanies the mysterious old man on an exploration of some caves in the neighboring mountains. After a time they encounter an aged hermit living deep in the heart of a mountain. While the others continue their explorations, Heinrich

[40] Friedrich von Hardenberg, *Schriften*, ed. Paul Kluckhohn and Richard Samuel, 2nd ed. (Darmstadt: Wissenschaftliche Buchgesellschaft, 1960), I, 255–65.

remains behind to leaf through the splendid old folios that fill the hermit's cave. By and by he comes across a volume written in an unfamiliar language—it turns out to be Provençal—and bearing no title. As he looks at the illustrations, they strike him as being somehow familiar. Gradually it dawns on Heinrich that the figures represent himself, his family, and his acquaintances—all clad in costumes from another culture and another era. In short: in those mysterious illuminations Heinrich finds outlined the course of his own life as foretold many years earlier. The ending of the manuscript is missing, as Heinrich learns from the hermit, and so only part of his life is actually prefigured. Since Novalis never completed his novel, not all the parallels are worked out in precise detail. Yet it is clear enough that here we are dealing with a series of portraits that are "haunted" in a different sense: painted in the past, they foretell or anticipate the life of the hero in some miraculous way, just as in "figural" or "typological" interpretation of the Bible the figures and incidents of the Old Testament are thought to "prefigure" the persons and events of the New Testament.[41]

Gérard de Nerval and Dante Gabriel Rossetti both wrote startlingly similar stories in which an artist discovers the circumstances of his love affair prefigured precisely in an old painting. Several of Nerval's *Contes Fantastiques* were inspired by E.T.A. Hoffmann; in fact, Nerval included a translation of Hoffmann's "A New Year's Eve Adventure" as one of the tales in that collection. In "The Devil's Portrait" (1839) we are not surprised to detect the influence of *The Devil's Elixirs* and "Arthur's Court."[42] A young English

[41] See J. R. Darbyshire, "Typology," in *Encyclopedia of Religion and Ethics*, ed. James Hastings, vol. XII (New York: Scribner, 1922), pp. 500–504.

[42] "Portrait du Diable," in *Nouvelles et Fantaisies*, ed. Jules Mersan (Paris: Champion, 1928), pp. 165–77; see also p. 298. Although Nerval never explicitly cites Novalis, it is taken for granted that as a French Germanophile he was familiar with his works. See Charles Dédéyan, *Gérard de Nerval et l'Allemagne*, vol. II: *L'Allemagne dans l'oeuvre littéraire de Nerval* (Paris: Société d'Éditions d'En-

painter named Eugene travels to Venice, where he hopes to recover from the rejection by his beloved Laura. In the ruins of a church he comes across a painting called *La Fiancée du Diable*, in which he detects an eerily precise resemblance to Laura. Shocked to learn that the painter had lost his mind and committed suicide because of the model for his painting, Eugene falls ill and dies, thus fulfilling the prophecy of the portrait.

Rossetti's fragmentary tale, "Saint Agnes of Intercession" (1849–50), offers a more complex variation on the same basic motif.[43] Rossetti, who was fond of *Melmoth the Wanderer* as well as of the less literary shilling shockers,[44] deals with his prefigurative picture in a manner that hovers ambiguously between the plausible and the supernatural. The narrator, a painter, recalls that his first interest in art was kindled during his childhood, when he became so infatuated with a painting of St. Agnes in Glory by a (fictitious) artist named Bucciuolo Angiolieri that he copied it repeatedly from a volume of prints in which it was reproduced. Now, years later, he has fallen in love with a girl named Mary Arden, whom he uses as the model for a painting that assures his first success at the exhibitions. A critic points out, however, that the style and head of the painting resemble the St. Agnes by Angiolieri—a likeness of which the painter had been wholly unaware. Since the old volume of prints has been lost, he becomes obsessed with the idea of seeing the original in order to ascertain to what extent the girl he loves resembles his childhood ideal. Using the money from his first sale and commission, he sets out for Italy to trace the old painting. His search leads him from Bologna to Rome to Florence—with no success. After several months a reference in a dictionary of art works sends him to Perugia,

---

seignement Supérieur, 1957), pp. 352–80 (on Hoffmann) and pp. 583–614 (on Novalis).

[43] *The Collected Works*, ed. William M. Rossetti (London: Ellis and Scrutton, 1886), I, 399–426 and 524–26 (Notes).

[44] Birkhead, *The Tale of Terror*, p. 86.

where the painting is supposed to hang in the Academy gallery. When he finally finds the painting, he is stunned. "The countenance was the one known to me, by a feeble reflex, in childhood; it was also the exact portrait of Mary, feature by feature." In an effort to comprehend the mystery he scans the catalogue notes on the artist. The painting of St. Agnes was allegedly the portrait of Bucciuolo's own beloved, painted while she was dying. "A woman had then lived four hundred years since, of whom that picture was the portrait; and my own eyes bore me witness that it was also the surpassingly perfect resemblance of a woman now living and breathing,—of my own affianced bride!"

Recovering from his bewilderment, he notices that a self-portrait of Bucciuolo is also displayed in the room. With a trembling sense of suspense he hastens to it and finds himself face to face with a portrait of himself. "I can recall my feeling at that moment, only as one of the most lively and exquisite fear." Distressed at this puzzling experience and by an ominous dream in which the various roles—himself, Bucciuolo, Mary, and the Renaissance model—are confused, he immediately goes back to London. His first inquiries assure him that Mary is quite well; but he himself falls into a fever that incapacitates him for several weeks. When he recovers sufficiently to recount everything to his parents, they begin to fear that his reason has been disturbed by brain-sickness. At last he is able to pay his first visit to Mary, but at this point the fragment ends. However, it is clear from the context, from the recollections of Rossetti's brother (in his notes to the story), and from etchings and paintings that Rossetti undertook to illustrate his narrative, that the story was to end with a re-enactment of Bucciuolo's destiny: the narrator-painter was to find himself painting a portrait of Mary on her deathbed.

In the works by Nerval, Rossetti, and Novalis we are dealing, respectively, with cases of single, dual, and multiple reincarnation, and the effect of this realization upon the affected viewer ranges from mortal shock through melancholy bewilderment to euphorious anticipation. Basically, all three writers share the romantic view of the prefigurative portrait: no rational explanation can really account for the mysterious analogies. In our next two cases, however, we can observe how the motif is altered as it moves out of the romance into the modes of the psychological tale and the ghost story.

Robert Louis Stevenson's tale "Olalla" (1887) is narrated by a wounded officer who goes to the mountains of Spain to recuperate from his injury.[45] Staying there with a family of shabby gentility in an isolated *residencia*, he is struck by a portrait on the wall of his bedroom depicting a beautiful, vivacious woman in a costume of former days: "her eyes, of a very golden brown, held mine with a look; and her face, which was perfectly shaped, was yet marred by a cruel, sullen, and sensual expression." As he contemplates the portrait the next morning, its beauty insinuates itself into his heart. "Day after day the double knowledge of her wickedness and of my weakness grew clearer." As the narrator becomes acquainted with the members of the household—the sensuous mother who lies around in a state of animal torpor, the faun-like brother Felipe, and the sister Olalla, with whom he promptly falls in love—he detects in all of them a family resemblance to the woman in the portrait. (Stevenson uses animal metaphors very skillfully to suggest the latent animality of the doomed family.)

Olalla tries in vain to send him away from the house without giving any reason. Matters become clear one day when the narrator cuts his hands and appeals to the mother for help. When she leaps at him, seizes his hand, bites it "with bestial cries," and sucks the blood, he finally realizes that the family is subject to an atavistic regression. Olalla and Felipe manage to rescue him from their mother, and this

[45] *The Merry Men and Other Tales and Fables*, Biographical Edition (New York: Scribner, 1921), pp. 158–220. For a good discussion of "Olalla" see Edwin M. Eigner, *Robert Louis Stevenson and Romantic Tradition* (Princeton, N.J.: Princeton Univ. Press, 1966), pp. 201–11.

time Olalla prevails upon him to depart. "Have your eyes ever rested on that picture that hangs by your bed? She who sat for it died ages ago; and she did evil in her life. But look again: there is my hand to the least line, there are my eyes and my hair. What is mine, then, and what am I?" Olalla is prey to a belief in a terrible fatalism, of which the portrait is the symbol. In her, the poles of bestiality and civilization are still in a precarious balance. "Man has risen; if he has sprung from the brutes, he can descend again to the same level." Seeing herself condemned to the affliction that has grown over her race for eight hundred years, she does not feel free to fall in love. "Shall I bind another spirit, reluctant as my own, into this bewitched and tempest-broken tenement that I now suffer in?" Vowing that the curse of her race shall die with her, Olalla sends the narrator away.

In "Olalla" Stevenson is concerned with the same phenomenon of schizophrenia he had depicted a year earlier in *The Strange Case of Dr. Jekyll and Mr. Hyde* (1886), but here the atavistic aspect of the personality is represented by the ancestral portrait, which embodies prefiguratively the state into which Olalla is condemned to degenerate. In Katherine Tynan's "The Picture on the Wall" (1895)[46] the portrait also foreshadows the fate of the heroine; but what was psychologically motivated in Stevenson's tale has here become purely supernatural. A young man named Annesley, paying his first visit to his fiancée's home, is given a bedroom dominated by the portrait of a strikingly handsome man. "The painting of the eyes was the painter's great achievement. As Annesley stood looking at the picture with a candle lighted the better to see it, he could have sworn the eyes looked back at him like those of a living man." At dinner no one in the family cares to discuss the portrait; when Annesley returns to his room he touches the painted canvas just to assure himself that there is nothing unnatural about the eyes. Awakened later by a cold breath on his forehead,

[46] *Victorian Ghost Stories*, ed. Montague Summers, pp. 314–30.

he sees in the dark "an evil face, swollen, distorted, malignant; the eyes, with a red gleam in them, looked furiously into his." When the apparition disappears he looks up at the portrait, which seems to peer at him with a changed expression. He notes with horror that its eyes resemble the apparition's. After a sleepless night, he speaks to his fiancée, who sends him to inspect the verso of the portrait in his room. On the back he sees painted the face that appeared to him during the night—the face of the handsome ancestor on the front, but painted during the madness that destroyed him after a wicked life. The engagement is broken off when Millicent tells Annesley that the same madness periodically afflicts members of her family.[47]

In the tales by Stevenson and Tynan the portrait bears a very close resemblance to the *genius loci* since, in both cases, it represents madness or degeneracy that threatens the entire family—a tendency that shows up especially in the animated eyes inherited from the portraits of the Gothic romances. Yet it is worth preserving a distinction. In the classic cases, the portrait as *genius loci* is concerned more with the house than with the family: the hanging judges, for instance, are intent upon protecting their domain against intruders, as is Colonel Pyncheon. In these other stories, by contrast, it is the psychological relationship between the portrait and the heroine that matters: the portrait prefigures the affliction that will devastate the heroine's life and ruin her happiness.

As a final example of the portrait as *figura* let us cite one of the most familiar instances from the nineteenth century, which suggests the extent to which the ghost story worked retroactively to impose a haunted portrait upon a work that originally had none. We have noted that E.T.A. Hoffmann

[47] In her story "The Eyes" (1910), which bears a striking resemblance to Tynan's tale, Edith Wharton inverts the motif: the eyes no longer come out of a portrait; they are clearly a projection of the story-teller's own evil conscience. Le Fanu introduces the motif of the portrait as *figura* in his well-known tale "Camilla" (from *In a Glass Darkly*, 1872), but fails to develop it.

tended to exclude the overtly supernatural from his works, preferring such rationalizations of the walking portrait as those in *The Devil's Elixirs* or "Arthur's Court." The same principle holds true in his "Councillor Krespel" (1816).[48] Krespel's lovely daughter, Antonie, has a strange malady in her chest: it has given her a splendid voice and, at the same time, means almost immediate death to her if she insists on raising that voice in song. In Hoffmann's original story, Antonie dies when, against the advice of her father, she is persuaded by her lover to sing. The story is another example of that romantic thesis, evident down to the works of Thomas Mann, that art and disease are inextricably interrelated.

Now, in the version of this story that is familiar to most people—Offenbach's *The Tales of Hoffmann* (1881)—the situation is quite different. Here it is not the lover, but the sinister Dr. Miracle who persuades Antonia to sing herself to death. In order to tempt her to forget her vow to her father, he conjures up the memory of her mother, formerly the most famous diva in Europe, who also died as a result of her singing. At this point the apparition of the mother actually steps forth from a life-sized portrait and joins Antonia in one of the most stirring arias of the opera. Here, of course, the walking portrait is a visual manifestation of Dr. Miracle's evocation of the mother's memory. The mother's destiny clearly prefigures the daughter's, for immediately after their duet Antonia dies. It is worth noting that in the French dramatization of 1851 upon which Offenbach's opera is based, this effect is still missing: the mother's voice is heard in the distance, off-stage, and the portrait does not move.[49] It was only when Barbier adapted his play for the libretto that he introduced the motif of the animated portrait—an alteration that may have been motivated by the technical need to get the singer of the mother's part on stage for the duet. But it may also be conjectured that the librettist,

[48] "Rat Krespel," in *The Serapion Brethren* (1819–21).

[49] Jules Barbier and Michel Carré, *Les Contes d'Hoffmann, Drame fantastique en 5 actes* (Paris: Michel Lévy, 1851).

along with his audience, had been prepared by the growing fascination with the supernatural in the second half of the nineteenth century to accept an effect that was still felt to be implausible in Hoffmann's original tale.[50]

WHEREAS the portrait as *genius loci* and as *figura* acts upon the heroes and heroines out of the past in which it was created, the portrait as *anima* represents an extension of the living hero's soul in the present. We can delineate this category quite precisely with reference to stories by three contemporaries whose works display a remarkable similarity: Gogol, Hawthorne, and Poe.

The first example, to be sure, is a transitional case that at first glance seems to bear a closer resemblance to the portrait as *genius loci* than as *anima*. Gogol's "The Portrait"—especially in its first version of 1833–34—is still close enough to romanticism to take its magic for granted.[51] Indeed, Gogol was fond of several of the works that we have already had reason to consider: notably *The Castle of Otranto, Melmoth the Wanderer*, and Washington Irving's "Adventure of the Mysterious Picture" (from *Tales of a Traveller*).[52] In addi-

[50] Opera seems to have a peculiar attraction for haunted portraits. We have already noted *Ruddigore* (1887) by Gilbert and Sullivan, which might be a direct parody of Offenbach's hugely successful opera. Another example occurs in Erich Wolfgang Korngold's *Die tote Stadt* (1920), where the portrait of the hero's dead wife steps from her frame and exhorts him to remain faithful to her memory (Act I, Scene 6). Interestingly, the novel upon which the libretto is based—Georges Rodenbach's *Bruges-la-Morte* (1892)—contains no such scene and no trace of the supernatural; the haunted portrait is inspired directly by Offenbach's opera. It looks almost as though the opera had its own autonomous tradition of the haunted portrait.

[51] I quote the first version according to the translation by Constance Garnett in *The Overcoat and Other Stories* (New York: Knopf, 1923), pp. 207–62. The second version is available in a translation by David Magarshack in *The Overcoat and Other Tales of Good and Evil* (1957; rpt. New York: Norton, 1965), pp. 93–159.

[52] Charles E. Passage, *The Russian Hoffmannists* (The Hague: Mouton, 1963), pp. 146–48.

tion, he seems to have been inspired directly by Hoffmann's "Fragments from the Lives of Three Friends" (1818), which opens with reports by two of the friends concerning apparitions that appeared to them at night.[53]

Gogol's story begins in Petersburg when a promising young painter, Chertkov, spends his last rubles to buy an unfinished portrait whose eyes exert a strange fascination for him. Terrified by the eyes, he leaves the painting in the shop; but soon after he arrives in his lodgings, he finds that it has mysteriously appeared there on the wall. As he studies the portrait in the moonlight, "the canvas disappeared, and the dreadful face of the old man stood out and seemed gazing out of the frame as though out of a window." At last Chertkov conceals the portrait behind a screen and goes to bed. But as he lies there—not asleep but in a trance-like state—"he saw the figure of the old man detach itself from the portrait and leave it, just as the upper foam is lifted from a frothing liquid, rise in the air, and float nearer and nearer to him, till at last it approached his very bedstead. . . . The old man's eyes glowed with a dull fire and were fastened upon him with all their magnetic power." The portrait figure advises Chertkov to renounce his dreams of artistic perfection and to paint portraits quickly for profit. It urges him to give up his garret and to rent an expensive flat, assuring him that it will provide the money. By the time Chertkov can sit up in bed, the image has again grown dim and retreated back into the frame.

Chertkov assumes that he has been dreaming. But the next day, when his landlord visits him with a policeman to collect the overdue rent, the policeman roughly seizes the frame of the portrait; it cracks open; a roll of gold coins falls out onto the floor. This money provides Chertkov with a new start. Setting himself up in an elegant apartment, as the portrait-figure had recommended, he tries to execute his

[53] Ad. Stender-Petersen, "Gogol und die deutsche Romantik," *Euphorion*, 24 (1922), 628–53. Hoffmann's tale—"Fragmente aus dem Leben dreier Freunde"—appears in *The Serapion Brethren*.

first commissions with some sense of artistic conscientiousness. But yielding gradually to the demands of his wealthy patrons, he forsakes his principles and becomes a fashionable society portraitist. After some years he is invited to judge the work of a Russian painter who has spent years in Italy, devoting himself patiently to his art. The beauty of the masterpiece so overwhelms and shames Chertkov that he rushes home intending to paint seriously again; but years of slovenliness have ruined his eye and his touch. In a wild reaction he begins buying up the works of promising young artists in order to destroy them. In his final madness he raves that all the walls of his apartment are hung with portraits whose eyes stare at him accusingly. He implores his visitors to take away the portrait of the old man with the living eyes. But the portrait has vanished; Chertkov dies in agony, and of his vast wealth nothing is left but the shreds of the masterpieces that he has torn to bits.

At this point, halfway through the story, matters are left unresolved. So far the plot has revealed no real direction or meaning: it seems to be little more than a weird anecdote after the fashion of the haunted portrait as *genius loci*, in which the supernatural events are capable, in theory at least, of a rational resolution. The portrait could have been delivered to Chertkov's rooms without his knowledge; he could have dreamed that the old man came down from the frame and spoke to him; the staring eyes of the portrait could be nothing more than projections of his own remorse; and so forth. But using a two-part structure familiar from several of his tales—e.g., "The Terrible Vengeance" or "The Overcoat"—Gogol appends a second section that explains and gives meaning to the seemingly senseless events of the first part. Paradoxically, by bestowing meaning on the events, the second part makes them appear more surely supernatural than they seemed before.

The setting and time are unrelated to the first part. The portrait has shown up again at an art auction, where it attracts a good deal of attention. Suddenly an elderly gentleman exclaims that he knows the history of the painting, and everyone listens eagerly to his account. Years earlier, in the poor section of Petersburg known as Kolomna, there was a money-lender named Petromihali—a dark-complexioned man with southern features who wore loose Asiatic attire. When he was about to die, he summoned a famous artist (the speaker's father) to his deathbed and implored him to paint his portrait. Since the unusual subject challenged the artist, he set to work immediately. As the dying money-lender saw that his features were being transferred to the canvas, "something almost like joy" gleamed in his terrible eyes. The artist, meanwhile, had been concentrating on the eyes; when he stepped back to appraise his work, he was smitten with horror to see that living eyes were glaring at him from the portrait. The money-lender begged him to finish, explaining that after his death he must go to the Devil and endure terrible tortures. "But I need not go to Him so long as our earth stands, if only you finish my portrait. I have learned that half my life will pass into my portrait, if only it is painted by a skillful artist." Overcome with repugnance, the painter refused to continue; the money-lender died with a curse on his lips for the artist.

Abandoning his paints and brushes along with the portrait, the artist rushes out of the room. But when he gets home he finds the portrait in his studio, and no one knows how it got there. He has it removed to the attic, but that night he distinctly sees the money-lender enter his room and tempt him to give "a fiendish direction" to his pious art. The next day he burns up the portrait along with its frame, but when he turns back to continue his work on an icon, he sees the portrait hanging once again in its now accustomed place. The artist resolves to confess everything to his priest, but when he makes his first attempt to do so, his wife swallows some needles and dies; the second time one of his sons falls out of a window and is killed. The painter sends his other son to a military school and he himself retires to a monastery in a remote town. Here he gradually wins back his serenity by painting Christian images. Ten years later, when his son visits him for the first time, the painter tells him the story just outlined. Then he goes on to describe a revelation that he received in a vision. The Antichrist seeks to be born into the world. At present he can force his way only into such sinners as the money-lender, men who are marked by their hatred of mankind and the Creator. If the painter had not created the portrait, the Antichrist would have withdrawn following the money-lender's death "because he cannot live longer than the body in which he has confined himself." But the devil crept into the living eyes of the portrait and will remain there for fifty years. At that time, if someone recounts the legend, the portrait's power will be extinguished. At this point the speaker remarks that those fifty years have now passed. When the listeners turn back to the painting, they notice that the eyes no longer have the eerie gleam of life. In fact, when they approach the painting, they see nothing but an insignificant landscape. As the story ends, many of the spectators wonder "whether they had really seen the mysterious portrait, or whether it was a dream and had been a momentary illusion of eyes exhausted by prolonged scrutiny of old pictures."

It has been necessary to recapitulate Gogol's story at unusual length because here the motif of the haunted portrait has been enlarged into the principal theme of the story. Anyone who has followed the argument so far can easily pick out the conventional devices that Gogol has adopted from the Gothic tradition and other sources. Folklore and popular belief contributed the notion that the soul of the deceased can enter the portrait. The Gothic romance supplied the image of the uncanny and lifelike eyes,[54] and *Melmoth the Wanderer* suggested that the accursed portrait cannot be consumed by fire. The devil's attempt to persuade the painter

[54] Gogol was obsessed with vision and seeing; see Leon Stilman, "The 'All-Seeing' Eye in Gogol," in *Gogol from the Twentieth Century: Eleven Essays*, selected, ed., and trans. Robert A. Maguire (Princeton, N.J.: Princeton Univ. Press, 1974), pp. 376–89.

to change his mode of art is familiar both from Southey's "The Pious Painter" and from the legend of the blacksmith and the devil, upon which Gogol based his earlier story, "Christmas Eve." But Gogol has revaluated the familiar elements, transforming his story into a profound statement on the precarious nature of art.[55] Two aspects of this problem can be singled out for our purposes, each linking Gogol to one of his American contemporaries. First, the artist has a huge moral responsibility since he is constantly subject to corruption by the forces of evil, which subvert his art. "Marvel, my son, at the terrible power of the devil. He strives to make his way into everything; into our deeds, into our thoughts, and even into the inspiration of the artist." This is the problem that was to obsess Hawthorne. Second, there exists the danger that even "good" art can have an insidious effect. As Chertkov reflects at the beginning of the story: "Does the highest art bring a man up to the line beyond which he captures what cannot be created by human effort, and snatches something living from the life animating his model?"—a thought that points the way to Poe. Both these elements are evident in Gogol's tale: both parts show an attempt to corrupt the artist, once successfully and once in vain; and the second part reveals that the life of the model can indeed animate the portrait.

In 1841–42 Gogol revised and substantially expanded his story in response to criticism of its fantastic elements.[56] To emphasize the fact that he considered it essentially a new story he changed the name of the hero from Chertkov to Chartkov. The later version has fuller narrative detail, more incidents, greater depth of characterization—but considerably less power. The original problem of the artist's respon-

[55] For a discussion of Gogol's complex and shifting attitude toward his art see Victor Erlich, *Gogol* (New Haven: Yale Univ. Press, 1969), esp. pp. 162–66.

[56] For a discussion of the revision see Vsevolod Setchkarev, *Gogol: His Life and Works*, trans. Robert Kramer (New York: New York Univ. Press, 1965), pp. 124–28 and 230–31.

sibility in the face of evil has been reduced to the problem of *l'art pour l'art* as opposed to commercialization. Above all, the supernatural elements have been completely disenchanted. Everything is explained, and as a result the magically ambivalent atmosphere of the original is sacrificed. Here there is no longer any mystery about the appearance of the painting in the artist's lodgings: he carries it home under his arm. Similarly, the old painter does not attempt to burn up the portrait; he gives it to a friend who appreciates its genius. Chertkov's vision of the portrait stepping out of its frame is unequivocally reduced to a dream—or, more precisely, to a series of dreams from which Chartkov thinks that he is awakening, only to discover that he is enmeshed in a new dream. In both versions, however, the relationship between the two parts is identical. The first part employs the motif of the haunted portrait in order to arouse our Gothic proclivities, and the second part exploits our interest to involve us in reflections concerning the near-magical relationship between the work of art and the reality it reflects and, in turn, the mortal responsibility of the artist.

Precisely this concern with moral responsibility lies at the center of Hawthorne's story, "The Prophetic Pictures" (written 1835).[57] Hawthorne tells us in a note that his story was inspired by an anecdote concerning Gilbert Stuart that he found in William Dunlap's *A History of the Rise and Progress of the Arts of Design in the United States* (1834).[58] Stuart was once engaged by Lord Mulgrave to paint the portrait of his brother, who was going abroad. When Mulgrave saw the completed portrait, he exclaimed that he could see insanity in the face. "I have painted your brother as I saw him," was the artist's reply. Soon after the brother's arrival in India he cut his throat in an attack of madness. "It is thus that the real portrait painter dives into the recesses of his sitters' minds, and displays strength or weakness upon the

[57] *Twice-Told Tales and Other Short Stories*, pp. 120–35.

[58] (Rpt. Boston: C. E. Goodspeed, 1918), I, 221–22.

surface of his canvas," Dunlap concludes. "The mechanic makes a map of a man."

It is no accident that stories concerning the portrait as *anima* begin just around this time. The daguerreotype was perfected in 1839, and soon thereafter the art of photography began to develop rapidly. But from the end of the eighteenth century there had been an increased demand for more effective mechanical means of visual reproduction—the physionotrace (1786), lithography (1796), heliography (1826), and so forth. This development gratified a public that, especially in the United States, demanded absolute resemblance in portraits; at the same time, it liberated painters, who had long chafed under what they regarded as "the burden of portraiture." These trends gradually enabled portrait painters of the early nineteenth century to shift their focus from "correct" reproduction to consciously subjective interpretation of their subjects[59]—a new emphasis that is reflected both in the anecdote about Gilbert Stuart and in Hawthorne's story.

"The Prophetic Pictures" concerns an (unnamed) European master who, having conquered all the challenges of conventional art, comes to the American colonies to explore their artistic possibilities before any of his colleagues. Because of his genius—"They say that he paints not merely a man's features, but his mind and heart"—he is compared to a wizard or a magician. Yet his skill is in great demand. When the young couple of the story, Walter Ludlow and his fiancée Elinor, visit the artist's studio to arrange for a pair of portraits, they find that his pictures bring out the character of persons so effectively that "the originals hardly resembled themselves so strikingly as the portraits did." When the painter approaches the couple, "his visitors were sensible of a kindred between the artist and his work, and felt as if one of

[59] Max J. Friedländer, *Landscape–Portrait–Still-life: Their Origin and Development*, trans. R.F.C. Hull (New York: Schocken, 1963), p. 262; Neil Harris, *The Artist in American Society: The Formative Years, 1790–1860* (1966; rpt. New York: Simon and Schuster–Clarion, 1970), pp. 56–88.

the pictures had stepped from the canvas to salute them." The young people are vaguely apprehensive because of a rumor that the painter takes possession of a subject's face and figure so fully that his paintings become prophetic. But they reach an agreement, and within a few days the portraits are finished. Walter and Elinor are strangely moved when they view the completed portraits. Although the features constitute a perfect likeness, the tone and mood are different in each: Elinor's eyes have a sad and anxious expression; Walter's portrait displays a spirit of unwonted liveliness. When Elinor asks the painter how he caught those expressions, he replies that "The artist—the true artist—must look beneath the exterior. It is his gift—his proudest, but often a melancholy one—to see the inmost soul. . . ." He tells her that he could retouch the portraits if she insisted but—and at this point he shows her a chalk sketch he has drawn of her and Walter—it would not influence the outcome.

Despite her fear inspired by the mysterious sketch, Elinor decides to leave the portraits unaltered. The painter soon leaves for a journey through the wilderness, while Walter and Elinor complete their plans and are married. On his return to Boston the painter hastens to see the portraits that have come to mean so much to him. Entering the house, he finds Walter and Elinor standing before their portraits, which they now resemble more closely than before: an expression of wild madness on Walter's face elicits a response of terror on hers. When Walter draws a knife to attack his wife, the painter recognizes the pose of the propetic sketch that he had shown Elinor months before. Advancing into the room, he "interposed himself between the wretched beings with the same sense of power to regulate their destiny as to alter a scene upon the canvas." When he reminds Elinor that he warned her of these developments, she acknowledges the fact, explaining that she went through with the marriage out of her love for Walter.

Hawthorne's tale has almost more implications than its brevity can sustain. First, the author appends a melancholy moralizing paragraph in which he asks if any of us would be deterred from any action if the results of our deeds could be set before us: "Some would call it Fate and hurry onward, others be swept along by their passionate desires, and none be turned aside by the PROPHETIC PICTURES." Second, he returns to the idea that art is timeless since it preserves beauty, or truth, for centuries after the original has perished: "it is the idea of duration—of earthly immortality—that gives such a mysterious interest to our own portraits." When Walter sees the completed paintings, he exclaims that now "No dark passions can gather on our faces," and Elinor remarks that "no dreary change can sadden us." The painter himself is intoxicated by the power of art, which makes the dead live again. "Thou snatchest back the fleeting moments of History. With thee there is no Past; for, at thy touch, all that is great becomes forever present. . . ." The conviction of Walter and Elinor that they can now no longer be affected by change is of course highly ironic, for the painter through his art has caught not the transient moment of their lives at the random moment of painting, but rather the essential quality of their souls: as a result, they grow inevitably toward the tragedy prefigured in the two portraits.

Finally, Hawthorne is obsessed with the problem of the artist. Whereas Gogol sees the artist as a simple craftsman constantly threatened by evil, Hawthorne shares the view that was prevalent in the United States before the Civil War: the artist as an exotic, demonic, Faustian magician, who is in touch with occult powers.[60] It is no accident that his painter is left nameless and is barely characterized: he is so totally committed to his art that he scarcely exists as a human being. Untouched by any love for his fellow man, he feels at most "the sort of interest which always allied him to the subjects of his pencil." This attitude has several implications. First, although he can look into other souls "with an acuteness almost preternatural," the painter is incapable

[60] Harris, *The Artist in American Society*, pp. 218–51; see also Millicent Bell, *Hawthorne's View of the Artist*.

of understanding how disordered and essentially inhuman his own soul has become. Second, because he lacks human emotions, the painter values his paintings more than the originals themselves. In fact, he comes to regard Walter and Elinor as creations of his art since he has lavished so much of his imagination upon them. At this point it is indeed possible for the painter to wonder if he is not "a chief agent of the coming evil which he had foreshadowed." Like Gogol, then, Hawthorne attributes supreme powers of creation to the artist, who is capable by his very virtuosity of bringing evil into the world. Yet the two contemporaries represent in their tales two radically different attitudes toward the theory of art for art's sake. Gogol argues for its necessity lest art be corrupted by the claims of material reality; Hawthorne, in contrast, depicts the dangers implicit in that attitude since the obsession with art can blind the artist to human life and reduce him to a problematic incarnation of the evil that regards human beings as no more than a means to the end of its art. In both cases the relationship between art and reality is embodied in the image of the haunted portrait, which stands in the relationship of *anima* to its original.[61]

Like Hawthorne, Poe is a fan of the Gothic romance. In addition, he is conscious of writing in the specific American tradition with which we have been concerned. In a review of *Twice-Told Tales* (1842) Poe writes: "We have very few American tales of real merit—we may say, indeed, none, with the exception of 'The Tales of a Traveller' of Washington Irving, and these 'Twice-Told Tales' of Mr. Hawthorne."[62] Like Hawthorne, Poe is obsessed with the problem of the artist who puts his art above human life. Yet the emphasis is different. Poe makes a point of establishing a Gothic at-

[61] In "The Portrait" (from *The Greater Inclination*, 1899) Edith Wharton gives yet another twist to the motif. The painter George Lillo, whose portraits capture the real character of his subjects, intentionally paints a falsely glorifying portrait of the shady politician Vard in order to spare his daughter's feelings.

[62] *The Complete Works of Edgar Allan Poe*, ed. James A. Harrison (New York: Crowell, 1902), xi, 109–10.

mosphere within the first paragraph of his brief tale, "The Oval Portrait" (1842).[63] The scene is a gloomy and deserted chateau in the Apennines—a neighbor of those Italian castles described so frequently in the novels of Mrs. Radcliffe, whom the narrator mentions in his first sentence. Indeed, the first half of the story follows the outline of a typical Gothic romance. With his servant, Pedro, the desperately wounded narrator establishes himself in an apartment in a remote turret of the chateau. In an incipient delirium from his wounds, the narrator lies reading a volume of commentary on the paintings that decorate the room. Suddenly his attention is caught by the portrait of a young girl—a vignette in an oval frame. At length he determines why the painting has such an impact. "I had found the spell of the picture in an absolute *life-likeliness* of expression, which at first startling, finally confounded, subdued and appalled me." At this point Poe departs from the Gothic tradition, for his portrait does not step down from its frame or otherwise seem to become animate. Instead, the catalogue gives an explanation that reminds us of Gogol's fear that the greatest painting "snatches something living from the life animating his model."

The young beauty in the portrait was married to a painter who, "having already a bride in his Art," neglected his wife. Eventually he prevailed upon his wife to sit for a portrait, failing to notice that the gloom in his turreted chamber withered her health and her spirits. As the portrait neared completion, it began to take on an uncanny resemblance to the original. The painter, "wild with the ardor of his work," rarely looked up from his canvas: "he *would* not see that the tints which he spread upon the canvas were drawn from the cheeks of her who sate beside him." At last he puts the final touch upon the portrait and, tremulous with wonder, cries out that "This is indeed *Life* itself"—only to perceive that his wife has in that instant died.

Both Poe and Hawthorne are cognizant of the essential

[63] *The Selected Poetry and Prose of Edgar Allan Poe*, ed. T. O. Mabbott (New York: Modern Library, 1951), pp. 223–25.

egocentricity of the artist, who pursues his work at the expense of human life. To this extent the nameless painters in "The Prophetic Pictures" and "The Oval Portrait" are kindred spirits. But there is a subtle difference in their interest, at least as far as the image of the haunted portrait is concerned. In neither case is the portrait haunted in any literal or Gothic sense although each stands in a magical relationship to its model. But whereas Hawthorne focuses his attention on the continuing relationship between portrait and model—notably, the degree to which the model comes to approximate the portrait, thus fulfilling the prophecy—Poe is fascinated by the extent to which the artist's ruthless exploitation of his human subject gradually drains the life out of her and bestows it upon his creation. It is these two aspects of the haunted portrait that become dominant a generation later when the image once again becomes almost thematically central in two novels of the later nineteenth century: Zola's *The Masterpiece* (1886) and Wilde's *The Picture of Dorian Gray* (1891).

This is not to imply that the portrait as *anima* disappears wholly during the intervening fifty years: but its occurrence is limited principally to such Victorian horror stories as Tom Hood's "The Shadow of a Shade" (1869), which make only the slightest concessions to rationalization.[64] Shortly before setting out on a lengthy Arctic expedition a young naval officer has his portrait painted for his fiancée. During his absence the portrait undergoes various remarkable changes: it becomes pale and moist; later it turns into a grinning skull; finally it appears with two drops of blood on its face. As it turns out, the officer has been murdered by the ship's surgeon, who has fallen in love with the fiancée. When the surgeon, upon the ship's return, visits the young lady to ask for her hand in marriage, the portrait falls from the wall and knocks him unconscious. During his delirium the surgeon confesses his crime and then commits suicide. The portrait, restored

[64] *Victorian Ghost Stories*, ed. Montague Summers, pp. 225–44.

to the wall but covered with a curtain, thereupon ceases performing its various supernatural miracles. Hood's story resembles a weird combination of Mérimée's parody "The *Viccolo* of Madama Lucrezia" and those tales of avenging statues that smash their enemies. Apart from confirming the tendency of magic images to lend themselves at a certain stage of their disenchantment to ghost stories, it contributes nothing to the growth of the genre. But the image of the haunted portrait was far from exhausted.

To MOVE from Poe's "The Oval Portrait" to Zola's controversial novel, *The Masterpiece* (1886), is not only to advance from a tale of four pages to an epic work of four hundred pages.[65] It is also to overleap the half-century separating late romanticism and full-fledged naturalism. Yet despite vast differences in scope, style, and intent, we can detect beneath Zola's novel precisely the same thesis and precisely the same view of the magical art-object that inspired Poe's tale, which Zola had read in the translation by Baudelaire.[66] *The Masterpiece* is in one sense a fictionalized history of the era of French impressionism. Combining his own autobiography with elements drawn from the lives of Manet and his childhood friend, Cézanne, exploiting the color theories of Monet along with a description of Manet's *Déjeuner sur l'herbe*, drawing on the scandal of the notorious Salon des Refusés of 1863 and various historical incidents of the period, Zola assembles a vivid panorama of the Parisian bohème in the 1860's.

We do not need to linger over the rich and often fascinating details of this densely woven fiction. The novel has basically two conflicting themes: the striving of the brilliant young painter, Claude Lantier, to remain true to his art de-

[65] *L'Oeuvre*, cited here in the translation by Katherine Woods (New York: Howell, Soskin, 1946), esp. pp. 374 ff.

[66] Robert J. Niess, *Zola, Cézanne, and Manet: A Study of L'Oeuvre* (Ann Arbor: Univ. of Michigan Press, 1968), p. 6.

spite the lure of commercial success and to incorporate his new theories into a definitive masterpiece; and the struggle of his wife, Christine, against the art that obsesses her husband and eventually wins him away from her. These two themes are interwoven from the first chapter on, but they reach their greatest density toward the end of the novel when Claude is working furiously to complete a huge symbolic painting that is meant, once and for all, to establish his reputation: a great nude Woman standing in the prow of a boat in front of the city (based on the Ile de la Cité). In a final attempt to win Claude away from the painting that she has grown to hate and to which they have sacrificed everything, including their livelihood and their child, Christine volunteers to pose for the principal figure. Claude is so deeply engrossed in his painting that he has even stopped sleeping with his wife. "For Claude, this was a deliberate abstinence: chastity on principle; the feeling that he must pour all his virility into his painting."

One night, awakening and missing Claude from the bed, Christine finds him in his studio working on his great nude. Suddenly Christine realizes that Claude is treating the painting as though it were a real woman. "He was rounding off some fleshy contours with sweeping strokes of the brush, and his movement was a caress . . . it was a scene of vast dark confusion, the brutal consummation of some tangled embrace." In an outburst of rage she screams that the painting is "the murderer that has poisoned my life." "She continued to shower reproaches upon his painting; it was true that he held back, to give to her preferred rival the virility that he refused to her." Claude, in turn, has become so blinded by his obsession that he fails to realize that he has created nothing but a grotesque and pathetic daub. The painting has turned into "the idol of some unknown cult," "an effigy of metals, of marbles, of gems, bringing this mystic rose of her sex to its burgeoning between the gold-encrusted pillars that were her thighs, under the sacred vault that was her abdomen." In a brilliant gesture Christine sweeps off her nightgown and stands before Claude in the pose of his painted image, begging for comparison. In her passion she seduces her husband from his art, urging him to blasphemy: that painting is all foolishness, that he will burn his pictures, that he will never work again. But after their passion is spent, Claude frees himself again from her sleepy embraces and returns to his studio, where he hangs himself from the platform, "face to face with his abortive and ruined work." When Christine discovers his body in the morning, she realizes that she has lost to the painted whore. "Above her, the Woman in the picture shone out in her symbolic idol's splendor."[67]

It is most conspicuously through his total internalization of the magic, which takes place wholly within the consciousness of the hero, that Zola has departed from the calculated ambiguities of Gogol, Hawthorne, and Poe. Yet thereby, paradoxically, Zola is able to restore to the image some of the primitive power that originally contributed to the superstition of the haunted portrait. In "The Oval Portrait" the painter's devotion to his art brought about the death of his wife. In Zola's novel that is also the movement of the plot until shortly before the end: Christine has been deprived of a happy family life, of her health, of her child, and of her husband's love by his consuming passion for his painting. But in a surprising reversal in the scene that we have just considered, Zola gives an unexpected Gothic twist to the motif: Christine emerges as the seductress who destroys the artist by tempting him from his art, like the Venuses who brought sweat to the brow of so many early German romantics.

If Zola, like Poe, is concerned principally with the ani-

[67] Balzac's story "Le Chef-d'oeuvre inconnu" (1831) is often cited as a possible source for Zola, and some of the parallels are indeed striking. Yet in our context it is worth noting that Balzac's hero-painter, Frenhofer, uses no human model for his painting. Hence the portrait is not strictly speaking an *anima* although Frenhofer attributes a soul to his painted woman and says that she would blush if any other eyes than his should see her.

mistic contest between the portrait and the model for the life-force that they must divide between themselves, Oscar Wilde shares Hawthorne's fascination with the growing approximation of the model to the painting. Wilde was no stranger to the Gothic novel: he was a great admirer of *Melmoth the Wanderer*, which was written by his great-uncle, and he was keenly aware of the tradition in which he wrote.[68] *The Picture of Dorian Gray* (1891) is obviously related to the many nineteenth-century works that employ the fashionable motif of the elixir of youth—from Hawthorne's parody in "Dr. Heidegger's Experiment" to Bulwer Lytton's remarkable novel *A Strange Story* (1862), in which the villain turns out to be an evil old man who has kept himself, by means of a magic potion, in the state of health and beauty of a youth of twenty. Principally, however, Wilde's novel belongs to the category of works in which the portrait functions as the *anima* of the original. Here, in fact, the motif has grown into the theme that dominates and characterizes the entire allegorical novel.

For all its virtuosity, *The Picture of Dorian Gray* is less complex and profound than the shorter works of Gogol and Hawthorne. Take away the epigrams and the witty conversation that fill Wilde's allegory, and the remaining structure is very simple, very mechanical indeed. A handsome young man of twenty, seeing his completed portrait, wishes that he could remain eternally young and that the portrait would age in his stead. This exchange seemingly takes place, and for eighteen years, as Dorian indulges himself in every pleasure and every vice, he remains unaltered in appearance while the portrait, carefully hidden away, turns old and ugly. Finally, out of a compulsion to share his secret, Dorian shows the painting to the artist, who reveals his dismay. Regretting his impulse, Dorian murders the painter. Then, although no finger of suspicion is pointed at him, Dorian is overcome with

[68] *The Picture of Dorian Gray*, ed. Isobel Murray (London: Oxford Univ. Press, 1974). In her Introduction (pp. xx–xxi) the editor discusses the question of Wilde's sources.

remorse and kills himself. When the servants finds his body, now withered with age, the portrait has been restored to its original beauty.

Wilde, writing at the end of the nineteenth century, has provided enough clues to enable the reader to rationalize almost the entire improbable action. From the day that it is completed until the day it is discovered by the servants in pristine condition, no one sees the painting but Dorian himself and Basil Hallward, the painter. The fact that the painting seems to have deteriorated in Dorian's eyes can be taken as a projection of his sense of guilt. Hallward, on the single occasion when he sees the portrait (in a poor light), tries to account for its condition by speaking of mildew and poison in the paints that he used. It is also conceivable that the portrait was never so perfect as he recalled it as being. In any case, it is quite possible to account rationally for the seeming senescence of the portrait. At the same time, although Dorian remains remarkably well preserved during the eighteen years covered by the narrative—to a degree that astonishes his friends—it is never said that he is absolutely unchanged. For instance, a prostitute whom he had corrupted years before says that in eighteen years "he hasn't changed much." In short, the seemingly preternatural circumstances of the novel can be explained as the unusually good physical preservation of a young man until his thirty-eighth year, combined with the projection of his personal guilt onto a defective portrait of his earlier innocence. In fact, in view of the potentially rational explanations for everything that happens, it could be argued that Wilde is relying very heavily indeed on the tradition of the haunted portrait to suggest to his readers that the mysterious changes actually do take place both in the portrait and in the model. Our own expectations delude us.

However, since Wilde wrote his novel quite frankly as an allegory, there is really no reason not to accept the supernatural for convention's sake and on its own terms. When Basil Hallward paints Dorian's portrait, he catches the young man at the last moment of unspoiled natural handsomeness. On the day the painting is completed, two things happen to corrupt Dorian's innocence. First, the sight of his own portrait produces in Dorian the first moment of self-consciousness along with the realization that he will grow old while the portrait remains eternally youthful. Second, the conversation of Lord Henry Wotton, who is also present in Hallward's atelier, awakens for the first time that curiosity about life that leads to Dorian's insatiable search for sensations and ultimately, when he has tried and discarded all normal sensations, to the belief that evil provides the only remaining access to beauty. On that day, therefore, Dorian makes the wish that—magically fulfilled or not—haunts him for the remainder of his life. "If it were I who was to be always young, and the picture that was to grow old! For that—for that—I would give everything! Yes, there is nothing in the whole world I would not give! I would give my soul for that!" (Ch. 2). Within a month—when Dorian causes the suicide of the actress, Sibyl Vane—the first touch of cruelty shows up around the mouth of the portrait. Whether real or imagined, it produces in Dorian the conviction that there could be "some subtle affinity between the chemical atoms, that shaped themselves into form and colour on the canvas, and the soul that was within him." Dorian begins to recognize the strange power of the painting: "As it had revealed to him his own body, so it would reveal to him his own soul" (Ch. 8). Eighteen years later, when he finally agrees to show the portrait to Basil Hallward, he warns him: "I shall show you my soul. You shall see the thing that you fancy only God can see" (Ch. 12). Like Hawthorne, then, Wilde credits the great artist with the ability to "see the inmost soul." In both cases the portrait is quite literally the soul or *anima*. But Wilde inverts the motif. Whereas in Hawthorne's tale the living models gradually approximate the vision rendered by the painter in the portraits, Wilde suggests that the portrait comes to resemble the spiritual image of the living model. Yet the implied magical relationship between model and *anima* is identical in both cases.

Wilde introduces a second important idea into the early pages of his novel. Like Hawthorne's painter, Basil Hallward becomes obsessed with his subject purely as an aesthetic phenomenon. To be sure, he is fascinated by Dorian and drawn to him; yet his idealization of the subject cuts him off from the living being. The "real Dorian," he remarks at the first sign of Dorian's changing character, is the one in the picture. Hallward is even reluctant to exhibit the painting, afraid that he has revealed in it too much of his own "curious artistic idolatry" (Ch. 1). Now this idea, so important in the opening chapters of the book, is soon displaced by the theme of the portrait as *anima*. It is clear that any elaboration of the artist-theme after the manner of Hawthorne would have interfered with the development of the Dorian-theme. For the point of the artist-theme concerns the profounder insights of the artist, who through the act of painting predicts the future of his subject. In Hawthorne's tale the young couple grows to resemble their own portraits. Here, however, there can be no such implied determinism: the portrait is supposed to be not prophetic, but simply an image of Dorian's soul. In the last analysis, however, it might be suggested that this is the psychological truth that underlies the whole allegory: Dorian, in his increasing self-awareness, begins to recognize in the portrait certain traits of evil that the painter, unwittingly or presciently, has painted into it. For in all the descriptions of the portrait—and the novel contains fewer than we seem to recall—the changes are alterations of expression. On the night of his death, for instance, Dorian is almost indignant because his one good deed has produced no dramatic change in the portrait. "He could see no change, save that in the eyes there was a look of cunning, and in the mouth the curved wrinkle of the hypocrite" (Ch. 20). From this point of view it could be argued that Hallward was murdered at the moment when

Dorian realized how deeply the painter had anticipated the development of his soul. In any case, Wilde like Zola is counting on the literary tradition of the haunted portrait to contribute the various magical implications that, upon close examination, are simply not present in his text since everything is amenable to rational explanations.

We notice in summary that all the treatments of the portrait as *anima*—in sharp distinction to the portrait as *genius loci* or as *figura*—involve the artist himself, who is entangled in the mysterious relationship that emerges between the model and its pictorial *anima*. In Hawthorne's story and Zola's novel this is clear from the beginning, for the works focus upon the artist himself. Gogol and Poe explore the artist's role only in the second part of their tales, as a retrospective explanation of mysteries in the first part. In the case of Wilde, as I have suggested, the theme of the artist was such a compelling one that Wilde was unable wholly to repress it although it conflicted to a certain extent with his main theme. All these works, finally, reveal a reverence for art that is virtually religious: hence the well-nigh magical power of the portrait in each case despite its secularization and disenchantment; it is the image of the aesthetic religion. But precisely because the image has been secularized, because it is clearly the product of a human creator, all these authors are keenly aware of the great moral responsibility incumbent upon the artist. The haunted portrait is not an antique relic left by an anonymous ancestry in the galleries of castles or ancient manors. For better or worse, for good or evil, it is the creation and responsibility of the painter, who thus enters the story with his huge burden of consciousness and conscience.

BY THE end of the nineteenth century and with the novels of Zola and Wilde we have reached the third of the four stages of disenchantment that we established in the preceding chapter. The haunted portrait that entered the Gothic romance with clearly supernatural associations went through a period of rationalization during late romanticism and then was internalized psychologically by writers of late realism. At this point we expect to find inversions of one sort or another. As a matter of fact, within the first decade of the twentieth century we can find interesting inversions of all three major forms of the haunted portrait: as *genius loci*, as *figura*, and as *anima*.

This is not to suggest, of course, that the motif in its conventional forms simply disappeared. In "The Ebony Frame" (1910) Edith Nesbit takes up the motif of dual reincarnation that we discovered in Rossetti's "Saint Agnes of Intercession" and exploits it for sheer horror.[69] The narrator, a young London journalist, has just inherited a house in Chelsea from his aunt. In the attic he finds two old portraits—one "a speaking image of himself" dressed in the fashion of James I, and another of a beautiful woman clad in the style of the same period. Infatuated with the woman in the portrait, he has the painting replaced in an ebony frame from which it had been removed and then hangs it over the mantelpiece. When he looks into her dark eyes, his gaze is held fixed "as by a strong magic," and he begs her to come down from her picture. It is important to note that the narrator asserts he was neither sleepy nor drunk. "I was as wide awake and as sober as ever was a man in the world." Yet as he regards the picture, he sees its eyes dilate, the lips tremble, the hands move slightly, and a smile flickers over her face. He rings for a lamp, but when he turns around the ebony frame is empty and the woman of the picture is moving toward him out of a shadowy corner of the room. At this point the author's intention becomes clear: not parody, not rationalization, but horror. "I hope I shall never again know a moment of terror as blank and absolute. I could not have moved or spoken to save my life. Either all the known laws of nature were nothing, or I was mad." The rest of the story is patently supernatural. It is explained that

[69] E. Nesbit [Bland], *Fear* (London: Stanley Paul, 1910), pp. 86–104.

in an earlier incarnation the narrator had been in love with the woman of the portrait. While he was away at war, she was burned as a witch. Prior to her death she sold her soul to the devil in return for the right to re-enter reality through the portrait (shades of Gogol) as long as it should remain in its ebony frame, which was "not carved by man's hand." The devil also agreed to permit her to remain a woman and remain in the world if her lover would consent to give up his own hopes of heaven. The young narrator, completely bewitched, is prepared to surrender his soul the following midnight. But on the appointed night he returns home to find that the house is on fire. It burns down, destroying once again the witch in her ebony frame, who escaped her first burning three centuries earlier. (Mrs. Nesbit does not seem to be aware of the superstition that such accursed portraits cannot be destroyed by fire.)

During the nineteenth century certain basic rules applied to the treatment of the supernatural—in Gothic romances, ghost stories, or literary adaptations. From Walpole through Gogol and Hawthorne down to Mrs. Nesbit it is always the Past that haunts the Present. The image of the past—the haunted portrait—can come down from its frame; but men from the present do not go up into the picture. In the twentieth century this one-way rule changes. In fact, on the very threshold of the century we encounter a remarkable work that in full consciousness inverts the familiar motif of the haunted portrait as *genius loci* as we know it from the Gothic romance and the ghost story: Henry James's novel *The Sense of the Past*. We are on safe ground when we assume that James was inverting a convention familiar to him. In her essay on "Henry James's Ghost Stories" (1921) Virginia Woolf observed that James was "a good deal attracted by the ghost story, or, to speak more accurately, by the story of the supernatural."[70] The fact is clearly borne out by Leon Edel's edition of *The Ghostly Tales of Henry James*,

[70] *Collected Essays* (London: Hogarth, 1966), I, 286.

for the anthology contains some of his finest prose. James was exposed from early youth to Gothic romances—notably *The Castle of Otranto* and *The Mysteries of Udolpho*—and he was an admirer not only of Hawthorne, to whose works he devoted a monograph, but also of Poe, Hoffmann, Le Fanu, and other nineteenth-century masters of horror and the supernatural.[71] In addition, like such contemporaries as Bergson, Freud, and his brother William, Henry James was profoundly interested in the movement of modern spiritualism.[72] In 1882 the Society for Psychical Research was founded for the specific purpose of investigating certain supernatural manifestations that the spiritualists insisted were authentic.[73] These interests of James's were intensified, toward the end of the century, by studies in the dissociation of personality, which suggested that man has a dual nature—a natural earthly self and a spiritual supernatural self—and thereby provided a psychological justification for the notion of double consciousness.

In the light of these tendencies of the times and James's own proclivities, it is hardly surprising that he responded so enthusiastically to what he called William Dean Howells' "really inspired suggestion" (in a letter of June 29, 1900) that he combine his two interests and write an "international" ghost story or tale of terror.[74] A few weeks later (August 9, 1900) James wrote to Howells that "it is not easy to concoct a 'ghost' of any freshness" but that he had managed to come up with an idea that was "less gross, much less *banal*

[71] Leon Edel, "Introduction," *The Ghostly Tales of Henry James* (New Brunswick, N.J.: Rutgers Univ. Press, 1948), p. x.

[72] Martha Banta, *Henry James and the Occult: The Great Extension* (Bloomington: Indiana Univ. Press, 1972), esp. pp. 9–36.

[73] Scarborough, *The Supernatural in Modern English Fiction*, pp. 4–5, argues that the Society for Psychical Research played a major role in the revival of interest in ghost stories at the end of the nineteenth century.

[74] On the circumstances of composition see Leon Edel, *Henry James: The Treacherous Years, 1895–1901* (Philadelphia: Lippincott, 1969), pp. 329–36.

and exploded, than the dear old familiar bugaboo." In earlier works, like "The Last of the Valerii," James had taken it for granted that the present is always burdened by the past, that Camillo is always haunted by the gods of his ancestors. Here, in contrast, James proposed through a brilliant inversion to depict a situation in which the present haunts the past. His hero, "plunging" or "diving" back into the past, "lives in an air of *malaise* as to the malaise he may, woefully, more or less fatally, find himself creating."

At the beginning of *The Sense of the Past* Ralph Pendrel, a thirty-year-old New Yorker of independent means, has just reached a turning-point in his life: his mother has died, leaving him with no family; he has been rejected by Aurora Coyne, a self-assured young widow with whom he is in love; and he has just inherited a house in London's Mansfield Square from the last of the English Pendrels.[75] Pendrel, an amateur historian who has written *An Essay in Aid of the Reading of History*, desires more than anything in life to arrive at what he calls "the sense of the past." By this he means that he wishes to enter, like the artist, into the very texture of the past: "to feel the stopped pulse," to grasp "the very smell of that simpler mixture of things that had so long served," to hear "the very tick of the old stopped clocks." As a result, he is delighted to have the house in London as his private access to that past that so far he knows only intellectually. In fact, he entertains "an underhand dream that his house might prove 'haunted.' " We recognize the classic formula of the haunted-house ghost story made familiar by Le Fanu, Bulwer Lytton, Bram Stoker, and other Victorian writers: a young man, out of a longing for adventure, enters a house that is rumored to be haunted. That James was fully aware of the convention he was exploiting is indicated by Pendrel's thoughts when he trifles with the idea of spending the first night in his London house: "Nights spent in peculiar houses were a favourite theme of the magazines, and he

[75] *The Sense of the Past* (New York: Scribner, 1922).

remembered tales about them that had been thought clever. . . . The real deterrent to sitting up at Number Nine would just be, he lucidly reasoned, its coincidence with the magazines. Nothing would induce him, he could at least fondly convince himself, to make the place the subject of one of the vulgar experiments that pass into current chatter."

"Vulgar experiments" notwithstanding, Pendrel encounters the obligatory ghost. As he wanders through the rooms on his first visit to the house, he feels himself strangely drawn back into its past. At length he notices in a small inner drawing room the portrait of a young man, dressed in the fashion of 1820, who is facing *into* the picture: "into the dark backward that at once so challenged and so escaped his successor." In his longing to experience that hidden past and, at the same time, to come face to face with the mysterious figure in the painting, Pendrel reminds himself of "the worshipper in a Spanish church who watches for the tear on the cheek or the blood-drop from the wound of some wonder-working effigy of Mother or of Son." Pendrel spends hours of that rainy evening and night exploring the fascinating old house and becoming, as he puts it, increasingly "disconnected" from the outside world of the present. Finally, at two o'clock in the morning, as he passes back toward the room with the strange portrait, he sees the light of his candle reflected in a mirror of the room. Coming nearer, he realizes that it is not a reflection after all. "It was like the miracle prayed for in the church—the figure in the picture had turned." As he stares at the features of the portrait that is now for the first time revealed, he realizes that he is looking into his own face.

So far James has followed the classic formula of the ghost story with a haunted portrait. At this point, however, the inversion takes over. As Pendrel explains a few days later to the Ambassador, the point of the whole affair turned out to be an exchange of identities—"an arrangement all the more easy that he bears an extraordinary resemblance to me." His double, the young man from 1820, is just as curious about the future (that is, Pendrel's time and world) as Pendrel is about the past. Pendrel has taken the Ambassador into his confidence so that someone will know the circumstances of his absence. After this singular interview the Ambassador accompanies Pendrel back to the house where, at the end of Book Three, he watches the young man pause at the doorway "with the supreme pause of the determined diver about to plunge" and then close the door behind him.

In 1900 James got no further than this point in his composition. It was not until 1914, when contemporary events made him long to immerse himself once more in the past, that he took up his novel again and began to write the account of Pendrel's adventures in the world of 1820, which he enters as soon as he closes the door upon the Ambassador. We have no need to sketch the plot of the novel of manners that James intended to insert at this point, since it remained fragmentary. We know from the remaining chapters and from James's notes for the continuation how the principal theme—the present haunting the past—was to work. As Pendrel enters the world of 1820, much about him strikes the inhabitants of that world as strange, indeed ghostly: not just his manner of speech, his air of "freedom," his unaccustomed experience, but also his seemingly clairvoyant ability to know things—such as the appearance of a particular blue pot—that he should not be in a position to know. It is in the artist who paints his portrait that the "malaise" of Pendrel's "queerness" first crystallizes. Pendrel, in turn, becomes increasingly ill at ease as he realizes how greatly he is "haunting" his companions. Matters reach their peak when his fiancée refuses to hang his portrait, which she finds so eerily disturbing, in the main drawing room and hides it away, instead, in the small parlor. This tension restores Pendrel to his own time, just as it summons his double back from the twentieth century. James intended to round off his novel by having Pendrel meet the Ambassador again just as he emerged from the house on Mansfield Square for the first time after his six-month absence. To complete the external framework, the Ambassador would bring him the news that Aurora Coyne had swallowed her haughty pride and come to London to be with him—summoned, ostensibly, by the awareness that Pendrel has now experienced adventures more profound than any she has ever known.

James's notion of transporting a contemporary into another historical age was anything but original. The popularity of such novels as Edward Bellamy's *Looking Backward* (1888), Mark Twain's *A Connecticut Yankee in King Arthur's Court* (1889), or H. G. Wells's *The Time Machine* (1895), indicates that this fictional device was quite fashionable around the turn of the century. By coupling this device with the equally familiar ghost story, however, James achieved an entirely unique effect. Through his surprising inversion he enables the reader to share the utterly original point of view of the haunting portrait figure. This shift in perspective permits him to play on a new and more sophisticated anxiety: not the conventional fear of encountering a haunted portrait, but the fear that obsessed James of being trapped in the past.[76] At the same time, he manages to avoid any preternatural effects by shifting all the "magic" into the consciousness of his hero. For here, as in all his "ghost stories," he is fascinated not with the supernatural *per se* but with the consciousness of the person who thinks that he is experiencing something supernatural. With James, in short, we

[76] Access to the ancestral past plus multiple reincarnations in the style of Rossetti are combined, probably unwittingly, in a recent novel by Noel B. Gerson, *Double Vision* (Garden City, N.Y.: Doubleday, 1972). Here a young painter shuttles back and forth between contemporary Connecticut and early eighteenth-century England. Despite its parallels to James's novel the book makes no attempt to explore similarly profound questions. The novel is a simple tale of the supernatural journey through time by means of a haunted portrait and a magic elixir. Inevitably, the same motif has made its appearance in children's literature. See Norma Kassirer, *Magic Elizabeth* (New York: Viking, 1966), in which a little girl re-experiences the life of her namesake by entering the haunted portrait in her aunt's house.

have reached the absolute inversion of a motif that entered European literature with *The Castle of Otranto*.[77]

Just when Henry James was struggling to rehabilitate for serious literary purposes the motif of the haunted portrait as *genius loci*, his friend and protégée, Edith Wharton, wrote one of the most remarkable inversions of the haunted portrait as *anima*. Like her mentor, Mrs. Wharton was obsessed both with art and with ghosts, topics to which she devoted many of her stories. Her most brilliant conflation of the two occurs in her tale "The Moving Finger" (1901),[78] which exploits various aspects of the haunted portrait and often reads like a gloss to *The Picture of Dorian Gray*. The portrait here—that of the lovely Mrs. Grancy by the artist Claydon—is commonly acknowledged to be a masterpiece. It seems to catch precisely that aspect of Mrs. Grancy's radiant charm that her own husband especially admires. After Mrs. Grancy's untimely death her husband goes abroad for five years on a diplomatic mission. When he returns to New York, the narrator goes to visit him and notes that he has aged as a result of his grief. At the same time, the narrator is shocked to discover that his wife's painted image, though not furrowed like Grancy's, seems to be clouded by "a veil of years." "The bright hair had lost its elasticity, the cheek its clearness, the brow its light: the whole woman had waned." It turns out that Grancy, on his return from Constantinople, had been unable to endure the encounter with her untouched beauty. "She smiled at me coldly across the distance that divided us. I had the feeling that she didn't even recognize me. . . . We were irrevocably separated by the five years of

[77] It is of course not only through portraits that the modern hero can enter the world of painting: several works permit the hero to escape from reality by stepping into landscape paintings. For examples see Hermann Hesse's autobiographical sketch, "Life Story Briefly Told" (1925), and C. S. Lewis' children's story, *The Voyage of the "Dawn Treader"* (1952).

[78] From *Crucial Instances* (1901); rpt. *The Collected Short Stories of Edith Wharton*, ed. R.W.B. Lewis (New York: Scribner, 1968), I, 301–13.

life that lay between us." He had prevailed upon the artist, Claydon, to retouch the portrait in such a way as to accommodate his wife's age to his own. Ten years pass. When the narrator again visits Grancy, now recuperating from a serious illness, he is dismayed to find that the portrait has changed yet again: "Line by line I saw my fear reflected in it. It was the face of a woman *who knows that her husband is dying*." Once again Claydon has touched up the portrait, and the prognostication turns out to be correct: despite the doctor's assurances Grancy dies within a short time.

Up to this point the author has focused primarily on Grancy's attitude toward his wife's portrait. Since he is in love with the memory of the real woman, he has no reverential attitude toward the portrait, which he regards as no more than "a beautiful mausoleum in which she had been buried alive: I could hear her beating against the painted walls and crying to me faintly for help." Hence it does not disturb him in the least to ask Claydon to alter the painting. The artist has a wholly different point of view. From the beginning it has been clear to everyone that the painting of Mrs. Grancy held a particular significance for him. It was even rumored that he "had been saved from falling in love with Mrs. Grancy only by falling in love with his picture of her." When people accused Claydon of visiting Mrs. Grancy merely in order to see the portrait, he replied that "the portrait *was* Mrs. Grancy." Grancy and Claydon represent two entirely different attitudes toward the work of art, even though both of them stand in a mystical relationship to the "haunted" portrait of Mrs. Grancy. The husband loves the painting only for the sake of the woman; the painter loves the woman only for the sake of the painting.

Only after Grancy's death does it emerge that the two men had been engaged for ten years in a contest over Mrs. Grancy—not the "real" Mrs. Grancy, who did not interest the painter, but the portrait into which he had sublimated his love. Grancy has bequeathed the portrait to Claydon, who immediately wipes away all traces of his retouching, restores the portrait to its original splendor, and hangs it in the place of honor in his studio. As Claydon explains, Pygmalion turned his statue into a real woman, but "I turned my real woman into a picture." Like Hawthorne's sorcerer-artist in "The Prophetic Pictures," Claydon is able to bring passion only to those elements of life that he has converted into art. "You don't know how much of a woman belongs to you after you've painted her," he insists. Indeed, there is at least the strong implication that Claydon, like the painter-heroes of Poe and Zola, weakened Mrs. Grancy and even precipitated her death by draining off her spiritual energy and strength into the animated portrait that he created. In any case, it is for the woman in the portrait that Claydon struggles with Grancy. When Grancy first requests him to alter the picture, "it was like asking me to commit murder." The painting is not a mere passive participant in this action: even in death Mrs. Grancy takes an active part. When Claydon looks at his painting, she seems to say to him: " 'I'm not yours but his, and I want you to make me what he wishes.' " After the initial alteration Grancy's friends are convinced that he "drew strength and courage from the sense of his wife's mystic participation in his task." Similarly, when Claydon is asked to make the final change before Grancy's death: " 'I swear it was *her* face that told me he was dying, and that she wanted him to know it! She had a message for him and she made me deliver it.' " Grancy himself is persuaded that his wife knows, better than the doctors, about his impending death. It is only after Grancy's death that Claydon is able to expose his own feelings. In accordance with Mrs. Grancy's wishes, he kept her and her husband together until the end by constantly retouching the portrait. "But now she belongs to me."

In the interest of realism and plausibility Mrs. Wharton has done away with all preternatural effects—even with the calculated ambiguity that characterized Wilde's novel only ten years earlier. Yet she has created a brilliant and absolute inversion of the motif of the haunted portrait as *anima* à la Hawthorne and Wilde. For here we have no living model that comes mysteriously to approximate its portrait; instead, we have a portrait that is touched up to resemble its deceased model. Mrs. Wharton is obviously playing with various implications of the haunted portrait: the portrait that magically "ages"; the Gothic portrait that communicates with the living; and the portrait that has absorbed the soul of the living model. The story acquires its texture and effect only against the background of supernatural tales of haunted portraits. Paradoxically, by shifting the mystery into the minds of the two principal characters, Grancy and Claydon, the author has succeeded in intensifying the impact of the old conventions and thereby in rejuvenating the haunted portrait as *anima* for the literature of the twentieth century.

Whereas James's novel and Mrs. Wharton's novella represent serious inversions of the haunted portrait in its aspects as *genius loci* and *anima*, our example for the inversion of the portrait as *figura* is purely comical. William De Morgan's novel, *A Likely Story* (1911), employs an inversion that seems inevitable—introduced for humorous effect in an excessively long and often ponderous novel.[79] Here much of the story is told from the point of view of the portrait itself, a *cinquecento* portrait of a beautiful young woman that hangs over the chimney-shelf in the library of an English country house. Although the portrait has its own consciousness and can talk, it does not come down from its frame. However, it witnesses certain complications in the lives of two families—that of the restorer who cleans the painting and that of the owner—and is able to clear up certain misunderstandings by telling them what it has seen. Instead of a portrait as *figura*, in other words, we have more precisely the portrait as chronicle or gossip columnist. And not only the portrait can speak. Even a photograph copy of the por-

[79] (New York: Henry Holt, 1911).

trait has the same magical ability—an intensification of the initial absurd inversion.

Just as the portrait is able to assist in the resolution of the two modern plots, the contemporary characters are able to help the portrait understand its own story. When the portrait first begins to speak in England (to a learned old antiquary named Mr. Pelly), it relates its story, beginning with the moment in sixteenth-century Italy when it gradually received the senses of sight, hearing, and speech. "The very first image I can recall is that of my artist, at work. He is the first human being I ever saw, as well as the first visible object I can call to mind. He is at work—as I am guided to understand by what I have learned since—upon my right eye. It is a very dim image indeed at the outset, but as he works it becomes clearer, and at last I see him quite plainly." The third of the three plots—a Gothic romance in miniature—concerns the events that the portrait witnessed as it was being painted: the love affair between the painter and the original of the portrait in an Apennine castle, followed by the terrible revenge of the woman's ugly old husband. Then for four hundred years, nothing: the portrait of the disgraced wife was hidden away in a storage room behind some old furniture.

It is only in the twentieth century, when it is discovered and sold away to England, that the portrait finally learns the conclusion of the story. An autobiographical manuscript by the painter turns up, and Mr. Pelly, who heard the first half of the portrait's tale and who knows of its ability to hear and talk, reads it to the portrait, thereby satisfying its curiosity of four hundred years. Apart from the inversion, it is characteristic that effects created originally for terrifying readers of Victorian ghost stories are now treated humorously. It is taken for granted, for instance, that the portrait talks. "Any picture can hear that is well enough painted," it points out. When the painting first speaks, Mr. Pelly is amazed not at that fact, but at the fact that for four centuries it had remained silent. "Mr. Pelly was dumbfounded at the unreasonableness of the position. A speaking picture was bad enough; but, at least, it might be rational."[80]

Now that we have followed all three principal categories of the haunted portrait through the four characteristic stages of their disenchantment—from conventional acceptance of magic through rationalization and psychological internalization to inversions of various sorts—we have reached the end of our survey. The haunted portrait does not disappear from literature by any means, but there are few significant new variations. The footnotes have already cited certain updatings of established forms, ranging from ghost stories through children's literature to popular fiction. To conclude our survey, let us briefly consider a recent novel that recapitulates the principal aspects of the haunted portrait that we have noted.

In *The Shape of Illusion* (1972) William E. Barrett rounds off the circle by referring quite explicitly to the oldest traditions of haunted portraits.[81] At one point, alluding to phenomena of the sort cited at the beginning of this chapter, one of the characters says: "There is magic in pictures, magic painted into them, that is white magic, serving God.

[80] It is not just portraits that can be prophetic or convey information. In Emile Erckmann-Chatrian's "L'Esquisse mystérieuse" (in his *Contes Fantastiques*, 1860) a young painter is arrested for murder when he paints, in meticulous detail, the scene of a crime that he did not witness; he then proves his innocence by painting in the portrait of the true murderer. Montague Rhodes James's "The Mezzotint" (in his *Ghost-Stories of an Antiquary*, 1920) deals with a mezzotint view of a manor house in Essex. During the course of two days a mysterious figure appears on the lawn, enters the house, and eventually departs. The incident turns out to be a re-enactment of the kidnapping of the artist's son, who had mysteriously disappeared in 1802. A comic version of the same motif is evident, finally, in Ruth McEnery Stuart's "The Haunted Photograph" (*Harper's Bazaar*, June 1909), when the widow of a hotel steward sees her deceased husband, in a photograph of the hotel above her mantelpiece, frantically rushing around the building performing various routine chores.

[81] (Garden City, N.Y.: Doubleday, 1972).

There are several Madonnas in Europe that have been known to weep, observed by many people with tears running from their eyes. The paintings have been examined by experts who found no trickery, nor trace of trickery. There are paintings of saints where the saint has bled. There are at least two Madonnas in paintings whose eyes have come to life and moved on occasion." The novel even refers to paintings of demons that answer questions by moving their lips. In other words, we are dealing with a writer who consciously chooses to relocate the motif of haunted portraits in the religious tradition in which it originated—with a writer, moreover, whose chosen genre is "fantasy fiction," which operates on the borderline between reality and the preternatural.[82] As the background for a story that deals with magic paintings and sorcerer-artists the author has chosen a small town in Germany, which still preserves a medieval-mystical atmosphere, where such occurrences are not inconceivable.

Barrett's novel begins in the least promising of settings for a tale of the supernatural—contemporary Manhattan. A twenty-nine-year-old painter named Kirk Donner is invited by his art dealer, along with a rabbi, a minister, and a priest, to inspect a mysterious painting that has come into his possession. The painting, by an otherwise unknown seventeenth-century German artist, depicts a motif unusual in religious art: the scene when Jesus, after the scourging, is being led through the courtyard of Pilate's palace surrounded by an angry, jeering crowd. What startles the viewers, however, is not the motif itself, but the uncanny fact that each of them, independently, recognizes himself in the hostile crowd depicted in the painting. It is no mere resemblance, we are assured, but a portrait—even though the similarity can be perceived by no one but the person represented.

At the suggestion of one member of the group, the editor of a Protestant journal, Donner goes to Germany to learn

[82] See Barrett's "Foreword" to *The Edge of Things* (New York: Avon, 1974), pp. 9–15.

what he can about the painter, Boniface Rohlmann. Although there is no record of other extant paintings by Rohlmann, it is known that he was born in 1619 in the town of Friedheim, where every ten years a Passion play is performed. The bulk of the novel deals with Donner's experiences during his week in the German village: the performance of the Passion play, his acquaintance with the village actors, the discovery that Rohlmann was burned at the stake for sorcery in 1661, and his love affair with the young woman representing an American news magazine at the Passion play. This framework enables the author to employ—by rationalization, intensification, or inversion—virtually every aspect of the haunted portrait that we have encountered.

Barrett achieves a modern effect of the animated portrait by introducing the old technique of the *tableau vivant.* In the course of the day-long Passion play the actors, from time to time and at important moments, freeze into tableaux easily recognizable as simulations of famous paintings—e.g., Leonardo's *The Last Supper*—and one of these scenes turns out to be based upon Rohlmann's mysterious painting. The motif of reincarnation (à la Rossetti, Henry James, and Mrs. Nesbit) occurs when Donner becomes acquainted with the actor who plays the role of the disciple John. This young man, a gifted wood sculptor with an undiscovered genius for painting, is at the same time the village simpleton: a child's mind in a man's body. After Donner has talked with him and seen his carvings and drawings, he realizes that the young sculptor amounts to a modern counterpart of the seventeenth-century Rohlmann: "Today I had walked on Kirschbaumstrasse with John Veit. It was like walking that street with Boniface Rohlmann, the street that he had painted. I had the feeling that this youth looked as Rohlmann had looked." The curious genius that distinguishes the young sculptor, who exclaims that he would gladly sell his soul for art materials, and that impels him to carve and draw weird monsters, is identical with the genius that Rohlmann's contemporaries regarded as sorcery when they burned him at the stake.

Barrett's novel involves no supernatural plunge back into the past: yet through Donner's researches into Rohlmann's life the seventeenth-century narrative is maintained along with the modern story. The most original invention concerns the painting itself, which is neither precisely a *figura* nor an *anima*. Yet since each viewer believes that he can distinguish in it his own features, it clearly belongs to the category of haunted portraits. Ultimately it is agreed that "the effect of that picture takes place in the human mind, which is mobile. Nothing changes in the painting, which is a fixed object; nothing at all." The painting, thus disenchanted, has simply become an image onto which men project their feelings of guilt, after the fashion of Dorian Gray. When Donner returns from his trip to Germany, he finds that he no longer recognizes himself among the figures in the painting. Instead, in the rabble attacking Jesus he now can make out the hate-contorted features of the girl with whom he had fallen in love in Germany. Overcoming his detachment—that reluctance to commit himself to any other human being that Hawthorne attributed to the artist—Donner realizes that he has projected onto his beloved that other aspect of himself. In short, the debilitating disengagement of the artist disappears as Donner is humanized through his experience with this contemporary version of the haunted portrait.

CHAPTER FOUR

Image as Symbol: The Magic Mirror

At several points in the fairy tale of Snow White the wicked stepmother approaches her mirror and utters words to the effect: "Mirror, mirror on the wall, who is the fairest of us all?" In each case the stepmother initiates decisive and violent action on the basis of the response because she knows that the mirror never lies to her. Now this is rather astonishing: not that an inanimate object can be a reliable and articulate source of information. After all, the fairy tale accepts magic as a convention. What is remarkable is the fact that a mirror—that is, a simple reflecting surface—should have this supernatural ability. Would it not be more reasonable to expect the stepmother to consult an animated statue or a haunted portrait? But as we have seen, animated statues rarely talk; they act. And the haunted portraits, though more garrulous, know little more than family history or the repressed thoughts of the viewer. The notion of informed and talking mirrors, in contrast, is widespread in folklore all over the world. The story of Snow White, for instance, exists in more than eighty variants extending from Iceland across Europe to the Balkans, Asia Minor, and Africa.[1] The mirror may consist of metal, glass, or water; but in every case the wicked queen addresses a reflecting surface with words approximating the formula that is familiar from the English version. But before we consider the origin of this singular notion and the literary uses to which it has been put, it will be useful to make certain initial discriminations. For man's

[1] Ernst Böklen, *Sneewittchenstudien* (Leipzig: Hinrichs, 1910–15).

perennial fascination with mirrors has produced at least three familiar metaphors that are culturally significant but not magic in our sense of the word: the mirror of art, the mirror of God, and the mirror of man.

In the tenth book of *The Republic* Socrates suggests that the artist is like a man who spins a mirror round and round: "You would soon enough make the sun and the heavens, and the earth and yourself, and other animals and plants, and all the other things of which we were just now speaking, in the mirror." For Plato, this analogy serves to express his contempt for the painter or poet, whose creations are at least twice removed from the true reality of Ideas. Unlike the carpenter, whose bed is a direct imitation of the original Idea of a bed, the artist who paints or describes that bed is making an imitation of an imitation, like the reflection in a mirror. This skeptical view of art was intensified by later Platonists. Marsilio Ficino, in his commentary on Plotinus' *Enneads*, argues that the artist is as remote from reality as the man who makes a statue of himself and paints it and then captures the reflection of the painting in a mirror.[2]

During the eighteenth century, when the imitative theory of art was held in great esteem, the analogy was highly popular.[3] Dr. Johnson could bestow no greater praise on Shakespeare than to assert that "his drama is the mirrour of life."[4] Even after the mimetic theory of art gave way to the

[2] *Marsilii Ficini Florentini opera* . . . (Basiliae, 1561), II, 1565 (Commentary on *Enneads* I, 4, 3): *perinde ac si artifex ipse vivens sui ipsius statuam simillimam fabricet, et hanc deinde referat in pictura, pictamque imaginem speculo rursus obijciat, unde ultima quaedam appareat specularis imago. Solus hic artifex homo est, nulla vero imaginum erit homo.* Quoted by Franz Koch, *Goethe und Plotin* (Leipzig: Weber, 1925), p. 246.

[3] M. H. Abrams, *The Mirror and the Lamp: Romantic Theory and the Critical Tradition* (1953; rpt. New York: Norton, 1958), pp. 30–46 ("Imitation and the Mirror").

[4] "Preface to Shakespeare" (1765), in *The Works of Samuel Johnson*, Yale Edition, VII (New Haven, Conn.: Yale Univ. Press, 1968), 65.

expressive theory during the romantic period and the image of the mirror was displaced, in England at least, by that of the lamp, the mirror continued elsewhere to provide a useful analogy. Stendhal was fond of the mirror-metaphor, which he frequently cited. The best-known example occurs in *Le Rouge et le Noir* (1831), where the author compares the novel to a mirror carried along a highway, reflecting at times the azure of the sky and at times the muck of the puddles in the road.[5] Edgar Lee Masters updated the analogy by motorizing it; one of the voices in his *Spoon River Anthology* (1915) recalls:

> "In youth my mind was just a mirror
> In a rapidly flying car,
> Which catches and loses bits of the landscape."[6]

The metaphor has also been inverted ironically. Oscar Wilde objected to it, reasoning that "it would reduce genius to the position of a cracked looking-glass."[7] His countryman, James Joyce, carried the analogy a step further at the beginning of *Ulysses* (1922), where Stephen Dedalus says that the proper symbol of Irish art is "the cracked lookingglass of a servant."[8] In Petersburg at the beginning of the century, a theater that staged parodies was called The Distorted Mirror. Yet the metaphor has remained vigorous, especially in realistic theories of art. The Marxist aesthetician Georg Lukács adduces the mirror hundreds of times as the symbol of an art that reflects a reality existing independent of our consciousness. But whether the analogy is used to designate the alleged artificiality of art, to praise its mimetic qualities, or to sug-

[5] Part II, Chap. 19.

[6] "Ernest Hyde," *Spoon River Anthology* (New York: Macmillan, 1919), p. 116.

[7] "The Decay of Lying" (from *Intentions*, 1891); rpt. *The Artist as Critic: Critical Writings of Oscar Wilde*, ed. Richard Ellmann (New York: Random House, 1969), p. 307.

[8] *Ulysses* (New York: Random House–Modern Library, 1946), p. 8.

gests its insufficiencies, all these examples have one thing in common: the mirror remains a simile or, at most, a metaphor; it has no real existence as an image but exists only as a figure of speech. Shakespeare's dramas are in no literal sense a mirror, any more than Stendhal's novels or the creations of Plato's artist. These creations may be *like* a mirror, for better or worse; but they are not mirrors.

A second important mirror-metaphor in Western thought descends from Plato and the Bible by way of Christian Platonism. This syncretic analogy, which was first publicized by Augustine and his commentators, is based principally on two passages in the New Testament. In one of his more cryptic utterances (1 Corinthians 13:12) St. Paul distinguishes between the obscure knowledge of God that is accessible to men on earth and the pure understanding that they will enjoy in eternity: "For now we see through a glass, darkly; but then face to face: now I know in part; then shall I know even as also I am known." (*Videmus nunc per speculum in aenigmate; tunc autem facie ad faciem.*) A second passage (James 1:23–24) introduces the mirror as a metaphor for the world of superficial appearances that distract men from divine truth: "For if any be a hearer of the word, and not a doer, he is like unto a man beholding his natural face in a glass: For he beholdeth himself, and goeth his way, and straightway forgetteth what manner of man he was."

Relying principally on these two texts, which they combined with ideas loosely adapted from Platonism, medieval Christian theologians developed the mirror-analogy into three rhetorical topoi.[9] Man's soul is a mirror in which God is reflected; Holy Scripture is a mirror that reflects the truth of God; and, negatively, man's mind is a mirror that reflects the illusory world of the senses. For instance, the unblemished mirror is a frequent metaphor for the Virgin Mary,

[9] Ritamary Bradley, "Backgrounds of the Title *Speculum* in Medieval Literature," *Speculum*, 29 (1954), 100–115.

whose purity is assured by the Immaculate Conception and by her perpetual virginity, as we read in the apocryphal Wisdom of Solomon (7: 26): "For she is a reflection of the everlasting light, and a spotless mirror of the activity of God."[10] It is not only in the theological writings of the time that these commonplaces occur. Indeed, "the mirror appears in the writing of nearly every author of the Middle Ages, and it reflects all the preoccupations of that time."[11] The mirror has been recognized as one of the more common figures in the works of Dante and Chaucer, in the *Roman de la Rose* of Guillaume de Lorris and Jean de Meun, in Ulrich von Lichtenstein's *Frauendienst*, as well as in much Provençal and Middle High German courtly lyric poetry—in short, in virtually every major literature of the later Middle Ages. As the metaphor of the mirror became increasingly familiar, it was turned upon the secular world, providing one of the most popular titles for encyclopedic works from the twelfth to the sixteenth century. Vincent of Beauvais' thirteenth-century *Speculum Majus*, which was to consist of four parts—Mirror of Nature, Mirror of Instruction, Mirror of Morals, and Mirror of History—furnished the model for works like Caxton's *Myrrour of the World* (a translation from Vincent of Beauvais), John Barclay's *The Mirrour of Mindes*, and Alexander Barclay's *Myrrour of Good Maners*—not to mention such items as the *Mirror for Magistrates*, Deschamps' *Miroir du Mariage*, or *A Looking Glass for London and England*. This usage still shows up in the titles of such newspapers as the London *Daily Mirror* or the German news weekly *Der Spiegel*. A group of young Americans recently published an anthology of contemporary culture in the United

[10] Edgar J. Goodspeed, *The Apocrypha: An American Translation* (1938; rpt. New York: Random House–Modern Library, 1959), p. 191. *Candor est enim lucis aeternae, et speculum sine macula Dei majestatis. . . .*" For this reason, in Christian iconography the Virgin is often depicted as holding a mirror.

[11] Frederick Goldin, *The Mirror of Narcissus in the Courtly Love Lyric* (Ithaca, N.Y.: Cornell Univ. Press, 1967), p. 8.

States, based explicitly on the pattern of the medieval *speculum mundi*, under the title *The Endless Mirror*.[12] But again, in all these cases the mirror is present not as an object, but as an analogy or metaphor: the soul is *like* a mirror that reflects God; the encyclopedic work is *like* a mirror that catches a reflection of the world.

The topos of the mirror-like soul, which more or less imperfectly reflects God, survived through late medieval mysticism down to eighteenth-century pietism.[13] Meister Eckhart intensified St. Paul's warning when he concluded (in Sermon LVI) that our view of God is as imperfect as our view of the sun reflected in a mirror lying in a pan of water (whereby the original image is refracted three times). But Thomas Aquinas, Heinrich Suso, and other scholars authenticated the mirror as a legitimate tool for self-reflection by declaring that *speculatio* is etymologically related to *speculum* (rather than to *specula*, "watchtower"). By way of Hildegard von Bingen, Jakob Böhme, Nicolas Cusanus, and Angelus Silesius the topos made its way down to the eighteenth century, when the pietist tradition expanded it to include the metaphor of God as the mirror of man's soul. A remarkable passage in Goethe's *The Sorrows of Young Werther* (1774) shows how prevalent both the Platonic and Christian pietist metaphors had become by combining them in one bold sentence. Claiming that he can often sense the presence of the Almighty, Werther exclaims: ". . . if only I could express it all on paper, everything that is housed so richly and warmly within me, so that it might be the mirror of my soul as my soul is the mirror of Infinite God. . . ."[14]

[12] Jack Folsom, *The Endless Mirror: Reflections on the Yestermorrow* (New York: Crowell, 1974).

[13] Hans Leisegang, "Die Erkenntnis Gottes im Spiegel der Seele und der Natur," *Zeitschrift für philosophische Forschung*, 4 (1950), 163–83; August Langen, *Der Wortschatz des deutschen Pietismus* (Tübingen: Niemeyer, 1954), pp. 316–19.

[14] The entry for May 10 (Bk. I); cited here in the translation by Catherine Hutter: *The Sorrows of Young Werther and Selected*

Until the end of the eighteenth century the mirror-metaphor in German literature—in contrast to the mimetic analogy prevalent in England and France—was determined primarily by this mystical view: namely, that the soul is a mirror that, if pure and unsullied, reflects the image of God.[15] But like many other religious ideas this metaphor was gradually secularized. Leibniz had already anticipated this development when, both in frequent letters and in such writings as the *Monadologie* (§63), he called his monads "miroirs vivants." It was notably the growth—indeed, the virtual discovery—of self-consciousness during the age of romanticism that provided the third important function for the venerable metaphor. Man's soul is the mirror no longer of God but of his fellow man and, implicitly, of himself. Concluding his first great letter to Goethe, Schiller noted that his communication had turned into a discourse: ". . . if you should fail to recognize your image in this mirror, then I beg you not to flee it for that reason."[16] German literature of the following decades teems with examples of the same topos: Schiller, Goethe, Jean Paul, Hölderlin, Novalis, Friedrich Schlegel, Hoffmann, Brentano—all are fond of the conceit that a human being is a "living mirror" that reflects the soul of the friend or beloved.[17] Goethe calls Frau von Stein "my dearest mirror."[18] Hölderlin's Hyperion regards himself as the mirror in which

---

Writings (New York: New American Library–Signet, 1962), p. 25. In this connection see Rita Terras, "Goethe's Use of the Mirror Image," *Monatshefte für deutschen Unterricht*, 67 (1975), 387–402.

15 August Langen, "Zur Geschichte des Spiegelsymbols in der deutschen Dichtung," *Germanisch-Romanische Monatsschrift*, 28 (1940), 269–80.

16 Letter of 23 August 1794; in *Der Briefwechsel zwischen Schiller und Goethe*, ed. Hans Gerhard Gräf and Albert Leitzmann (Leipzig: Insel, 1955), I, 7.

17 Hans Peter Neureuter, *Das Spiegelmotiv bei Clemens Brentano: Studie zum romantischen Ich-Bewußtsein* (Frankfurt am Main: Athenäum, 1972), esp. pp. 23–73.

18 Letter of 8 January 1781, in *Goethes Briefe an Frau von Stein*, ed. Jonas Fränkel, rev. ed. (Berlin: Akademie, 1960), I, 264.

the rays of Diotima's light are caught.[19] Novalis' Heinrich von Ofterdingen sees himself as the mirror of Mathilde's "unfragmented existence."[20] By the time Ferdinand Raimund wrote his late-romantic miracle play *The King of the Alps and the Misanthrope* (1828) the metaphor was so well established that it could be reified on the stage: Astragalus, the king of the Alps, assumes the physical shape of the misanthropic Rappelkopf in order to show him, as his "soul mirror," how unattractive Rappelkopf's irritability and paranoid suspicions appear to others.[21] He literally becomes a mirror-image of the other. This romantic analogy recurs in later writers as well. We shall return in another connection to Hermann Hesse's *Steppenwolf.* But it should be pointed out here that Hermine is employing the metaphor of the mirror in the conventional romantic sense when she tells Harry Haller that "I please you and mean so much to you because I am a kind of looking glass for you, because there's something in me that answers you and understands you."[22] In *A Room of One's Own* (1929) Virginia Woolf intensifies the metaphor ironically: "Women have served all these centuries as looking-glasses possessing the magic and delicious power of reflecting the figure of man at twice its natural size." Attributing the entire growth of civilization to this function, so soothing to the male ego, Woolf concludes: "The looking-

[19] *Hyperion oder der Eremit in Griechenland* (1797 and 1799), in Hölderlin, *Sämtliche Werke,* ed. Friedrich Beissner, III (Stuttgart: Kohlhammer, 1958), 63: "in welchem Spiegel sammelten sich, so wie in mir, die Strahlen dieses Lichts?"

[20] *Heinrich von Ofterdingen* (1802), in Friedrich von Hardenberg, *Schriften,* ed. Paul Kluckhohn and Richard Samuel, 2nd ed. (Stuttgart: Kohlhammer, 1960), I, 277: "Gehört nicht ein eigenes ungeteiltes Dasein zu ihrer Anschauung und Anbetung? und bin ich nicht der Glückliche, dessen Wesen das Echo, der Spiegel des ihrigen sein darf?"

[21] *Der Alpenkönig und der Menschenfeind* (Act II, Scene 1), in Raimund, *Sämtliche Werke,* ed. Friedrich Schreyvogl (Munich: Winkler, 1961), p. 378: "Seelenspiegel."

[22] *Steppenwolf,* trans. Basil Creighton and rev. Joseph Mileck and Horst Frenz (New York: Holt, Rinehart and Winston, 1963), p. 108.

glass vision is of supreme importance because it charges the vitality; it stimulates the nervous system" (Ch. 2). Yet in all these cases, for a third time, the mirror is not an image that actually exists in the fictional reality of the work, but a metaphor or analogy: one figure functions *as* a mirror for another.[23] No one thinks for a moment, as did "The Glass Graduate" in Cervantes' *Exemplary Novels*, that he has literally turned to glass.

All three of these metaphors—the Platonic mirror of art that reflects the phenomenal world, the Christian mirror of the soul that reflects God, and the romantic mirror of the self that reflects another human being—had a powerful effect on thought and literature for many centuries, and their familiarity no doubt helped to prepare audiences for literary mirrors of another sort. But they do not constitute images in the strict sense of the word as defined in the Introduction. The mirror as *image* began to play a conspicuous role in literature precisely at the moment when romantic subjectivism began to discover its own consciousness: when the mirror, in other words, was no longer directed figuratively at the world or at God or at one's fellow man, but was held up quite literally by the hero to his own countenance.

In this capacity as an autoscopic tool, the mirror of self-scrutiny shows up repeatedly in literature. It is no accident that the theme of Narcissus reappears in European literature along with the discovery of consciousness. The legend of the young man who scorns the love of Echo and is punished for his disdain by falling irremediably in love with his own reflection has been employed—from Ovid's *Metamorphoses* down to Gide, Valéry, Rilke, and Freud—as a vehicle for the widest variety of interpretations, from the Platonic

[23] Ralph Freedman, *The Lyrical Novel: Studies in Hermann Hesse, André Gide, and Virginia Woolf* (Princeton, N.J.: Princeton Univ. Press, 1963), develops the romantic notion of the individual as the mirror of another person into a refined critical tool for the analysis of the lyrical novel, whose authors are concerned with techniques whereby the hero can mirror himself on his road to self-awareness.

through the Christian to the romantic and the psychoanalytical.[24]

But since that same romantic age also rediscovered the ancient Edenic truth that consciousness almost invariably produces conscience, the mirror simultaneously becomes the instrument that exposes the horrors of the self; as a result, it is often broken when it reveals truths that are hard to bear. In Klinger's drama *The Twins* (1776) Guido smashes his mirror in a symbolic gesture of self-annihilation when he is unable to face himself after having slain his brother Ferdinando.[25] In Jean Paul's novel *Titan* (1803–04) the tutor Schoppe gradually goes mad because, unsettled by his study of Fichte's philosophy, he feels that his "pure Self" is constantly pursuing his "empirical Self." At first, identifying his mirror-image with the inescapable Fichtean "Ego" that torments him, Schoppe simply covers up all the mirrors in his vicinity; when he is finally put into the madhouse, he smashes every mirror in sight. Similarly, in Raimund's *The King of the Alps and the Misanthrope*, before Rappelkopf is finally cured by seeing his unattractive self reflected in the "soul-mirror" provided by Astragalus, he smashes his looking glass—"the world-seducing mirror"—in disgust.[26] At the other end of the century, Oscar Wilde's Dorian Gray finally shatters the carved oval mirror, decorated with a frame of white-limbed ivory Cupids, that reflects the pernicious beauty that has corrupted his soul. For more than a century broken mirrors bestrew the pages of a literature obsessed with the problem of consciousness and the terrible sense of guilt it entails. Yet even these mirrors, although

[24] Frederick Goldin, *The Mirror of Narcissus*; Robert Mühlher, "Narziß und der phantastische Realismus," in *Dichtung der Krise: Mythos und Psychologie in der Dichtung des 19. und 20. Jahrhunderts* (Vienna: Herold, 1951), pp. 407–540; and Louise Vinge, *The Narcissus Theme in Western Literature Up to the Early 19th Century* (Lund: Gleerups, 1967).

[25] Maximilian Klinger, *Die Zwillinge* (Act IV, Scene 4).

[26] *Der Alpenkönig und der Menschenfeind* (Act I, Scene 14), p. 354: "der weltverführende Spiegel."

they have reality as images in the fictional world, cannot occupy our attention. For whether they reflect the joy or the despair of consciousness, whether they are cherished or smashed, they are in no sense of the word "magic" images and hence cannot be disenchanted.

WORLD folklore, however, is full of mirrors that are conspicuously magical. A quick glance at the *Motif-Index of Folk-Literature* reveals dozens of legends concerning clairvoyant mirrors and transforming mirrors, mirrors that render the viewer invisible or that rejuvenate him, mirrors that cause blindness or in which the devil appears, mirrors that answer questions and that make wishes come true, mirrors that turn black or that reveal hidden treasures.[27] The belief in all forms of magic mirror is based on two sets of assumptions, one concerning their spiritual properties and one concerning their physical properties.

The spiritual properties of mirrors are associated with the theory of the material origin of the soul.[28] From India to Egypt, from Africa to China, from Aztec Mexico to New Guinea, primitive men believed that a man's shadow—and, by extension, his reflection—*is* his soul. Anthropologists have discovered that some peoples—e.g., certain Canadian Indian tribes, the Patagonians of South America, the Melanesians and Tasmanians of the South Pacific—use the same vocable to designate both "soul" and "reflection." A late cultural derivation of this primitive notion can be seen in the fact that the French term for a large standing mirror is *psyché*. This belief explains why, in folklore and literature, the devil

[27] Stith Thompson, *Motif-Index of Folk-Literature*, VI, 509.

[28] Julius von Negelein, "Bild, Spiegel und Schatten im Volksglauben," *Archiv für Religionswissenschaft*, 5 (1902), 1–37; M. Weynants-Ronday, *Les Statues vivantes*, pp. 66–96; G. F. Hartlaub, *Zauber des Spiegels: Geschichte und Bedeutung des Spiegels in der Kunst* (Munich: Piper, 1951), p. 23. Despite its title, Pierre Mabille's *Le Miroir du merveilleux* (Paris: Minuit, 1962) has almost nothing to do with our topic or with mirrors at all; it amounts to a running commentary on various texts representing the marvelous.

is so eager to lay his hands on a man's shadow or reflection —not because it *symbolizes* his soul but because it *is* his soul. By the same token, the gods in Indian mythology and the devil in Western folklore often cast no shadow—because the soul is a human attribute. According to legend and Bram Stoker's *Dracula*, vampires are not reflected in the mirror for the same reason: when they lose their souls they lose their reflections. This fundamental belief that the mirror-image is the soul accounts for virtually all the powers attributed to magic mirrors.[29]

Since the mirror-image is the soul, the mirror represents the realm of souls, spirits, and the dead. The mirror therefore speaks with the authority of the spirit world about things past, present, and future—a fact that accounts for the mirror's powers of temporal and spatial clairvoyance.[30] Since, collectively, these spirits know everything, they can tell the viewer what is happening elsewhere in the world of the living and the dead; since they know what is buried beneath the surface of the earth, they are widely consulted for the purpose of divining metals and water. Mirrors can be conjured to prophesy the future—especially if they are approached with lighted candles and the proper formula at midnight on special nights of the year—say, on New Year's

[29] For the next two paragraphs see *Handwörterbuch des deutschen Aberglaubens*, ed. Hanns Bächtold-Stäubli, vol. IX: *Nachträge* (Berlin: De Gruyter, 1941), cols. 547–77. See also Géza Róheim, "Spiegelzauber," *Imago*, 5 (1917), 63–120 (separately printed: Leipzig and Vienna, 1919), which analyzes numerous examples of mirror-magic according to Freud's theory of narcissism.

[30] This view of the soul is not, of course, limited to primitive man. See C. G. Jung's letter of 10 January 1939 to Pastor Fritz Pfäfflin: "the psyche does not exist wholly in time and space. It is very probable that only what we call consciousness is contained in space and time, and that the rest of the psyche, the unconscious, exists in a state of relative spacelessness and timelessness. For the psyche this means a relative eternity and a relative non-separation from other psyches, or a oneness with them." Jung's *Letters*, ed. G. Adler and A. Jaffé and trans. R.F.C. Hull, I (Princeton, N.J.: Princeton Univ. Press, 1973), 256.

Eve. The mirror also functions as an effective apotropaic against the evil eye (cf. the legend of Perseus and Medusa); it can ward off various illnesses and peasants even use it to drive away hailstorms. For these reasons mirrors are sometimes worn as amulets. But great caution must be exercised, because any such potent magic can also be dangerous.

Since the soul remains in the mirror after the death of the body, it is advisable to drape the mirrors in the room of a dead person to prevent the soul of the deceased from emerging to haunt the living (or, according to a different theory, to prevent death from doubling itself in the mirror and claiming another life). The soul of the deceased can be conjured up from time to time for purposes of divination. But there is always the danger that the soul thus summoned may not be content to remain quietly within the mirror; it may emerge from the glass in the form of a ghost. Moreover, since the conjurations generally take place at night, there is always the risk that the person consulting the mirror—that is, standing at night, alone, before the realm of death—will lose his own reflection in the glass (for instance, if the candle goes out unexpectedly) and, as a result, die. Or perhaps the devil himself will appear in the mirror, which is the doorway to his realm, and carry away the soul of the foolhardy conjurer. Because of such perils, in many cultures children under a certain age are not permitted to look into mirrors lest the influence of the dead or the devil cause the child to become ugly or to stammer, to fall ill or even to die.

These ancient superstitions continue to show up in modern variations. Hans Christian Andersen's familiar cycle of stories, "The Snow Queen," revolves around the delusions that affect the young hero, Kay, when his eye is pierced by a splinter of glass from the devil's mirror, which causes everything good to appear bad and vice versa. In Kurt Vonnegut's *Breakfast of Champions* (1973), Kilgore Trout, a writer of science fiction, calls mirrors "leaks" or "holes between two universes." "If he saw a child near a mirror, he might wag his finger at a child warningly, and say with great solemnity, 'Don't get too near that leak. You wouldn't want to wind up in the other universe, would you?' "[31]

Folklorists have found it convenient to divide magic mirrors into two categories: cognizant (*wissend*) and causative (*wirkend*). These categories suffice to subsume most of the common superstitions cited above. For purposes of literary analysis, however, a different principle of organization is more useful. Literature, of course, makes extensive use of motifs borrowed from folklore. But literature is concerned primarily with the relationship of a character to the magic mirror. These relationships can be defined more easily with reference to the physical properties of mirrors than to their spiritual properties of cognition and causation.

For anyone with a natural capacity for wonder, there is something inherently mysterious about mirrors. First, the mirror knows more than the viewer knows since it can see what is happening behind our backs. This property, in conjunction with the theory of the soul, has yielded the art of catoptromancy, or divination by mirrors. Second, the mirror has the disturbing ability to double everything. As the heresiarch of Uqbar puts it in Borges' fable of "Tlön, Uqbar, Orbis Tertius," "mirrors and copulation are abominable, since they both multiply the numbers of men."[32] Third, the mirror contains within itself a strange world in which everything is inverted or backward, from the parting of one's hair to the print in a book. Leonardo's secret writings share much of the mystery of the mirrors before which they must be held to be deciphered.

These three properties suggest the three principal categories of magic mirror that we find in literature: the catop-

[31] *Breakfast of Champions* (New York: Delacorte, 1973), p. 19.

[32] Jorge Luis Borges, *Ficciones*, ed. Anthony Kerrigan (New York: Grove, 1962), p. 17. Borges' obsession with mirrors, which constitute one of his most frequent images, goes back to "the earliest fears and wonders of my childhood, being afraid of mirrors, being afraid of mahogany, being afraid of being repeated." See Richard Burgin, *Conversations with Jorge Luis Borges* (1969; rpt. New York: Avon-Discus, 1970), p. 31.

tromantic mirror that the viewer consults for information; the doubling mirror from which the reflected figure emerges to confront the viewer as his own "double"; and the penetrable mirror that the viewer can enter in order to experience at first hand its reflected world. Whereas the catoptromantic mirror tends to remain at the level of a minor motif, the doubling and the penetrable mirror easily develop into symbolic images: of the self and of an alternative world-model.

THE oldest and most familiar of these categories is the catoptromantic mirror, which we have already encountered in the story of Snow White. It does nothing but speak; no figures emerge from it, and there lurks behind it no world that one might be tempted to enter. Cognitive mirrors of this sort are known from folklore all over the world. Evidence suggests that the belief in magic mirrors was quite extensive during the Middle Ages. The medieval passion for order, which systematized all existing knowledge into encyclopedias, also applied itself to magic, including the so-called *magia specularia.* In his *Polycraticus* (1159), for instance, John of Salisbury described the various techniques of the *specularii,* those who practice divination by means of reflecting surfaces. Any competent sorcerer was expected to be able to make a magic mirror, and every really important ruler was reputed to own one. (The dream of efficient technological intelligence-gathering antedates modern secret services by many centuries.) Magic mirrors are always associated with reports concerning the palace of Prester John, the legendary Christian potentate of India. According to one version, Prester John's mirror was set with three precious stones, which sharpened the senses of the viewer, and it was kept under constant scrutiny by three learned men, who could make out everything that was going on in the world.[33]

[33] See the account by Johannes Witte de Hese (1389), in Friedrich Zarncke, *Der Priester Johannes,* Zweite Abhandlung (Leipzig: Hirzel, 1876), p. 167: *item ibi est speculum, in quo sunt positi tres*

Other documents attest to catoptromantic experiments by historically more valid figures like Dr. Faust, Nostradamus, and Catherine de Medici. Friar Bacon is said to have manufactured a magic mirror at Oxford in which one could see what people were doing anywhere on earth; but he subsequently destroyed his invention because it proved to be too great a distraction to his students.[34] At its most sophisticated level, the art of catoptromancy distinguishes various kinds of magic mirror depending on the materials used and the process by which each is fabricated: the theurgic mirror, the mirror of Cagliostro, the Swedenborgian mirror, the Galvanic mirror, the cabalistic mirror, and various others.[35] But basically all are identical to the extent that they are consulted for divination only. In the twentieth century, magic has been largely replaced by science, but the goals are often the same. An American industrial engineer recently patented a mirror trademarked "Select-a-Size," which has found an eager market among weight-watchers and clothing designers.[36] The upper part of the mirror remains flat, providing a true reflection of the head, and the curvature of the lower section can be adjusted to present a more flattering view of the body. Have we really come so far from "Mirror, mirror on the wall . . ."?

The catoptromantic mirror shows up widely in literature as well. In Mme Leprince de Beaumont's moralizing fairy tale, "Beauty and the Beast," Beauty's room in the Beast's

---

lapides preciosi, quorum unus dirigit et acuit visum, alter sensum, tercius experienciam. Ad quod speculum sunt electi tres valentissimi doctores, qui inspiciendo speculum vident omnia, quae fiunt in mundo, ut ibidem dicitur.

[34] E. M. Butler, *The Myth of the Magus* (Cambridge, England: Cambridge Univ. Press, 1948), p. 149; see also Carl Kiesewetter, *Faust in der Geschichte und Tradition* (Leipzig: Max Spohr, 1893), pp. 459–92. Kiesewetter reproduces some of the conjuration formulas used by Renaissance *specularii.*

[35] *The Encyclopedia of Occult Sciences* (New York: Tudor, 1968), pp. 328–30.

[36] Reported in *The New York Times* for 31 August 1974.

palace has been thoughtfully equipped with a magic mirror in which she can see how her family is faring back at home. Especially during the age of romanticism, which rehabilitated folk culture, the magic mirror appeared with increasing frequency in serious literature. In Goethe's *Faust* (1808), for instance, the aged scholar is first exposed to the ideal of womanly beauty when he peers into a magic mirror in the "Witch's Kitchen" (ll. 2429–30):

> Was seh' ich? Welch ein himmlisch Bild
> Zeigt sich in diesem Zauberspiegel!
> (What do I see? What a heavenly image
> Reveals itself in this magic mirror!)

The motif of catoptromancy is also closely associated with the medieval legend of Genoveva, who is rejected by her husband after having been falsely accused of infidelity. In Ludwig Tieck's version (*Leben und Tod der Heiligen Genoveva*, 1800) the mirror is used for evil purposes: the villain, Golo, bribes the witch to make her magic mirror depict an act of infidelity that, in fact, never took place. In Friedrich Hebbel's drama (*Genoveva*, 1843), in contrast, the magic mirror proves Genoveva's innocence. Friedrich de la Motte Fouqué's *The Magic Ring* (*Der Zauberring*, 1813), one of the most popular romances of the Napoleonic period in Germany, also tells of a magic mirror that displays to the innocent observer all the delights of kingdoms far and wide. But as so often is the case in fairy tales, the mirror is governed by a taboo. When the heroine, Berta, draws the curtain away from the mirror in violation of a specific prohibition, it becomes prophetic and reveals to the horror-stricken girl her own future image, covered with blood. And we recall that in Willibald Alexis' "Venus in Rome" (1828) Hubert is bewitched when the priest Palumbus casts a spell on his image in the magic mirror.

It was no doubt inevitable that a magic image as firmly established in romantic literature as the catoptromantic mirror would be not discarded but retained under the prevailing laws of adaptation. By 1830 we find clear examples of rationalization. In "My Aunt Margaret's Mirror" (1828) by Sir Walter Scott, a writer profoundly indebted to German romanticism, a matron of Edinburgh consults a "Paduan Doctor" to learn what has happened to her husband, who is with Marlborough's troops in Flanders.[37] In the wizard's magic mirror she sees what is later confirmed as true: her husband has abandoned her for a younger woman and, moreover, murdered his reproachful brother-in-law. Scott presents the tale as a true story told him by his great-aunt, Mrs. Margaret Swinton; but he carefully includes within the narrative the possibility of rationalization. For the level-headed sister of the more gullible wife suggests that the Italian "man of skill," recently arrived from the continent, would have had the opportunity to learn the circumstances of the case in advance and to prepare his phantasmagoria accordingly. (Scott's manipulation of credulity and skepticism reminds us again of his treatment of the walking portrait in "The Tapestried Chamber.")

Hawthorne, a brilliant manipulator of magic images appropriated boldly from romanticism, always added a qualification that protected him, as author, against charges of naïveté or mysticism. In his "Legends of the Province House" (1842) he tells the tale of "Old Esther Dudley," the last descendant of an eminent but improverished Loyalist family, who remains as caretaker of Province House after the last governor of the province of Massachusetts has departed.[38] Hawthorne is fascinated by Esther Dudley principally as an archetype of blind conservatism who, failing

[37] *Castle Dangerous. Chronicles of the Canongate*, Standard Edition (Boston: Dana Estes, 1894), pp. 243–96. For a discussion of Scott's sources and revisions see Parsons, *Witchcraft and Demonology in Scott's Fiction*, pp. 217–20.

[38] From Part Two of *Twice-Told Tales* (1842); cited according to *Twice-Told Tales and Other Short Stories*, ed. Quentin Anderson (New York: Washington Square Press, 1960), pp. 221–33.

to perceive that the revolution has transformed history, remains true to the king. During the years between the departure of Sir William Howe and the arrival of Governor Hancock, the old woman lives alone in the Province House with no company but her memories, the neighborhood children, and—ghosts. (The ghosts constitute a fitting image for a conservatism tied superstitiously to the past.) "Many and strange were the fables which the gossips whispered about her," Hawthorne observes, characteristically introducing a supernatural motif while carefully dissociating himself from it. Among the articles of furniture in the mansion is an antique mirror with a tarnished gold frame and a "surface so blurred, that the old woman's figure, whenever she paused before it, looked indistinct and ghost-like." It was the general belief that the old woman could conjure up from the mirror not only the former governors and their ladies or the clergymen but even the Indian chiefs who had come to Province House: "all the figures that ever swept across the broad plate of glass in former times. . . ." Rumors of this sort make Mistress Dudley the object of fear and pity alike, but also assure her of her privacy. Yet she is never lonely. "Whenever her chill and withered heart desired warmth, she was wont to summon a black slave of Governor Shirley's from the blurred mirror, and send him in search of guests who had long ago been familiar in those deserted chambers." The spectral messenger would go forth to the graveyard, where he would knock at the tombs and summon the dead to Mistress Dudley at Province House at midnight.

In certain contexts the romantic image was preserved as a convention with all its magical associations. In Act II of Wagner's *Parsifal* (1882) Klingsor watches the hero's approach toward his castle in a magic mirror. But more often the image is rationalized by psychological internalization, as in the "nighttown" chapter of Joyce's *Ulysses* (1922), where the drunken Stephen Dedalus and Leopold Bloom peer into the mirror in Bella Cohen's brothel and see, jointly, the face of a beardless William Shakespeare, who addresses them angrily[39]—an apparition justified by the allusions to Shakespeare earlier in the day.

In all these representative cases the catoptromantic mirror of folklore has been appropriated as a requisite for literary purposes, but it seems to have no deeper meaning: its function, in the works that accept magic as a convention, is simply to reveal certain information. In the other cases it supplies little but atmosphere. To this extent it can be said that the image of the catoptromantic mirror, when it occurs in literature, remains on the level of a motif, never achieving the significance of a theme or symbol.

BEFORE we turn to the category that made the main contribution to nineteenth-century literature, we need to consider two works that stand outside the categories, yet, to the extent that they transform the magic mirror into a theme, clearly attest the romantic fascination with the image. E.T.A. Hoffmann, perhaps the finest fiction-writer of German romanticism and certainly the one who had the greatest influence on subsequent writers in Germany and abroad, adopted the motif of the catoptromantic mirror in several works—notably in his tale *The Golden Pot* (1814), where the polished surface of the pot acts as a mirror that magically reveals the poetic realm of Atlantis to Anselmus, the hero of the story.[40] In his "Tale of the Lost Reflection" Hoffmann goes much further than simple divination by mirror. The story, which has become widely known as the Giulietta-scene in Offenbach's *Tales of Hoffmann*, was originally an encapsulated episode in Hoffmann's framework narrative, "A New Year's Eve Adventure" (1815).[41] Following a dis-

[39] *Ulysses*, pp. 553–54.

[40] Robert Mühlher, "Liebestod und Spiegelmythe in E.T.A. Hoffmanns Märchen 'Der goldne Topf,'" in *Dichtung der Krise*, pp. 41–95.

[41] "Die Abenteuer der Silvester-Nacht," from *Fantasies in the Manner of Callot* (1814–15); cited according to the translation by Alfred Packer in *The Best Tales of Hoffmann*, ed. E. F. Bleiler (New York: Dover, 1967), pp. 104–29.

astrous New Year's Eve party the narrator, a "Travelling Enthusiast," takes refuge in a beer cellar, where he meets a man who turns out to be none other than the unhappy hero of Adalbert von Chamisso's story *Peter Schlemihl* (1814), the man who sold his shadow to the devil. While they are chatting, another man enters the cellar, after having instructed the tavern-keeper to cover up all his mirrors. Within a few minutes Schlemihl gets into a quarrel with the newcomer, who rushes back out of the room. Later that evening, when the Travelling Enthusiast finds lodgings, he is put into a room in which all the mirrors have been draped. His roommate proves to be none other than the mysterious stranger from the beer cellar. When the stranger steps up to the mirror, which the narrator has uncovered, it becomes evident that he has no reflection. The next morning, when the narrator wakes up, he finds that the stranger, named Erasmus Spikher, has left behind a manuscript containing the story of his life, in which he recounts how he lost his mirror-image.

Although the details differ, the story generally approximates the version made famous by Offenbach. In Hoffmann's original the hero is a young married man, who leaves his wife and child for a time in order to fulfill his lifelong dream of a *Bildungsreise* to Italy. (Although his profession is not specified, he seems to be another of the Christian artist-figures who are tempted to forsake their art and their faith for the sake of erotic passion.) Arriving in Florence (not Venice, as in the operatic version), Spikher attends a garden party, where he meets and falls in love with the seductive courtesan, Giulietta. Though warned by his friend Friedrich and repelled by Giulietta's associate, the sinister "miracle-doctor" Signor Dapertutto, Spikher accepts an invitation to a festival given by Giulietta. There, after quarreling with a young Italian who is also bewitched by the enchanting courtesan, he kills him. In despair because he must flee and leave behind his beloved Giulietta, Spikher agrees to let her keep as a memento his mirror-image, which Giulietta calls "this dream of your ego." "No power—not even the Devil—can take it away from you," he promises her, "until you own me, body and soul." After a passionate embrace, he watches in astonishment as his image steps out of the mirror, glides into Giulietta's arms, and disappears with her in a cloud of mist.

Signor Dapertutto helps Spikher to escape, but things go badly for him from that moment on. Soon discovering that everyone mocks him for having no reflection, he insists that all mirrors be covered in his presence. Shortly after Spikher's return to Germany, his young son is horrified when he notices that his father has lost his reflection, and his wife drives him out of the house. Eventually, when Spikher has reached a nadir of despondency, Dapertutto and Giulietta show up, promising to restore his precious mirror-image if only he will poison his wife and child and thus break the churchly bonds tying him to them. Spikher is seriously tempted—especially when he sees his one-time reflection, now wholly independent of him, embracing Giulietta in the mirror. He has already dipped his pen into his own blood, ready to sign, when a vision of his wife appears. Appalled at the sacrilege he was about to commit, Spikher resigns himself to a life with no reflection, no family, no happiness—but with his immortal soul still intact.

In several senses Hoffmann's tale turns out to be a witty "mirroring" of the story of Peter Schlemihl. First, Schlemihl serves as a *Seelenspiegel* for Spikher, a "soul-mirror" reminding him of his own foolishness and despair. Second, the plot of Hoffmann's tale clearly "mirrors" that of Chamisso's story: both men sign away to a representative of the devil something that subsequently reveals itself to be unexpectedly dear to them. In both cases this loss compels them to renounce familial bliss and personal happiness. Third, both writers make use of the primitive belief in the identity of the soul and the shadow or reflection; but in both cases the original identity is weakened. Schlemihl's shadow and Spikher's reflection are no longer, literally and materially, their souls, but merely a precious part of them that can be used by the devil for purposes of spiritual blackmail.[42]

However, there are significant differences as well. Above all, although Hoffmann's tale depends on a supernatural incident, it is not essentially a supernatural tale like Chamisso's. Peter Schlemihl not only loses his shadow; he receives a magic purse in return for it and goes on to acquire Seven League boots, to travel under a cloak that makes him invisible, and to witness a whole repertoire of magic tricks performed by the devil. Hoffmann, in contrast, is concerned principally with Spikher's response to this single intrusion of the supernatural into his life. To be sure, the loss of one's reflection is clearly a supernatural happening; yet if we accept that absurd premise, then the denouement is psychologically just as rational and consistent as it is, say, in Kafka's "The Metamorphosis," whose protagonist thinks that he has been transformed into a huge beetle. In addition, the public reaction is just as reasonable as the community response to the scarlet letter that Hester Prynne wears on her dress: both the deprivation and the addition of an image can symbolize a moral condition. In other words, in Hoffmann's tale only the premise is supernatural, but not the story itself. Hoffmann has gone far beyond those romantic writers who were content to use the catoptromantic mirror as a simple motif. In his tale the image has clearly achieved the level of a theme: the story of Erasmus Spikher is inconceivable without the image of the lost reflection.

Although Hoffmann's tale does not fit into any of the three principal categories, it exerted a profound influence on other writers.[43] We shall take up in another connection Dos-

[42] Gogol, who was profoundly influenced by Hoffmann, used the same motif for parodistic effect in "The Nose." See Charles E. Passage, *The Russian Hoffmannists*, p. 167.

[43] Although there is no question of any direct influence, Hawthorne's notion in his *American Notebooks* (17 October 1835) sounds almost like a response to Hoffmann: "To make one's own

toevsky's novel *The Double*, which was directly affected by Hoffmann's tale. However, the influence of the tale is evidenced just as clearly by a parodistic imitation. In "Onophrius, or the Fantastic Vexation of an Admirer of Hoffmann" (1832), Gautier tells the story of a young poet-painter who is so exaggeratedly committed to the cultivation of his imagination that he eventually goes mad.[44] At night he does not dare to look into a mirror lest he see there something other than his own reflection. Finally, he takes the tale of Peter Schlemihl and "A New Year's Eve Adventure" so much to heart that he insists he is unable to see his own reflection in mirrors or his shadow on the floor.

Shortly after Hoffmann's story appeared, the poet Clemens Brentano wrote a letter to the author. He begins by confessing that he is often tempted to extinguish candles so as not to see his shadow and to curtain the mirrors so as not to be confronted with his own reflection. "This reflection of myself in your book," he continues, frightens him so much that he is unable to comprehend how Hoffmann could stand to expose his own reflection so frankly. "For a long time now I have had a certain horror of all writing that reflects itself and not God."[45] Brentano's letter was never sent. But as a document it suggests not only the fascination of Hoffmann's story for a generation obsessed with mirrors, but also the depth of Brentano's own feelings about the mirrors that occur with such frequency in his works.

---

reflection in a mirror the subject of a story." Just as Hoffmann wrote about a man without a reflection, Hawthorne's allegorical fantasy "Monsieur du Miroir" (1837; in *Mosses from an Old Manse*, 1846) deals with a reflection without a man: though it cannot talk, it can go anywhere, move rapidly through obstacles, float upon water, etc. Its "whole business is REFLECTION," Hawthorne concludes.

[44] From his collection of ironic tales, *Les Jeunes-France* (1832), in Théophile Gautier, *Oeuvres*, XVI (Paris: Charpentier, 1883), 25–70.

[45] *E.T.A. Hoffmanns Briefwechsel*, ed. Hans von Müller and Friedrich Schnapp, II (Munich: Winckler, 1968), 82.

Brentano's attitude displays a curious ambivalence.[46] On the one hand, he frequently uses the affirmative romantic metaphor of the individual who mirrors another. On the other hand, he early discovered the agony of consciousness as reflected in mirror-images. In one of his most famous poems, "Lurelay," the sorceress, whose beauty destroys men yet who is incapable of love, cannot bear to gaze into mirrors because of her wretchedness:

Vor Jammer möcht ich sterben,
Wenn ich zum Spiegel seh.

But despite Brentano's characteristically romantic obsession with the mirror as a metaphor, he seems to have used the image of a magic mirror only once in his works.

We do not know precisely when Brentano wrote the relevant section of the first version of his *Chronicle of the Travelling Scholar*—perhaps as early as 1810 but possibly only after reading Hoffmann's "Tale of the Lost Reflection," which terrified him so.[47] In any case, the story displays Brentano's growing preoccupation with religion, which eventually led to his conversion to Christian mysticism. The mystical context becomes clear long before the young scholar, Johannes, relates the legend of the master artisan, whose skill in constructing wondrous artifacts was so great that he was often considered a sorcerer.[48] Among other things, he had fashioned of metal such subtle mirrors that even invisible spirits could be seen in them as visible figures.

[46] This ambivalence is one of the central topics in Hans Peter Neureuter, *Das Spiegelmotiv bei Clemens Brentano.*

[47] For a comparison of the two pieces see Ernst Fedor Hoffmann, "Spiegelbild und Schatten: Zur Behandlung ähnlicher Motive bei Brentano, Hoffmann und Chamisso," in *Lebendige Form: Festschrift für Heinrich E. K. Henel*, ed. Jeffrey L. Sammons and Ernst Schürer (Munich: Wilhelm Fink, 1970), pp. 167–88.

[48] "Die Chronika des fahrenden Schülers" (Urfassung), in Clemens Brentano, *Werke*, ed. Freidhelm Kemp, II (Munich: Hanser, 1963), esp. pp. 567–69.

His mirrors magnified distant speech and song, and intensified the rays of the sun so powerfully that metal could be melted in their reflection. The master built his finest mirror in awe of the glory of God. But gradually, as more and more people came to admire his work, he devoted himself increasingly to the mirror and neglected his other duties. Finally, becoming rich and proud, he lost sight of God and immersed himself in sinful passion. One day, when the sky was cloudy, he put his child to rest near the mirror and went off on a brief errand. During his absence the sun came out, and its intensified rays struck and killed the child. When the master returned and saw what havoc he had wrought, and recognized that he had forsaken the consolation of God, he lay down upon his child and was himself consumed by the flames, which then moved on to burn his house and eventually to destroy the entire sinful city.

Like Hoffmann, Brentano has gone well beyond the romantic writers who limited themselves to the motif of the catoptromantic mirror: Brentano is interested not so much in the fact of magic itself as in the moral reactions of the master craftsman; the image has been transformed into a symbol notably consistent with the remark in his letter to Hoffmann, which expresses "a certain horror of all writing that reflects itself and not God." The magic mirror constructed by Brentano's *specularius*, though originally meant to reflect the glory of God, was corrupted to gratify the illusory world of appearances and, ultimately, to reflect nothing but the vanity of the master himself. Brentano is talking generally about his own shift from an attitude of aesthetic autonomy during his early years to his later writing in the service of the Church. In the image of the mirror, which had long provided metaphors for his work, he found the perfect image on which to build his anecdote.

In the last analysis, however, Brentano's tale contributes nothing to the history of the image because it does not depend for its effect upon the physical or spiritual properties of the mirror. What Brentano required was any artifact that can become autotelic and distract the artist from his devout purposes. It is imaginable, for instance, that the story might just as well concern a sculptor who wrought a statue of Jesus or Mary and then became infatuated with his work as pure art until, one day, it fell on his child and crushed it. Both Hoffmann and Brentano attest the romantic catoptromania and the sense, around 1815, that the magic mirror might well serve as more than a simple motif in literary works. But the image was not destined to become truly symbolic until writers were able to exploit the traditional properties of magic mirrors to express a compulsive generational concern.

THE FIRST significant advance of the mirror-image beyond the essentially private stage represented by Hoffmann and Brentano can be seen in connection with the obsessive nineteenth-century motif of the *Doppelgänger*. The belief in ghostly "doubles" of living people, which originated during the same murky period that regarded shadows and reflections as material manifestations of the soul, had already showed up frequently in literature.[49] But generally the eerie aspect was subordinated, for comic purposes, to the confusions that arise when an actual physical double appears. Think of the multiple confusions that enliven the various treatments of the Amphitryon theme from Plautus to Molière, or Plautus' *Menaechmi*, or *A Comedy of Errors* and other comedies by Shakespeare. Around 1800, however, the

[49] Otto Rank, *Der Doppelgänger* (1925; *The Double: A Psychoanalytic Study*, trans. and ed. with an introduction by Harry Tucker, Jr. [Chapel Hill: Univ. of North Carolina Press, 1971]); Ralph Tymms, *Doubles in Literary Psychology* (Cambridge, England: Bowes and Bowes, 1949); Robert Rogers, *A Psychoanalytic Study of the Double in Literature* (Detroit: Wayne State Univ. Press, 1970); C. F. Keppler, *The Literature of the Second Self* (Tucson: Univ. of Arizona Press, 1972). It should be clear from these representative titles that most of the vast literature on doubles in literature is psychologically oriented; none of the studies traces the images —e.g., shadow, mirror, portrait, etc.—systematically from the literary point of view.

ancient motif began to acquire new values. It is symptomatic of this revaluation that, in the hands of Heinrich von Kleist, the traditionally comic theme of Amphitryon becomes tragic, as the confusions of identity undermine Alkmene's faith in all cognition, causing her to question meaning altogether.

It has been suggested with considerable cogency that the motif of the double tends to appeal especially to periods of "subjective realism"—that is, to such periods as romanticism and expressionism, whose writers, fascinated with phenomena of the unconscious, seek literary means of externalizing that unconscious "second self."[50] Among the multiple and complex factors that came together to produce the historical phenomenon we designate as "romanticism," at least three contributed to the contemporary obsession with doubles. The first was Fichte's philosophy, which in the decade following the publication of the *Wissenschaftslehre* (1794) had an unparalleled influence on thought in Germany.[51] An act of radical self-consciousness stands at the beginning of Fichte's system, which denies the existence of any reality apart from the Absolute Self: first the Ego posits itself; then this Ego posits the non-Ego (external reality), upon which it can exercise its powers of cognition. For early romantic writers, many of whom reduced the subtleties of Fichte's theory of knowledge to grand oversimplifications, this act of splitting consciousness into an observing and an observed self provided a philosophical basis for the popular belief in doubles. The individual goes through life happy and untroubled until he discovers, suddenly and accidentally, that he is not an independent human being but merely the empirical self linked to a more powerful absolute self represented by a double. Jean Paul, who coined the term *Doppelgänger*, was fascinated by the phenomenon of twins and look-alikes, and his works are peopled with doubles who constitute complementary halves: e.g., the twins Walt and Vult in *Years of*

[50] Ralph Tymms, *Doubles in Literary Psychology*, pp. 121–22.

[51] Wilhelmine Krauss, *Das Doppelgängermotiv in der Romantik: Studien zum romantischen Idealismus* (Berlin: Emil Ebering, 1930).

Indiscretion (*Flegeljahre*, 1804). But the motif, which in many of Jean Paul's works is natural and comic, acquired a tragic potential as a direct result of his study of Fichte. In *Titan* (1800–03) Jean Paul depicts in fictional form the perils of a Fichteanism that, in a philosophically untrained mind, can degenerate into pure solipsism. Schoppe, already ravaged by the pursuit of the "pure" self that he detects in the mirrors surrounding him, drops dead of fright when he encounters what seems to be his double, his other self, in the flesh. It turns out to be his old look-alike friend, Siebenkäs; but the effect of a double's appearance on this mind deranged by Fichte is no less lethal. And the affinity of the two motifs—mirror and double—is effectively established.

Whereas Jean Paul thought of the double chiefly in Fichtean terms, other romantic writers found a justification for the phenomenon in the theory of animal magnetism, which was popularized around the turn of the century by German scientific thinkers under the impact of Anton Mesmer.[52] Essentially, animal magnetism was nothing but hypnotism. But at the beginning of the nineteenth century it was believed that a magnetic and physical force actually emanated from the hands of the hypnotist and acted upon the mind of the patient. This widely accepted theory provided a "scientific" basis for doubles, which was more tangible than the philosophical basis provided by Fichte. According to Mesmer's teaching, two people could actually be bonded together in a magnetic union. G. H. Schubert concluded his influential *Views on the Nocturnal Aspects of Natural Science* (1808) with a chapter on animal magnetism, in which he discusses "the intimate union of two human beings" made possible by hypnotism.[53] The familiar relationship between the "Magne-

[52] See Oskar Walzel, *German Romanticism*, trans. Alma Elise Lussky (1932; rpt. New York: Capricorn Books, 1966), esp. Chap. III ("The Third Stage of the Early Romantic Theory").

[53] *Ansichten von der Nachtseite der Naturwissenschaft* (Dresden, 1808; rpt. Darmstadt: Wissenschaftliche Buchgesellschaft, 1967), p. 350: "eine solche innige Vereinigung zweyer menschlicher Wesen."

tiseur" and the "Somnambulist" parallels and foreshadows other more profound relationships. "We envisaged the possibility that two separate human beings are capable in a certain sense of being one." As a result of such speculations, the doubles in the works of Hoffmann, an assiduous student of Schubert's writings, are tied together by firmer and more sinister bonds than the wild imaginings that motivate Jean Paul's Schoppe. The plot of Hoffmann's novel *The Devil's Elixirs* (1815–16) is almost too complicated to follow, let alone to recapitulate. Suffice it to say that much of the action depends upon confusions of identity produced by the half-brothers Medardus and Viktorin: one shows up unexpectedly in situations where the other is expected, or they confront each other without warning, and so forth. But what distinguishes Hoffmann's work from earlier works involving doubles is the implication, indeed the argument, that a terrible "magnetic" power binds the brothers inescapably and tragically together, compelling one of them as the demonic and sinful part to drag the other ever more deeply down into perdition. (Very much the same relationship exists between the brothers in James Hogg's *The Private Memoirs and Confessions of a Justified Sinner* of 1824.)

Although Fichteanism and Mesmerism provided a powerful yet temporary justification for the double from the standpoint of philosophy and natural science, a third and ultimately far more lasting basis emerged from the romantic interest in psychology.[54] In a series of studies ranging from G. H. Schubert's *Dream Symbolism* (*Die Symbolik des Traumes*, 1814) to Carl Gustav Carus' *Psyche: A Genetic History of the Soul* (*Psyche: Zur Entwickungsgeschichte der Seele*, 1846) romantic thinkers refined the notion that the soul consists of two aspects: one conscious and the other unconscious. The unconscious, which expresses itself in dreams,

[54] See Ricarda Huch, *Die Romantik* (1899 and 1902); rpt. 2 vols. in 1 (Tübingen: Rainer Wunderlich-Hermann Leins, 1951), pp. 413–25 ("Neue Wissenschaften") and pp. 433–57 ("Der Mensch in der romantischen Weltanschauung").

myth, and folktales, constantly strives to assert itself; but it does so only at the expense of consciousness. Therefore a constant struggle is waged in the human soul between the dark forces of the unconscious and the light forces of consciousness. Since the romantics at this early stage in the history of psychology lacked any rigorous terminology to describe this obsessive concern, they returned to it again and again in the indirect language of symbols. In Fouqué's tale *Undine* (1811), for instance, the water sprite who marries a knight in order to acquire a human soul represents the impulse of the unconscious (nature) to strive upward towards consciousness. Conversely, the pervasiveness of mines and mining as symbols in romantic literature (e.g., Novalis' *Heinrich von Ofterdingen* and Hoffmann's "The Mines at Falun") suggests the romantic impulse to explore the unconscious with all its depths and dangers. The familiar motif of the double soon lent itself as an appropriate image for the newly discovered unconscious, embodying the dark and suppressed aspects of the individual personality. In the course of the nineteenth century, as Fichteanism and Mesmerism went out of fashion, the psychological justification for the motif of the double became increasingly effective.

THE obsession with *Doppelgänger* did not immediately involve the image of the mirror. As long as we are dealing with fiction in which two look-alike figures actually appear, as in the works of Jean Paul and Hoffmann, there is little need of mirrors. The confusion of identity, along with the horror of self-confrontation, is guaranteed simply by the fact that one character sees, or thinks that he sees, himself in another: Schoppe in Siebenkäs, Medardus in Viktorin. But when the physical double, for one reason or another, disappeared from the scene, other means had to be found to depict the encounter with one's double, which had become so important to the romantic mind. In the course of the nineteenth century, for at least two reasons, the physical double did gradually take his leave from literature. First, it was felt increasingly that physical doubles were improbable: magic would almost be a more acceptable explanation than the sudden appearance of a look-alike relative. More important: the literary conventions changed. Rather than seeking to externalize the unconscious after the fashion of the romantics, later writers tended to internalize their motifs, making them psychological rather than physical. As they began to seek other means for rendering the effect of the popular motif of the double, the mirror began to come into its own. At the same time, as the image of the mirror comes increasingly to stand for the double, it takes on more symbolic force. We can observe the beginnings of the shift from exteriorization to internalization, from magic to psychology, from motif to symbol, in two works of the 1840's, whose authors maintain an ambivalent attitude toward the problem of the double: Poe's "William Wilson" (1839; 1845) and Dostoevsky's *The Double* (1846).

Poe's story, the first-person narrative of a great reprobate, is not "a record of my later years of unspeakable misery" but a retrospective account of their origin. William Wilson, whose very name suggests the untrammeled volition and willfulness that characterize him, is chagrined to discover among his classmates only one who refuses to submit to his will: paradoxically, the recalcitrant boy, who is also named William Wilson, was born on the same day and entered school on the same day.[55] In fact, apart from the fact that a defect in his "gutteral organs" prevents him from raising his voice above a low whisper, he is in every respect the twin of the other William Wilson. This double, who follows Wilson to Eton, Oxford, and finally to the continent, infuriates him through "his frequent officious interference with my will." But Poe adds a twist that clearly distinguishes his treatment of the double from that of Jean Paul and Hoffmann: for this double exists only in Wilson's own eyes. "I saw that we were of the same height, and I perceived that we were even

[55] *The Selected Poetry and Prose of Edgar Allan Poe*, ed. T. O. Mabbott (New York: Modern Library, 1951), pp. 131–49.

singularly alike in general contour of person and outline of feature." Yet at no time does anyone else—schoolmates, teachers, fellow students, or companions—note or comment upon the allegedly striking similarity.

In their next two encounters—at Eton and at Oxford—no one else witnesses the appearance of the second Wilson, who always shows up just as the first Wilson is engaging in some shameful activity. In Rome, finally, when Wilson sets out to seduce the wife of his host at a masquerade ball, he feels a hand on his shoulder and hears "that ever-remembered, low, damnable *whisper* within my ear." Despite the costume and mask of the stranger and despite the lapse of so many years, Wilson believes that he recognizes in him his double. Dragging the intruder into a nearby antechamber, he challenges him to a duel and "plunged my sword, with brute ferocity, repeatedly through and through his bosom." At this moment Wilson is distracted by a sound at the door, and when he looks back, he is astonished and horrified at the sight.

> The brief moment in which I averted my eyes had been sufficient to produce, apparently, a material change in the arrangements at the upper or farther end of the room. A large mirror,—so at first it seemed to me in my confusion—now stood where none had been perceptible before; and, as I stepped up to it in extremity of terror, mine own image, but with features all pale and dabbled in blood, advanced to meet me with a feeble and tottering gait.
>
> Thus it appeared, I say, but was not. It was my antagonist—it was Wilson, who then stood before me in the agonies of his dissolution. His mask and cloak lay, where he had thrown them, upon the floor. Not a thread in all his raiment—not a line in all the marked and singular lineaments of his face which was not, even in the most absolute identity, *mine own!*

Poe's story has been variously interpreted. As far as its general meaning is concerned, there is a consensus that the double represents the muted voice of Wilson's conscience, which Wilson finally succeeds in destroying. But at least three different interpretations have been advanced to account for the double. The supernatural: that the double actually exists and that the murdered man is in fact physically identical with the double whom Wilson had known in his boyhood. The psychological: that the double and the murdered man are simply a figment of Wilson's deranged imagination. The equivocal: that the various doubles have a physical existence as persons, as innocent victims upon whom the crazed Wilson projects the features of his own physiognomy. Poe's own position is unclear. But however we read the ending, the mirror plays an essential role—the mirror from which it seems to Wilson that his double advances to meet him. Whether there is a mirror or not, Poe introduced that familiar motif into his story for the purposes of horror. If we commit ourselves to an interpretation, it seems most reasonable in the light of the text to assume that Wilson is a schizophrenic who projects the "good" side of his character onto others. The second Wilson, as a boy, can easily be rationalized as a double existing only in Wilson's own imagination; on the next two occasions no one else sees the alleged double; and on the final occasion he hears the familiar whisper "within my ear." Wilson kills an innocent man, whom in his mask he confuses with his ancient imagined double; when, after a brief interruption, he turns back to the room and confronts his own features in a mirror, he transfers these features to the face of the stranger he has just slain. We have come quite some distance from Jean Paul and Hoffmann, who take the physical double for granted, even if they account for the psychic kinship in different ways. But once the physical double begins to disappear, the mirror must enter the fiction to supply the physical appearance of the missing double.

The close parallels between "William Wilson" and *The Double* suggest a generational similarity in Poe and Dostoevsky that goes beyond their common indebtedness to Hoffmann. Dostoevsky, one of the principal "Russian Hoffmannists," uses doubles in several of his works—but nowhere more effectively than in his early novel *The Double* (1846), which is specifically indebted to *The Devil's Elixirs* and "A New Year's Eve Adventure."[56] Here, however, we find a more intensified portrayal than in any of the preceding cases because, rather than narrating the story of extended encounters with a double, Dostoevsky depicts only the four critical days during which his protagonist's paranoia reaches the delusional stage. When we first meet the minor bureaucrat Golyadkin, he is already so profoundly deranged by a persecution complex that he is under a doctor's care. "I have enemies," he tells his doctor, "deadly enemies who have sworn to ruin me" (Ch. 2).[57] But he has no enemy worse than himself, for he spends long hours of solitude talking to himself and taunting himself for his various shortcomings.

On the first day of his final breakdown Golyadkin, who is ridiculed even by his own servant, performs a variety of totally irrational acts, which culminate when he goes to a birthday party to which he has not been invited—for the daughter of a superior, with whom he has fallen in love—and then, after disgracing himself thoroughly, is thrown out of the house. It is at this moment of utter humiliation, despair, and confusion that Golyadkin first encounters his double, who not only has the same name and comes from the same province, but who is like an inverse mirror reflection of all of Golyadkin's characteristics. Rather than being meek, submissive, good-natured, and frank, the second Mr. Golyadkin is brazen, self-assertive, malicious, and ambitious. Obtaining a position in Golyadkin's office, where he sits facing him, the double gradually insinuates his way into the favor of Golyadkin's associates, undermines him both professionally and socially in the eyes of his friends and superiors, and makes fun of him publicly. Convinced that his forebodings have all come true, Golyadkin spends two days in wild dreams and frantic er-

[56] Passage, *The Russian Hoffmannists*, pp. 197–201.

[57] I refer to the translation by George Bird (1958), rpt. in *Great Short Works of Fyodor Dostoevsky* (New York: Harper & Row Perennial Classic, 1968), pp. 1-144.

rands. He talks to himself, writes letters to himself, and persuades himself that he is being poisoned. Finally he comes to the conclusion that the double is responsible for keeping him apart from the girl he loves. On the fourth day, believing that he has received a letter from the girl, Golyadkin forces his way into her house with the intention of eloping with her. But he finds that the double has anticipated him. What seems to be at long last a reconciliation between Golyadkin and his double turns out to be a kiss of betrayal: the doctor arrives and takes Golyadkin away to the madhouse while his double skips along beside the carriage, gleefully throwing goodbye kisses with his hands.

It rapidly becomes clear to the reader that the alleged double, having no physical reality whatsoever, is the realistic externalization of Golyadkin's inner state. Though possibly at first a projection onto actual figures, during most of the story the double exists entirely as a hallucination of Golyadkin's warped imagination, which has progressed, as a result of his worry and mortification, from an incipient persecution mania to a severe case of schizophrenia. For instance, when Golyadkin wakes up after a long evening's conversation with his double, "imagine his amazement to find not only the guest but also the bed on which he had slept, gone from the room!" (Ch. 8). Golyadkin, who is capable of great feats of the imagination even before he first encounters his double—he carries on extended conversations and envisions detailed scenes—puts his feverish fancy to work in all the scenes in which the double appears. The double, in short, is nothing but an extension of suppressed aspects of his own personality—those traits of self-assurance that Golyadkin wishes he possessed.

Under these circumstances the mirror required in order to lend physical reality to the double since he exists only in the mind; and it turns out that mirrors are indeed frequently mentioned in the text. In the opening paragraph, when Golyadkin awakens in the morning, the first thing he does is to look into the mirror: "he bounded out of bed, and ran to a small round mirror standing on the chest of drawers. Although the sleepy, weak-sighted and rather bald image reflected was of so insignificant a character as to be certain of commanding no great attention at a first glance, its possessor remained well pleased with all that he beheld in the mirror." Similarly, at dinner that same day, "after reading a few lines he rose, looked at himself in the mirror, righted his dress, and smoothed his hair" (Ch. 3). In other words, we are dealing with a man who needs mirrors simply in order to assure himself of his own existence.

But after the appearance of the double, the looking-glass of which Golyadkin has hitherto been so fond becomes his enemy because it now mirrors not his accustomed self but the *other* Golyadkin. After a snack in a restaurant, for instance, Golyadkin pays for the fish patty that he ordered. To his astonishment the attendant claims that he has consumed not one, but eleven patties. After a brief argument Golyadkin realizes what has happened. "Standing in the doorway of the next room, almost directly behind the waiter and facing Mr. Golyadkin—standing in the doorway, which till then he had taken to be a mirror—was a little man. It was Mr. Golyadkin, not Golyadkin the elder, the hero of our tale, but the other, the new Mr. Golyadkin" (Ch. 9). On another occasion, when Golyadkin, driven by his despair, calls on his superior to complain about the conspiracy against him, the same phenomenon occurs. "Mr. Golyadkin began to feel uneasy. Shifting his gaze, he caught sight of yet another strange visitor. In a doorway, which till then our hero had as on a previous occasion taken for a mirror, *he* appeared, the *he* who is already familiar to the reader, Mr. Golyadkin's very intimate friend and acquaintance" (Ch. 12).

For all the differences between Poe and Dostoevsky, these two stories from the 1840's are remarkably similar. Both deal with cases of radical schizophrenia in which the hero projects half of his character—in one case his conscience and in the other his aggressive traits—onto others or into the void.[58] At this stage in the development of the double-motif both writers find it useful to employ the familiar romantic image of the mirror at crucial points in order to reify this projection of the double. In neither case do we find what could be called a magic mirror: both William Wilson and Golyadkin confuse the image in the mirror with their mysterious doubles, and there is only a hint of the supernatural. What first seems to be an apparition turns out to be the reflection of one's self. Yet for their effects of horror and the grotesque, respectively, both Poe and Dostoevsky exploit the associations of the magic mirror from which the reflection emerges. As a result of half a century of romantic catoptromancy they are able to count on the proper conditioned response in their audiences.

Despite his initial satisfaction with his novella, Dostoevsky conceded some thirty years later in *The Diary of a Writer* (1877) that he had failed in his execution of the tale. "Its idea was quite lucid, and I have never developed anything in literature that is genuinely more serious than this idea. But the form of the story was an utter failure."[59] With reference to a writer of Dostoevsky's stature the term "failure" is relative. But it seems likely that Dostoevsky had in mind here the narrative inconsistencies produced by the conflict of tone between Golyadkin's delusions and the ironic stance adopted by the narrator. In the works of Jean Paul and Hoffmann

[58] Dostoevsky's double anticipates with considerable precision that hidden, repressed, inferior, and guilt-laden part of the personality that Jung called the "shadow." See C. G. Jung, *Aion: Research into the Phenomenology of the Self*, trans. R.F.C. Hull (Princeton, N.J.: Princeton Univ. Press, 1959), pp. 8–10, where Jung speaks of projections of the shadow: "The effect of projection is to isolate the subject from his environment, since instead of a real relation to it there is now only an illusory one. Projections change the world into the replica of one's unknown face."

[59] Cited in Konstantin Mochulsky, *Dostoevsky: His Life and Work* (1947), trans. Michael A. Minihan (Princeton, N.J.: Princeton Univ. Press, 1967), p. 50.

this problem does not arise because the double is accepted as physically real both by the narrator and by the characters within the fiction. But as soon as the double is shifted out of the realm of fictional reality and into the mind of the hero, the problems become different: the narrative can move easily to the extremes of pathos or farce, depending on the narrator's attitude. Poe avoids the difficulty by employing a first-person narrator: the man who suffers the delusion tells his story with the appropriate seriousness, and the reader is permitted to make his own judgments concerning the state of his mind. In Dostoevsky's account, however, the seriousness of the psychological analysis, which critics have admired since the publication of the novel, is constantly undercut by the sly winks and disclaimers of the narrator.

WE SEE how well the lesson of narrative stance was learned when we move ahead to two remarkable works that appeared in 1877: Robert Louis Stevenson's "Markheim" is recounted in a dispassionate third-person that identifies itself with the consciousness of the hero; Maupassant's "The Horla" narrates itself in the form of a journal. In both cases, therefore, the mirror seems to be truly magical because the appearance of the double in the mirror is narrated from the point of view of the hero, who accepts it as such.

"Markheim" is the story of a man who visits an antique dealer on Christmas Day under the pretext of buying a gift for a lady.[60] At the first opportunity he kills the dealer with a dagger and goes upstairs to the drawing-room in search of money, with which he plans to recoup his huge losses on the Stock Exchange. Here, as he is sorting out the keys, he hears footsteps coming up the stairs of the empty house. A hand takes the knob, the lock clicks, and the door opens. A face looks into the room, smiles "as if in friendly recognition," and then withdraws, closing the door behind it. When the startled

[60] *The Merry Men and Other Tales and Fables*, Biographical Edition (New York: Scribner, 1921), pp. 116–41.

Markheim cries out, the visitor enters the room. As Markheim stares at him, "the outlines of the new-comer seemed to change and waver like those of the idols in the wavering candle-light of the shop; and at times he thought he knew him; and at times he thought he bore a likeness to himself; and always, like a lump of living terror, there lay in his bosom the conviction that this thing was not of the earth and not of God." In the ensuing conversation the stranger warns Markheim to speed up his activities, for the maid is returning sooner than expected. Playing the devil's advocate in the subtle dialectics that follow, the stranger urges Markheim on to crime. "For six-and-thirty years that you have been in this world, through many changes of fortunes and varieties of humour, I have watched you steadily fall. Fifteen years ago you would have started at a theft. Three years ago you would have blenched at the name of murder. Is there any crime, is there any cruelty or meanness, from which you still recoil?" Although he offers to show Markheim where the money is hidden, Markheim delays until the doorbell announces the returning maid. Even at this moment he could still escape with a lie; but he resolves that there is still one door of freedom open to him from his life of corruption: "I can cease from action." Now it becomes evident that the stranger has been, all this time, the personification of Markheim's conscience. As the visitor's features brighten and soften with a tender triumph, Markheim descends the stairs and sends the maid to summon the police, confessing that he has killed her master.

As in "William Wilson," the mysterious stranger, the voice of conscience, is reified through his appearance in a mirror. But in Stevenson's story the reflection assumes a much more vivid and independent life than was the case in Poe and Dostoevsky: there the motif of the mirror simply reinforced the initial delusion; here the motif is magnified into the symbol of the story. The author introduces the motif in the first scene, when Markheim is still pretending to be interested in a gift. The dealer suggests a fifteenth-century hand-glass; but when he shows it to Markheim a shock passes through him, "a sudden leap of tumultuous passions to the face." Rejecting the mirror as a possible gift, he exclaims: "Why, look here—look in it—look at yourself! Do you like to see it? No! Nor I—nor any man." It is only later that we realize that Markheim resists the mirror, at this first encounter, because it presents to him the image of his guilty soul: the mirror is established, in other words, in its traditional role as image of the soul. "I ask you for a Christmas present, and you give me this—this damned reminder of years, and sins and follies—this hand-conscience!"

Creeping up the stairs after the murder, he is haunted by the thought that something in the house is watching him: "a faceless thing, and yet had eyes to see with; and again it was a shadow of himself." By the time he reaches the landing he feels so observed that he longs to be at home, "girt in by walls, buried among bedclothes, and invisible to all but God." All this—the fear of mirrors as a "hand-conscience," the sense of guilt, and the growing dread of being observed—prepares us for the inevitable mirrors in the drawing-room upstairs: "several great pier-glasses, in which he beheld himself at various angles, like an actor on a stage." In short, Markheim becomes, in the reflection of those mirrors, an actor on the stage of his own guilty conscience. The dialogue with the stranger turns out to be a discussion with his own double as reflected in the great mirrors of the drawing-room. Everything else—the footsteps on the stairs, the hand on the doorknob—can be accounted for by his overwrought conscience and imagination. When Markheim leaves the room to confront the maid downstairs, the stranger merely fades away after his features—Markheim's, of course—undergo a wonderful transfiguration.

To the extent that Poe and Dostoevsky were interested in the growth of schizophrenia, the episodes with the mirror were reduced in importance to passing moments in an extended process. To the extent, in contrast, that Stevenson is obsessed with the crucial moment of confrontation with conscience, so vivid that it becomes hallucinatory, the mirror can be used almost in its original magical force: for the course of several minutes Markheim's conscience assumes such eidetic reality that it seems literally to have emerged from mirrors become magical. Paradoxically, this use of the image of the magic mirror is possible only when the psychological realism of the narrative has progressed to a point at which it is clear that no hint of the supernatural is intended. Although the motif with all its eerie implications is clearly a borrowing from romantic sources with which Stevenson was intimately familiar, we do not for an instant suspect any supernatural happenings; the magic is nothing but the product of Markheim's over-excited imagination. But we feel it precisely because the narrator restrains his own commentary and lets Markheim speak for himself.

If Stevenson's tale stands, like Poe's, in the tradition of the double as an allegory of conscience, Maupassant's "The Horla" reminds us unmistakably of Dostoevsky's realistic analysis of a worsening persecution mania.[61] But Maupassant, rather than restricting himself to the critical four days depicted in *The Double*, traces the paranoia over a six-month period from its inception to the narrator's imminent suicide. In this case the narrator-hero is pursued not by his own visible *Doppelgänger*, but by a mysterious and undefinable power that he comes to call the "horla"—a word presumably related to the French words *horrible, hors* ("outside"), and *hurler* ("to scream"). Although Maupassant did not believe in the supernatural, he was conspicuously interested in psychology and madness from his first stories on; the motif of "The Horla" shows up in an earlier version entitled simply "The Letter of a Madman" ("Lettre d'un fou," 1885). During this first great period of psychology, which was characterized by studies on the dissociation of the personality and by a renewed interest in animal magnetism, Maupassant regularly attended lectures by J. M. Charcot at

[61] Guy de Maupassant, *Selected Short Stories*, trans. Roger Colet (Baltimore: Penguin, 1971), pp. 313–44.

the Salpêtrière on hysteria and hypnosis. Much of this went into his story, which includes its own theory of psychopathology.

According to the narrator and the various sources he cites, the universe is full of invisible, unknowable forces that affect our mood and our welfare. In the course of several months the narrator comes to believe that he is being invaded by a creature that drinks water and milk, picks flowers, reads books, and spies on him constantly. As he reconstructs events, this spirit arrived on a Brazilian three-master he observed off the coast one day in May (the first entry in his journal). As matters go from bad to worse, the narrator goes completely mad. Locking the Horla in his house, he burns it down, servants and all. Yet in the last sentence he decides that the Horla has not, after all, been destroyed in the fire. Realizing that the Horla's existence is inextricably linked to his own, as parasite to host, he has no recourse left but to kill himself.

The mirror-motif occurs close to the end of the story when the narrator determines to catch sight of the mysterious being that is taking over his mind. Lighting two lamps and eight candles, he sits down at his desk and pretends to write until he senses that the Horla is peering over his shoulder. Rising quickly and turning around to face the looking glass in the wardrobe, he is overcome by horror. "It was as bright as day, but I could not see myself in the mirror! It was empty and bright, and full of light to the very depths. My reflection was nowhere to be seen, yet I was standing right in front of it! I could see the whole limpid piece of glass from top to bottom. I stared at it with panic-stricken eyes . . . knowing that he was there, that his invisible body had swallowed up my reflection." As he watches, a change begins to take place in the mirror. "I began to see myself in a mist at the back of the mirror, as if I were looking through a sheet of water." As this shapeless and opaque transparency becomes clearer, the narrator realizes that he has been looking at the Horla.

Here Maupassant brilliantly exploits various motifs borrowed from folklore and legitimated in part by contemporary scientific theory, for their sheer horror value. We share the terror of the man who looks into the mirror and, like Hoffmann's Erasmus Spikher, fails to see his own reflection. Just as folklore informs us that a man who looks into a mirror at night may see the devil (and lose his own image in the process), the narrator here perceives his nemesis—the Horla. Like Stevenson, Maupassant is able to make use of a purely magical motif because he renders it psychologically reasonable. The narrator has been primed by his readings in superstition and psychology to see the Horla in the mirror. Since there are no other witnesses to the events described, the narrator can render the impression of his own senses directly in his journal, which traces the stages of his dissolution into total madness.

To appreciate the virtuosity of Maupassant's psychological masterpiece, we might pause for a moment to compare one of Villiers de l'Isle-Adam's *Contes Cruels* (1883), which uses many of the same narrative motifs as "The Horla"—notably the magic mirror, ghosts, arson, and a seaside setting—but in a configuration vastly inferior to Maupassant's classic of horror. In "The Desire to Be a Man" an old tragedian named Esprit Chaudval, the scion of a family of Saint-Malo pilots, is about to quit the stage and accept a post as lighthouse attendant near his family home.[62] He has spent his entire life playing out other men's passions on the stage. Now that age is forcing him to rejoin mankind, he must discover some genuine feelings of his own if he is to be a man. Deciding that he is too old for love and having no ambition left, he settles upon remorse—even if he must commit a crime in order to savor that sensation. On the evening of his departure from Paris he sets a huge fire in a warehouse district, in which almost a hundred people die. Then, having retired to his solitary lighthouse with a large

[62] "Le Désir d'être un homme," in *Cruel Tales*, trans. Robert Baldick with an Introduction by A. W. Raitt (London: Oxford Univ. Press, 1963), pp. 137–46.

mirror in which to study the expressions on his face, he waits for the ghosts of remorse to haunt him. He finally dies of a stroke, disappointed because he has not experienced any human emotion. He fails to realize that he is himself the phantom that he had vainly awaited; he has become such an empty shell of a man, incapable of feeling, that he even manages to forget his act of arson until he happens to read about it in an old newspaper.

The main action of the story is preceded by a scene in which the old actor sees himself reflected in the large window of a restaurant. After greeting his familiar image, he enters a trance-like state in which he sees, in the catoptromantic mirror, scenes from his childhood. Realizing that he has lost that past, he shatters the glass with a stone so that it can never again reflect anything else. Villiers' ironic tale of a man who longs to be haunted in order to demonstrate his humanity to himself is not particularly good. Despite its unique twist, its elements are not made credible. Apart from its use of the mirror-image—both the shattered mirror at the beginning and the magic mirror in which, paradoxically, the ghosts fail to appear—it is of interest chiefly because its motifs so precisely anticipate the elements out of which Maupassant constructed one of his finest stories.

THE INCREASINGLY compelling association of madness with the image of the magic mirror, which has been evident from Jean Paul and Hoffmann through Dostoevsky to Maupassant, reaches its greatest intensity in two stories published just after the turn of the century: "L'Ami des miroirs" by the Belgian symbolist Georges Rodenbach, and "In the Mirror" by the Russian symbolist Valerii Briusov, the translator of Poe. Rodenbach's tale (posthumously published in 1901) is ostensibly an account by the friend of a man who died in a madhouse under strange circumstances.[63] This man had always been fascinated by mirrors, which he regarded as "win-

[63] "L'Ami des miroirs," *Le Rouet de brume: Contes posthumes*, 2nd ed. (Paris: Ollendorff, 1901), pp. 27–35.

dows opened upon the infinite" (anticipating by three-quarters of a century Kurt Vonnegut's Kilgore Trout and his "leaks" between universes). From time to time this catoptromania is intensified into catoptrophobia, as when he flees from his apartment lest the mirrors close over him like water. Gradually his obsession becomes more severe. He is particularly afraid of large shopwindows: "ces maudits miroirs! Ils vivent de reflets." You walk past them unsuspectingly and they steal away your complexion and color, leaving you pale and wan. His friend consoles him, assuring him that everyone appears bloodless and deformed in the cheap shop windows. The catoptromaniac finally decides that the only solution is to furnish his apartment with a number of flawless looking glasses, in which he can compare perfect images of himself, and to stop looking into the shop windows, for which he has nothing but contempt: "miroirs hypocrites, miroirs malades." Gradually he accumulates a splendid collection of beautiful mirrors from many periods of history and with the most varied frames and glasses. To avoid the vulgar street-mirrors he begins to stay at home more and more, where he finds the most enchanting entertainment by undertaking imaginary voyages through the mirrors into the past or the future. When his concerned friend asks him what he does for female company, the "ami des miroirs" assures him that the mirrors are like streets, in which many women appear whom he can pursue. Increasingly losing all sense of identity, he fails to recognize himself in the mirrors that cover his walls and takes the images to be physical reality rather than mere reflections. During their last conversation he tells his friend that, whereas he had formerly felt isolated and lonely in the world, he now lives amidst a friendly crowd in which everyone is just like him and where he feels happy and secure. At this point the mirror-friend has become so deranged that he must be committed to a madhouse, where his room has only one mirror. But he has become so accustomed to living in the realm of the looking glass that the single mirror provides him with everything he requires: lovely vistas, beautiful women whom he can love, congenial company. The mirror-world becomes so much more attractive than reality that he finally decides to enter it once and for all. The next morning he is discovered dead in his room, his skull cracked and blood-soaked from his attempt to penetrate the mirror.

Rodenbach makes explicit use of many supernatural motifs associated with magic mirrors: mirrors observe us and sap our vigor, they are spatially and temporally clairvoyant, the images can emerge from the glass and assume physical reality, and they constitute the entrance to a mysterious world that mortals can enter. But we are willing to accept all this because it is presented in a psychologically plausible manner. In fairy tales we accept magic mirrors because, for the duration of the narrative, we agree to suspend our disbelief and to take magic as one of the premises of the genre. Here, in contrast, there is no question of magic at all: it has been wholly internalized and put into the mind of the observer. As far as the "ami des miroirs" is concerned, the magic world of mirrors exists, at least until his ill-fated attempt to enter that realm—and perhaps even then he dies too soon to be disillusioned. But for the narrator and the reader this "magic" is nothing but the manifestation of a gradually disintegrating consciousness, which becomes increasingly incapable of distinguishing between reality and the fairy-tale world of his childhood.[64] We are not expected even for a moment to accept magic as a convention or to hover uncertainly between credulity and reason. The magic image has been wholly disenchanted by psychology.

Few modern writers have conjured with magic images in their fiction more enchantingly than Valerii Briusov. In "The

[64] It might be debated, of course, whether the mirrors were the symptom or the cause of his madness. Otto Rank, *The Double*, p. 73, note 8, relates a case that occurred in 1913 in London: a jealous young lord, to punish his unfaithful mistress, locked her up for a week in a room walled with mirrors; by the end of eight days she had gone incurably mad and smashed all the mirrors.

Marble Bust" a man is arrested for attempting to steal a fifteenth-century Italian statue that appears to be an actual likeness of his former beloved, "a sort of re-creation of life in marble." In another tale ("Protection") a young officer hopes to seduce a beautiful widow by dressing up like the portrait of her dead husband. The ruse almost works; but when the startled woman faints, the scheming officer encounters what seems to be the phantom of her husband (actually his own reflection in a mirror), who threatens him into desisting from his shameful designs. Whereas these stories play with motifs that are familiar from other contexts—notably the portrait as *figura* and the avenging statue—at least one story goes beyond existing conventions to add a new element. "In the Mirror" (written from 1902 to 1906) deals, like Rodenbach's tale, with a psychiatric case of catoptrophilia.[65] As we learn at the end, the first-person account by a young woman who has "loved mirrors from my very earliest years" is composed while she is a patient in a home for the mentally afflicted. Since her girlhood she has surrounded herself with looking glasses and spends whole days in the "separate universes" of the mirrors. "This protracted actuality, separated from us by the smooth surface of glass, drew me towards itself by a kind of intangible touch, dragged me forward, as to an abyss, a mystery." Irresistibly attracted by "the apparition which always rose up before me when I came near a mirror and which strangely doubled my being," she comes to realize that each of her mirrors—the small handmirror, the circular boudoir mirror, the oblong mirror of the wardrobe door, the folding gold-framed triptych, etc.—reproduces a different double of herself, which according to circumstances she loves, hates, despises, fears, mocks, or pities. "I knew that they were all hostile toward me, if only for the fact that they were forced to clothe themselves in my hated likeness." When a mirror

[65] Valery Brussof, *The Republic of the Southern Cross and Other Stories,* with an Introductory Essay by Stephen Graham (London: Constable, 1918), pp. 55–72.

is particularly offensive, she hides it, gives it away, or even breaks it, only to be stared at reproachfully by the faces in "the broken fragments of the world I had destroyed."

The title refers to a large pier-glass that the narrator acquires at a sale one autumn. Responding at once to the haughty challenge in the eyes of her reflected double, she has the mirror placed in her boudoir, where she immediately engages in a struggle of wills with her rival. On that first day the contest ends when she tips the mirror "so that it began to swing, rocking the image of my rival pitifully to and fro." On the following day the second duel begins, "a duel of eyes—two unyielding glances, commanding, threatening, hypnotising." The struggle goes on for days and weeks until the woman, unwilling to acknowledge defeat by fleeing or smashing the mirror, feels herself coming increasingly under the control of her mirror-image. "Little by little I lost the possibility of letting a day pass without once going to my mirror. *She* ordered me to spend several hours daily in front of her." On one December day the contest of wills lasts into the twilight. In the darkened room the reflected woman rises from her chair and moves forward, forcing her rival to do the same, until their hands touch on the glass and their faces meet in a monstrous kiss. The narrator faints; "and when I came to my senses after this swoon I still saw in front of me my own boudoir on which I gazed *from out of* the mirror."

Her life as a mere reflection continues for several months. At first she is miserable and submissive in her new role, simply responding in her soundless world to the commands of the woman outside. But gradually, as she sees her rival living her life, wearing her dresses, being considered as her husband's wife, the humiliations stir a thirst for revenge. Deceiving her enemy by affording her all the satisfactions of apparent victory, she learns how to control the other and force her to carry out her wishes. One day men come into the boudoir with tools to pack and move the mirror. Concentrating her will, the woman in the mirror summons her rival and forces her first to send the men out of the room and then to exchange places with her once again. "I cried out loudly and victoriously and fell just here, in front of the pier-glass, prone from exhaustion." When her husband and the servants rush in, she asks them to remove the mirror and then collapses in a feverish faint. Her friends and relatives, already fearing that she was demented for spending so many hours and days before her mirror, are convinced of her madness when she tells them about all that has allegedly happened during the past weeks. She is sent away to the mental institution, where she is now setting down her weird account. But the last paragraph introduces a new ironic uncertainty: the author of the memoirs is beginning to wonder whether she is indeed herself or, perhaps, her own reflection. To dispel her last clouds of doubt, she wants to peer once more into the depths of the fateful mirror in order to assure herself that the impostor, her enemy, is still imprisoned there.

In many respects the stories by the two symbolist poets are so similar that Briusov's version might fittingly be called "L'Amie des miroirs." Together, the tales represent the culmination of the nineteenth-century tradition of the psychological study of the double. But Briusov goes even a step further than Rodenbach, thereby achieving a final inversion of the motif: whereas Rodenbach's hero is killed in his attempt to enter the mirror, Briusov actually follows the consciousness of his narrator into the mirror—"that mysterious world into which I had gazed from my childhood and which up till now had remained inaccessible to me"—and tells part of the story from the standpoint of the mirror-image looking out at reality.

A curious example combining the effects of the two symbolist stories can be found in the works of Rilke, who was familiar with Rodenbach's writings. Rilke's lifelong obsession with mirrors is evident in his poetry from the beginning down to his last poems—notably in one of the most famous of his *Sonnets to Orpheus* (1922; Part II, Sonnet 3). Here, as in most of his poems, Rilke celebrates mirrors as a symbol of impenetrability (*Unbetretbarkeit*): they reveal to our eyes a beautiful world that we can never enter. But in his novel-like prose work, *The Notebooks of Malte Laurids Brigge* (1910), Rilke uses the mirror much more after the fashion of Rodenbach and Briusov. Here he is interested not in the inviolable world lying behind the mirror but in the mirror-image itself as the symbolic projection of a more powerful, even tyrannical, aspect of human consciousness.

Here again there is no assumption of magic on the part of the narrator, the twenty-eight-year-old Malte looking back at a scene from his childhood. But the *child* Malte still believes in fairy-tale magic and takes it for granted that mirror-images can come to life. The scene in question takes place in the Brigge family manor at Ulsgaard, whose upper story consists of unoccupied and rarely visited guest rooms.[66] On one occasion Malte slips upstairs and discovers a room full of masks and costumes, which he has never seen before. In the adjoining room there is a narrow wall-mirror made of many fragments of green glass.

> Ah, how one trembled to be in there, and how ravishing when one was. When out of the dimness something drew near, more slowly than oneself, for the mirror did not, so to speak, believe it, and did not want, sleepy as it was, to repeat promptly what had been said to it. But naturally it had to in the end. And now it was something very surprising, strange, altogether different from one's expectation, something sudden, independent, which one rapidly surveyed, only in the next instant to recognize oneself after all, not without a certain irony which came within a hairsbreadth of spoiling all the fun.

From the start, then, the child attributes a certain magical animation to the mirror, which resents his intrusions and exhibits the greatest reluctance to return his reflections. But the mirror eventually exacts its revenge for these intrusions.

[66] *The Notebooks of Malte Laurids Brigge*, trans. M. D. Herter Norton (1949; rpt. New York: Norton, 1964), pp. 91–95.

One day, as Malte is parading before it in one of his masks and costumes, he knocks over a small table, spilling some old aromatic essence on the parquet floor. As he tries to wipe away the spot, he becomes confused and finds himself hampered by the bulky costume.

> Hot and angry, I rushed to the mirror and with difficulty watched through the mask the working of my hands. But for this the mirror had just been waiting. Its moment of retaliation had come. While I strove in boundlessly increasing anguish to squeeze somehow out of my disguise, it forced me, by what means I do not know, to lift my eyes and imposed on me an image, no, a reality, a strange, unbelievable and monstrous reality, with which, against my will, I became permeated: for now the mirror was the stronger, and I was the mirror. I stared at this great, terrifying unknown before me, and it seemed to me appalling to be alone with him. But at the very moment I thought this, the worst befell: I lost all sense, I simply ceased to exist. For one second I had an indescribable, painful and futile longing for myself, then there was only he: there was nothing but he. (pp. 95–96)

Malte is finally rescued from the power of the malevolent mirror when, in his terror, he rushes down the stairs and is discovered by the servants, who get a good laugh from the child's discomfiture.

Rilke's handling of the magic mirror reveals that he belongs to the same literary generation as Rodenbach and Briusov: in all three cases the "magic" is made quite credible because it is filtered through the consciousness of an observer who believes in its powers. In one sense, however, Rilke goes beyond the two symbolists. In the two earlier stories the image of the mirror-reflection reaches symbolic status; but in both cases the symbolism is subordinated to the psychological interest of the narrators. The reflection is a symbol, but only as a projection of the personality within the restricted context of madness. Rilke also uses the reflection as a projection of Malte's *persona*. But, beyond that, he has adapted the image of the magic mirror as the fictional embodiment of a thought that concerns him immensely in his novel: the conviction that human beings are gradually becoming depersonalized in our society while, in a compensating movement, things and objects take on human characteristics. Thus at the end of the mirror-scene, the mirror-image becomes real and Malte feels that he has been reduced to the function of the reflecting surface, merely reflecting the other. Technically Rilke is doing exactly what Briusov did in his story; but as a symbol Rilke's image has broader implications than Briusov's.

The image of the magic mirror as symbolic double, which we have traced in progressive stages from Poe and Dostoevsky through Maupassant and Stevenson to Rodenbach, Briusov, and Rilke, reached an impasse at the beginning of the twentieth century. It would be difficult to carry the psychological analysis of the image much further than Rodenbach and Briusov did. Even Briusov's device of shifting the observing consciousness "magically" into the mirror suggests that the time had arrived for inversions of the image. We sense this discomfort if we consider a work that seems on the surface to be nothing but a straightforward psychological rationalization of the image.

J. E. Poritzky's *Ghost Stories* (1913), which take place on the borderline between realism and the seemingly supernatural, seem at first reading to mark a simple return to the manner of their ostensible model, E.T.A. Hoffmann. In all his tales Poritzky stresses rationalism and modernity in order to make the effect more startling when a "ghost" appears in contemporary Berlin. In the tale "One Night" the narrator is joined by an older man—"a Doctor Faustus in age and wisdom"—for a conversation.[67] The evening before, the old man relates, while dreaming of his youth he suddenly recalled the superstition that prohibits looking into a mirror at

[67] "Eines Nachts," *Gespenstergeschichten* (Munich and Leipzig: Georg Müller, 1913), pp. 113–25.

midnight. When he stepped before the mirror to test the superstition, he was prepared to see himself as he had appeared as a boy since he was so wholly absorbed by visions of his youth. It was with the greatest distaste that he saw, instead, the wrinkled face that peered out at him from the mirror as though it were "an evil sorcerer"—an ironic inversion of the conventional motif, since he expected the mirror to be magic and was disappointed to find that it was perfectly normal. The old man explains this unusual experience scientifically on the basis of theories concerning the dissociation of consciousness, citing cases of "psychic cleavage which cannot be explained away simply as hallucinations." Just as he was confronted with a vision of his own past, it is also possible for a young person to catch a glimpse of future modes of existence. He asks the narrator if he has never had the sensation of feeling old, but the young man denies it. When the older man takes his leave, the narrator is offended that his guest neglects to take his extended hand. "I was alone, and opposite me was a mirror which held me captive." The entire conversation, he concludes, was an encounter with a projection of himself some thirty-five years hence.

Here again the image of the magic mirror is justified in the manner conventional since Dostoevsky and Poe: it is represented as being a particularly vivid, almost eidetic projection of the dissociated personality into the mirror, and the text contains explicit references to contemporary psychological theories, notably those of Ribot, as a rational justification. At the same time, Poritzky achieves an intensification of the conventional motif that bears a curious resemblance to James's notion in *A Sense of the Past*: that the present (or future) can haunt the past (or present). For the symbolic image that the narrator sees in the mirror is not the double of his present dissociated consciousness; it is a projection of his consciousness into the future. To intensify the inversion even more: that projection, in turn, relates his own thoughts of the past as well as his experience with the projection of his own (present) dissociated consciousness into the mirror.

By 1913, then, the magic mirror was still a popular literary image, whose reputability was vouched for by the list of major European writers who, in one fashion or another, had employed it. But the image was close to the point of exhaustion. The subtle inversions by Briusov, Rilke, and Poritzky show that the straightforward psychological internalization of the image was no longer felt to be viable. Just at the moment when its usefulness for the analysis of the psyche seemed outlived, however, a new generation of writers concerned with the exploration of consciousness appropriated the image for their own purposes. The experimental exuberance of twentieth-century art enabled writers to make free and playful use of the image with no compulsion to justify it rationally or psychologically in every case.[68] As their name suggests, the expressionists were concerned with externalizing their inner visions, and therefore in their rejuvenation of the mirror-image they reversed the nineteenth-century trend toward psychological internalization that had begun with the post-romantics.

The new function of the magic mirror was widely publicized by the early German film classic, *The Student of Prague* (1913), based on a scenario by Hanns Heinz Ewers.[69] Ewers, along with Poritzky a leading representative of the

[68] This liberation did not occur only in literature, of course. In the history of art the mirror was long a popular device for adding surprising dimensions to a painting. But modern painters often use "magic-mirror" effects for other purposes: e.g., Picasso's *Girl before a Mirror* (1932; Museum of Modern Art, New York) or M. C. Escher's *Magic Mirror*. From serious art the device has penetrated into advertising on television, in newspapers, and on dustjackets of novels.

[69] This film provides the starting point for Rank's analysis in *The Double*. See also the discussion in Siegfried Kracauer, *From Caligari to Hitler: A Psychological History of the German Film* (1947; rpt. Princeton, N.J.: Princeton Univ. Press, 1966), pp. 28–31. Kracauer argues that the film introduced an element that was to become an obsession of German cinema: "a deep and fearful concern with the foundations of the self." He suggests that the hero's split personality reflects a dualism in the German national consciousness.

so-called German *Spukliteratur* of the early twentieth century, was the author of a book on Poe, editor of the German translation of *Dorian Gray*, translator of Villiers de l'Isle-Adam, and compiler of a popular anthology entitled *A Gallery of Fantasts.* Not surprisingly, his film script shows many influences and resembles a pastiche of motifs from "William Wilson," Goethe's *Faust*, Hoffmann's tales, and Wilde's novel. Balduin, a student at the university of Prague, is practicing fencing positions in front of his mirror when the sinister Scapinelli (a linear descendant of Hoffmann's Dapertutto) appears, offering him a fortune if Balduin will sign over to him anything in the room that Scapinelli wishes. The impoverished student happily signs the contract, assuming that his bare room contains little of value. He is dumbfounded when Scapinelli points to his reflection in the mirror. Shock gives way to horror when the reflection actually steps out of the mirror and follows the sorcerer out the door. The remainder of the film depicts a series of complications in which Balduin is constantly thwarted by his malevolent double, who has assumed all the evil aspects of his personality and who consistently intervenes in his love affair. Finally, when his beloved discovers that he has no reflection and expresses her horror at the fact, Balduin hastens back to his room with the intention of committing suicide. When his double appears in the locked room, Balduin seizes the pistol and, instead, shoots the double, who promptly disappears. Overjoyed at his apparent liberation, Balduin uncovers the mirror and, for the first time since its initial departure, sees his image back in the mirror where it belongs—only to discover, à la William Wilson, that his shirt is soaked with blood and that he has been shot in the heart. When he falls to the floor, dead, Scapinelli appears and tears up the contract, scattering the pieces over Balduin's corpse.

The intellectual and literary pedigree of Ewers' film is instantly apparent to anyone who has read the texts discussed thus far. The scenario is in one sense a dictionary of motifs associated with the image of the magic mirror in nineteenth-century literature. What is interesting, however, is the fact that Ewers makes frankly supernatural use of the mirror-image as a double and rejects psychological rationalization in order to project symbolically an inner world of dream and the imagination. To this extent Ewers' film anticipates several major works of the twenties, which restore to the disenchanted image the magic it has lacked since the tales of Hoffmann.

Mirrors occupy a place of honor in the poetry of Rilke's younger contemporary from Prague, Franz Werfel. One of his earliest poems is called "The Fat Man in the Mirror": the disgusting fat man the young poet sees when he looks in the mirror represents his consciousness suddenly awakened to maturity and a grim reality.[70] In many of his poems during the war years the encounter with one's self in the mirror provides an incentive for speculation on the vanity of the poet's calling. Werfel's obsession with mirrors comes to its peak in his so-called magical trilogy, *Mirror-Man* (1920),[71] an allegorical play that is related, on the one hand, to such symbolic dramas of self-discovery as Goethe's *Faust* and Ibsen's *Peer Gynt* and, on the other, to the Viennese tradition of the *Zauberposse*, or comic fairy tale, as represented by Raimund's *The King of the Alps and the Misanthrope*. His hero is also a linear descendant of those mirror-smashing solipsists of romanticism—but with a characteristically expressionist twist.

When the play begins, the thirty-year-old Thamal has just arrived at a mysterious monastery in the mountains, where he begs to be admitted to the order. Feeling that he is too weak to resist evil and yet longing for purity, he has fled the crime and vice of the city in the plains below. The abbot, after trying to dissuade Thamal, agrees to test him. A monk begins the initiation by outlining the three stages of human

[70] "Der dicke Mann im Spiegel" (from *Der Weltfreund*, 1911); rpt. *Gedichte aus dreißig Jahren* (Stockholm: Bermann-Fischer, 1939), pp. 16–17.

[71] *Spiegelmensch: Magische Trilogie* (Munich: Kurt Wolff, 1920).

consciousness. The first stage is the level of solipsistic self-consciousness at which the individual recognizes nothing but himself in everything that he sees:

> Denn was auf der Erde, unterm Himmel sich
> Ihm zeigt und begegnet ist ewig: sein Ich!

Some men progress beyond this stage of distorted reality to the level of dissociated consciousness: existence becomes a struggle with the other half of one's being, which drags man through evil and guilt:

> Von Stund an ist er entzweit,
> Und muß blutig und mit zerrissenen Händen ringen,
> Zu bezwingen sein Geleit,
> Das ihn schleppt durch Mord und schuldige Taten.

The man who succeeds in transcending this dissociation of consciousness reaches a state of mystical unity—with himself and with all creation:

> Er ist nicht mehr entzweit,
> Er atmet in Frieden,
> Und ist ganz mit sich vereinigt.
> Die Dinge sind von seiner Selbstsucht gereinigt,
> Aus allen Wesen winkt ihm zu
> Unzählig seiendes wirkendes Du,
> Das sich ihm jubelnd ergibt.
> Er aber sieht—und liebt.

The three parts of the play correspond to these three levels of consciousness. The Thamal who arrives at the monastery is still at the first level. After the monk has left him alone for the night, he notices a veiled frame in the corner of the room. Approaching it with his lamp, he tears off the cover and exposes a large mirror. Disgusted at the sight of himself, which he has been trying to escape, he decides to rid himself once and for all of this hated self. Seizing a pistol, he shoots at the mirror, which crashes to the floor in fragments. But out of the frame leaps Mirror-Man. In dithyrambic language Mirror-Man informs Thamal that, far from destroying him, the vain and megalomaniac side of his personality, the shot has liberated him from the confining mirror. Playing Mephisto to Thamal's Faust—the play contains frequent allusions to the language of Goethe's *Faust*—he tempts the repentant Thamal to have confidence in his own power. In a lengthy dialogue with the vacillating Thamal, Mirror-Man persuades him that he, Thamal, has the capacity to liberate mankind as well as himself through his bold deeds. Succumbing to these blandishments, Thamal follows Mirror-Man into the adventures that constitute the long second part of the play.

The details of the plot need not hold us up. In eight scenes Thamal experiences the entire range of human depravity: he causes the death of his own father, seduces his best friend's bride, permits himself to be proclaimed the living god of a populace that he liberates from the snake-demon Ananthas, and so forth. In the last part, Mirror-Man has grown swollen with power and influence whereas Thamal, the residue of his own conscience, is reduced to a shadow of himself and eventually brought to justice for his crimes against humanity. Sick of himself and his own degradation, Thamal resolves to rid himself of Mirror-Man in the only possible way: by killing himself. Ignoring the energetic protests of his second self, Thamal drinks a gobletful of poison. As he does so, Mirror-Man sinks gradually into the glittering surface of a huge mirror that materializes beneath his feet. At the moment of Thamal's death the stage is suddenly transformed, and Thamal finds himself once again in the monastic setting of the first scene. The monk takes Thamal by the hand and leads him up to a vast mirror that covers the entire rear wall of the hall. As Thamal watches, a procession of aged monks passes across the surface of the mirror. Then he notices with horror that his own image is missing. But when he touches the mirror in response to the monk's command, it is transformed into a gigantic window that looks out upon a beautiful world representing a higher reality. By voluntarily destroying his own individuality, Thamal has reached the third level of consciousness at which all being co-exists in unity and harmony. Putting on a golden belt, he is admitted to the order—with the warning that he is still so close to Maya, the phenomenal world of illusory appearances, that he will need much time and effort to reach the ultimate stage of pure love.

Werfel's modern miracle-play is conventional in several senses. The birth of the New Man is perhaps the dominant dream of expressionism, a dream shared by dozens of Werfel's contemporaries. Moreover, we recognize many familiar motifs in his treatment of the mirror-image. The appearance of Mirror-Man is based on the superstition that a man who peers into a mirror late at night, with candles or lamp in hand, can sometimes see the devil or evil spirits appear. The wasting away of the real Thamal while his reflection thrives is a motif that has already been explored by Briusov and Rilke. The notion that only suicide can liberate a man from his double occurs in Maupassant, Wilde, and Ewers. But Werfel has succeeded in amalgamating these and other traditional motifs into a symbolic image that constitutes an immensely effective vehicle for the expressionist message of the play. In fact, here the mirror-image has clearly become the symbol that characterizes the play. Above all, there is absolutely no attempt to rationalize the existence of Mirror-Man. Obviously, he is Thamal's "double," his "second self." But Werfel, as a member of a literary generation that put images at the center of their art, is perfectly willing to accept this vivid image at face value without resorting to rationalization, psychological internalization, or any kind of disqualifying inversion.

The theory of the three levels of consciousness underlying Werfel's play is an ancient one that was revived by many of Werfel's contemporaries. In Hermann Hesse's novel *Steppenwolf* (1927), the image of the mirror-reflection as the hero's double is again used to illustrate this triadic rhythm of humanization.[72] The "Treatise" that is handed to Harry Haller near the beginning of the book explicates virtually the same theory that the monk outlines for Thamal: that human consciousness moves from an original sense of child-like unity with all being through a second stage of dissociated consciousness to a third stage of reunification with the All. The third stage is embodied by what Haller learns to call "the Immortals," and the dissociation of his own consciousness is represented by the division of his personality, as he sees it, into the two poles of "bourgeois" and "wolf from the steppes." But in *Steppenwolf* the image of the reflection as double is refracted into *multiples.* Simple dissociation, Haller learns, does not encompass the varied aspects of human consciousness. It requires a whole Magic Theater of mirrors to contain these multiple aspects.

On November 6, 1809, E.T.A. Hoffmann made the following entry in his journal: "A strange notion at the ball on the sixth. I imagine my Ego as seen through a multiplying-mirror—all the figures moving around me are aspects of my ego and I am annoyed by their activities. . . ."[73] Hesse was a devoted admirer of Hoffmann, whom he considered the most brilliant of romantic narrators. One of his earliest stories, "Lulu" in the volume *Hermann Lauscher* (1901), was "dedicated to the memory of E.T.A. Hoffmann." Throughout his lifetime he referred to Hoffmann in his fictions, letters, and essays. It is more than conjecture that Hesse was acquainted with the passage cited above, for at least twice—in 1916 and 1919—he reviewed the new edition of Hoffmann's *Tagebücher* (1915), in which the entry was printed. It is not unlikely that this passage catalyzed the poetic vision in which, ten years later, *Steppenwolf* culminat-

[72] *Steppenwolf,* trans. Basil Creighton and rev. Joseph Mileck and Horst Frenz (New York: Holt, Rinehart and Winston, 1963).

[73] E.T.A. Hoffmann, *Tagebücher,* ed. Friedrich Schnapp (Munich: Winckler, 1971), p. 107. Hoffmann's term for "multiplying-mirror" is *VervielfältigungsGlas* (*sic*).

ed. To be sure, Hesse had often used the image of the magic mirror in earlier works. At the end of the novella *Klein and Wagner* (1919) Friedrich Klein, who has deserted his family and embezzled money from his company, looks into a mirror and sees the ravaged features of "Wagner"—a composite image representing both the composer and a notorious murderer of that same name. But the example is a rather conventional projection of a single double. It has none of the multiple projections of *Steppenwolf*.

The high point of the novel follows a masquerade ball that Harry Haller attends with his friends, Pablo and Hermine. In the Magic Theater, under the influence of drugs that Pablo has shared with him, Haller is privileged to see his simple mirror reflection refracted into a multiplicity of figures embodying different aspects of his personality. The mirrors of the Magic Theater are carefully anticipated in the course of the novel. As we noted at the beginning of this chapter, Hermine realizes that she functions as "a kind of looking glass" for Haller. Appropriately, mirrors provide one of her characteristic attributes. Shortly after Haller meets Hermine for the first time, for instance, she takes out a tiny pocket-mirror to powder her face; later it occurs to Haller that her face was in fact "like a magic mirror." There are many other references to mirrors. Early in the work, when Haller is still obsessed with the simple duality of bourgeois and wolf contending within his personality, the mysterious "Treatise on the Steppenwolf" notifies him that he is oversimplifying his psychic situation. In order to resolve the conflict of his being, he reads, "a Steppenwolf must once have a good look at himself. He must look deeply into the chaos of his own soul and plumb its depths." To attain this insight, the tract continues, there are at least three ways. It is possible that Harry will encounter the Immortals, or perhaps enter one of the Magic Theaters—or that he will obtain one of the little mirrors. But Haller, it continues, is already aware of these possibilities: "he is aware of the existence of that mirror in which he has such bitter need to look and from which he shrinks in such deathly fear." In one sense, then, the novel depicts Haller's progress toward the magic mirrors mentioned early in the treatise: that is to say, his progress from the mirror as a metaphor or analogy for the soul or the person to the reified metaphor of the mirror as a tangible image in the fictional reality of the novel.

On the night of the Magic Theater Pablo prepares Haller for the encounter with his selves by holding up a round pocket-mirror, in which Harry sees himself reflected as always before: a fluid movement in which an amorphous and only half-shaped wolf flows through the image of Harry Haller. If Haller wants to enter the illusory world of the Magic Theater, Pablo tells him, he must commit an illusory suicide by destroying that image of himself. Once again he takes out his pocket-mirror and holds it up before Haller, assuring him that he can extinguish that image simply by laughing at it, by refusing to take it seriously. When Haller finally bursts into laughter at the pathetic "Harrywolf" in the mirror, "the mournful image in the glass gave a final convulsion and vanished. The glass itself turned gray and charred and opaque as though it had been burned." After this act of self-extinction, through which he has rid himself of his "problematic personality," Haller is now ready to look into what Pablo calls "a proper looking-glass." As he gazes at his reflection in the huge wall-mirror, the image disintegrates into countless Harrys or aspects of Harry—some young, some old; children, schoolboys, youths; middle-aged and elderly Harrys of every appearance. No sooner has Harry recognized these various facets of himself than they run off to the right and left, into the depths of the mirror and right out of it. One runs up to Pablo, embraces him, and dashes off with him while another, a boy of sixteen or seventeen, disappears into a booth on which is written "All Girls Are Yours."

The magic mirror not only provides the central image for the Magic Theater by enabling Harry to break down the various aspects of his personality, it also plays a role in the sideshows within the Magic Theater. When Harry enters a booth proclaiming "Guidance in the Building Up of the Personality," he finds a chessmaster, vaguely resembling Pablo, sitting on the floor in a yoga position. As he holds a mirror up to Haller, the reflection again disintegrates into countless figures; but this time the figures, instead of being life-sized, are shaped like chessmen, which the chessmaster places on his board. Then he shows Haller how many different games can be played with the same group of figures—not just the single simple game that Harry has hitherto been content to call his life.

After various adventures in the Magic Theater, Haller returns to the huge mirror at the entrance, where he again confronts his reflection, a pale and exhausted Harry, with whom he has a brief dialogue before they are interrupted by the appearance of one of the Immortals, Mozart. Some time later Haller finds himself in the corridor once again. "In the great mirror, Harry stood opposite me. He did not appear to be flourishing." Disgusted at the sight of his own reflection, Haller spits at the image and then kicks the mirror until it shatters. That act of violence marks the end of Haller's experiences in the illusory world of the Magic Theater. For in the next instant he destroys the entire illusion when he comes upon Pablo and Hermine in an embrace: in an access of rage and jealousy he stabs Hermine to death. (It is not clear from Hesse's text whether Harry stabs the real Hermine or simply her mirrored image—presumably the latter, though it is a matter of interpretation.)

Unlike Werfel, whose play he reviewed enthusiastically in 1921, Hesse does not ask us to accept the magic mirror as a literary convention. He justifies the image, or images, by presenting them as the projection of Haller's drugged consciousness, which has been stimulated by frequent allusions to mirrors as a metaphor and by the many actual mirrors that have flashed symbolically through the novel. However, psychological credibility is not the point in Hesse's novel, as it still was for Rodenbach and Briusov. In fact, the scene in the Magic Theater is calculatedly surreal, borrowing many of its effects from contemporary expressionist literature, theater, and film. Hesse, an heir of romanticism, has taken the image of the magic mirror familiar to him from many sources, and has converted it into a powerful symbol for the multiple aspects of the human personality. Thus he carries the image a step further than the many other writers from the early nineteenth century on, who used the mirror simply for the representation of a single "double."

Two postwar examples can conclude our discussion of the mirror-image as double. Hermann Kasack's surrealist novel, *The City beyond the River* (1947),[74] one of the major literary works of the immediate postwar period in Germany, stands explicitly in the tradition of Hesse, who is mentioned in the text. The "city" of the title refers to an intermediate realm between life and death, a sort of purgatory in which the dead reside for a time, mere shadows of themselves, before they pass over into the absolute nothingness of death. Kasack meant this ghostly necropolis as a symbolic representation of the hollowness of Western civilization. The plot deals with a young man, Robert Lindhoff, who has been engaged from the land of the living to bring order into the archives of the city. At one point Lindhoff is inspecting some factories on the city's edge. Annoyed by his guide and anxious to get back into the city, Lindhoff hurries off on a side-path, expecting to find a short cut. Instead he gets lost in a "labyrinth of mirrors," a "mirror prison" that was originally designed to prevent inhabitants of the city from escaping. The scene rapidly becomes surreal. First he sees walking toward him a figure that to his astonishment turns out to be a *Doppelgänger*. A moment later the single figure has split into a dozen small images, only to return in the form of a gigantic face grinning at him. As he tries to escape the labyrinth, he is surrounded at every turn by distorted images of himself. Sometimes these selves escort him on either side,

[74] *Die Stadt hinter dem Strom* (Frankfurt am Main: Suhrkamp Verlag vorm. S. Fischer, 1949), pp. 282–89.

sometimes extended to a bizarre height and at other times grotesquely contracted. Lindhoff has begun to doubt the reality of his own existence when suddenly a new effect strikes his eyes. In the mirrors he sees, instantaneously realized, every thought that comes to his mind. Like Harry Haller in the Magic Theater, Lindhoff sees himself strangling a man, raping a woman, working in his archives: "All the figures executed whatever he thought in that very instant as a mirror-act. All his suppressed wishes and curses, the most hidden stirrings of his emotions, hate and love, were brought visibly before his eyes. The images of his soul hastened past as though in a film that runs faster and faster." Eventually Lindhoff is released from the "prison of mirrors" —not by his own efforts but because someone else turns on the lights. The multiple mirrorings of his *persona* that Lindhoff perceives in the magic mirrors of the labyrinth amount to symbols for the various facets of his human personality, the "dross" (as he is told) that must be shed before any deceased person is ready to enter the world of the dead. This mirror scene, which constitutes only a passing episode in a long novel, does not have the focal significance of the Magic Theater in *Steppenwolf*. But in the explicit surrealism of his technique and in his intensification of the mirror-image from "doubles" to "multiples," Kasack clearly continues in the tradition of Werfel, Hesse, and other writers of the twenties.

Our final example occurs in a novel by Heinrich Böll, who is generally considered to be a reasonably sober and realistic writer. The heroine of *Group Portrait with Lady* (1971), Leni, gradually emerges as a secularized Virgin Mary, a modern madonna. Many of the details of characterization, along with several of the central episodes of plot, are typologically based on legends dealing with the Holy Mother.[75] We are clearly, in other words, in a religious

[75] Theodore Ziolkowski, "The Author as *Advocatus Dei* in Heinrich Böll's *Group Portrait with Lady*," *University of Dayton Review*, 13 (1976), 7–17.

realm—despite all the secularization of effects. One of the details used early in the novel to introduce this theme concerns Leni's peculiar relationship to the Virgin. "She is on intimate terms with the Virgin Mary, receiving her almost daily on the television screen, and she is invariably surprised to find that the Virgin Mary is also a blonde, by no means as young as one would like her to be; these encounters take place in silence, usually late at night when all the neighbors are asleep and the TV stations—including the one in the Netherlands—have signed off and switched on their test patterns. All Leni and the Virgin Mary do is exchange smiles."[76] On a purely rational level, of course, the author is suggesting that these encounters with the Virgin Mary are nothing more than Leni's own reflection on the lighted television screen: the Virgin reflects Leni's physical appearance precisely. Yet between this rational explanation and the miraculous appearance of the divine double on the screen that Leni accepts as a miracle, Böll leaves room for the ambiguity that characterizes so many depictions of the magic mirror. For there seems to be no satisfactory way of accounting, after all, for the reflection on the television screen. Almost the last words of the novel, put into the mouth of one of the most skeptical characters, deal with this vision: " 'It is herself, Leni herself, appearing to herself because of some still unexplained reflections.' " The narrator concludes with the laconic comment: "Well, there remain the 'still unexplained reflections. . . .' " In other words, Böll uses the strategy of ambiguity that we have often encountered in writers on the boundary between romanticism and realism, between faith and skepticism. At the same time, by locating the motif of the magic mirror in a specifically religious context, Böll brings us almost full circle back to the cultic realm in which such magic images initially got their start. For a third time, then, we have seen a magic image go through the four stages of disenchantment. The mirrored image of

[76] *Gruppenbild mit Dame*, cited according to the translation by Leila Vennewitz (New York: McGraw-Hill, 1973), p. 13.

the double entered romantic literature bearing the clearly magical associations of its mystical source; in the works of Poe and Dostoevsky it was rendered ambiguous through rationalization; in the works of Stevenson and Maupassant and then especially of Rodenbach, Briusov, and Rilke it was internalized and wholly disenchanted by psychology; and finally it experienced its purely literary revival in the twentieth century.

THE MIRROR in which the double appears and from which he sometimes emerges, singly or multiply, is the principal category of magic mirror in nineteenth- and twentieth-century literature. Yet this category has contained hints, from time to time, of a third important category that still needs to be mentioned. Rilke was frustrated by the "impenetrability" of mirrors, which prevented him from entering the more beautiful world that he saw reflected in them. Rodenbach's "ami des miroirs" dies as a result of his attempt to penetrate the mirror. The finale of Werfel's miracle-play shows us how the magic mirror, which at first reflects the illusory world of everyday reality, finally becomes a transparent window opening out onto an ideal world, the spiritual kingdom of eternal reality that Thamal is now privileged to enter. Werfel leaves it to our imagination to follow Thamal into that realm behind the mirror, to which he presumably retreats after the curtain falls. A few writers, however, take the representation of the mirror-realm as their chief subject: the double does not emerge from the mirror; instead, the human being enters the mirror, which becomes the symbol of a different reality of an altogether different order.

The most familiar example is no doubt Lewis Carroll's classic, *Through the Looking Glass* (1872). We have already noted an inherent characteristic of reflecting surfaces that from the start contributed to the mystery of mirrors: the fact that the mirror inverts everyday reality, making everything appear in reverse. To construct the fictional world of his fantasy, Lewis Carroll simply applies this principle with the utmost rigor. Given the premise that it is possible to pass through a mirror to the other side, the world beyond the looking glass is depicted according to a strictly logical pattern. In that realm all books—e.g., the poem of the Jabberwocky—are printed in reverse so that Alice must hold the text up to the glass in order to decipher it. When Alice sets out in pursuit of the Red Queen, she immediately loses sight of that regal personage until it occurs to her that she must walk in the opposite direction in order to catch up with her. However, if we accept the initial absurd premise—that it is possible to penetrate a mirror—the appeal of *Through the Looking Glass* is not so much to our sense of magic and mystery as it is to the child's fascination with the seemingly miraculous laws of nature. Its laws are less literary than logical. In the final analysis Lewis Carroll is a captive of his rational generation: it turns out that Alice has simply fallen asleep and dreamed her entire adventure. To rediscover the "magic" of magic mirrors we must turn to the symbolic fantasies written by one of Lewis Carroll's close friends, the Scottish romancer, George MacDonald.

MacDonald, who was exposed at an impressionable age to German romanticism and who even translated Novalis' *Twelve Spiritual Songs* (1851), was a veritable catoptrophile. In his "faerie romance," *Phantastes* (1858), for instance, the narrator remarks that "all mirrors are magic mirrors. The commonest room is a room in a poem when I turn to the glass."[77] This romance, which is patently based on Novalis' *Heinrich von Ofterdingen*, contains an interpolated tale (Ch. 13) that the narrator discovers in a mysterious old

[77] George MacDonald, *Phantastes and Lilith*. With an Introduction by C. S. Lewis (Grand Rapids, Mich.: Eerdmans, 1964), p. 73. The thought expressed here recapitulates the impulse behind the "Claude-glasses" popular among eighteenth-century travelers: small tinted mirrors in a frame in which one looked at the landscape, which was rendered as though in a painting by Claude Lorrain. For a discussion of MacDonald's debt to German romanticism see Robert Lee Wolff, *The Golden Key: A Study of the Fiction of George MacDonald* (New Haven, Conn.: Yale Univ. Press, 1961).

volume. The story concerns Cosmo von Wehrstahl, a student at the University of Prague, who buys a beautiful old mirror from an antique dealer. The following evening Cosmo admires his purchase and thinks to himself: "What a strange thing a mirror is! and what a wondrous affinity exists between it and a man's imagination! For this room of mine, as I behold it in the glass, is the same, and yet not the same." As he watches, he sees with amazement the graceful form of a woman, clothed in white, glide into the reflected room and lie down on the couch. Yet when he turns to his own couch, it is vacant. For several hours Cosmo observes the sleeping beauty, until at last she leaves the reflected room. For several weeks the girl returns each evening to the room in the mirror, and as Cosmo studies her reactions and tastes, he rearranges his own room to suit her, disposing of a skeleton that frightens her and adding an elegant couch and screens of Indian fabric. One evening, as he stares at the girl in the mirror, he detects a blush of self-consciousness on her face, and she leaves earlier than usual. When she fails to return for several days, Cosmo is plagued by uncertainty and jealousy. Consulting his books of sorcery, he prepares some powerful charms whereby he succeeds in drawing the girl first back into his reflected room and then from there into his real room. She implores him to liberate her by shattering the mirror. When he tries to smash it with his sword, a great clap of thunder knocks him senseless. When he recovers, both the girl and the mirror are gone. Some days later Cosmo hears rumors concerning the strange illness of the Princess Hohenweiss, which resulted from a witch's curse and which was somehow related to the loss of an antique mirror from her dressing-room. Shortly thereafter he learns that an acquaintance, the reckless and fiery Steinwald, recently acquired a mirror similar to the enchanted one that he lost. Cosmo goes to Steinwald's house to fulfill his promise by smashing the mirror, but in the process he is mortally wounded by his opponent. At that moment, in another part of the city, the princess suddenly recovers from her mysterious affliction and rushes out into the night, where she finds the dying Cosmo and embraces him as a final gesture of gratitude.

This lengthy encapsulation in *Phantastes* gives ample evidence of MacDonald's early obsession with mirrors, and it displays, moreover, a new refinement in the treatment of the image: for Cosmo's mirror is not simply a catoptromantic mirror that shows what is happening somewhere else, nor is it a doubling mirror; it casts a true reflection of his room, and the lovely princess enters that reflected reality, which is more beautiful than ordinary reality. But not until we get to his *Lilith: A Romance* (1895) does this image become the dominating symbol of an entire book. The story begins, as do many of MacDonald's fictions, in the library of a great estate, where the narrator, who has just completed his studies at Oxford, is improving his knowledge of science, both ancient and modern. One summer evening he seems to perceive a tall figure at the other end of the library, reaching up to remove a book from a shelf; in the next instant the vision has disappeared. Several days later the experience is repeated even more vividly: he recognizes a slender old man in a long dark coat leaving the library, but when he follows, the old man disappears again. When he asks the butler for information, he learns that the library was long considered haunted by a Mr. Raven, the librarian of his ancestor, Sir Upward: they had both been reputed to read "strange, forbidden, and evil books" (p. 190). A week later the old librarian appears once more, and this time the narrator follows him through the house up to the main garret. There he finds a tall, old-fashioned mirror in an ebony frame, on top of which stands a black eagle with outstretched wings. "I had been looking at rather than into the mirror, when suddenly I became aware that it reflected neither the chamber nor my own person. I have an impression of having seen the wall melt away, but what followed is enough to account for any uncertainty:—could I have mistaken for a mirror the glass that protected a wonderful picture?" (p. 192).

Leaning forward to examine the landscape, he stumbles and finds himself on a houseless heath, nose to beak with a large raven.

The narrator enters and leaves the mirror-world several times accidentally before he learns its secret: it constitutes a "region of the seven dimensions" (p. 202), where most of the physical and many of the mental laws of this world are different. "As for moral laws, they must everywhere be fundamentally the same" (p. 220). It is this last qualification that enables the narrator to become the hero in the romantic quest that takes place when he enters the mirror again of his own volition. In brief: the world beyond the mirror turns out to be the New Jerusalem, where an eternal mythic struggle continues between Good and Evil, represented by Adam (Mr. Raven) and Eve in opposition to Lilith, Adam's first wife, who roams destructively through this world in the shape of a great white leopardess. After various adventures, in the course of which he falls in love with Lona, Lilith's daughter, and then loses her through death, the narrator returns to the "real" world. The long romance concludes with a quotation from Novalis suggesting the meaning of the fantasy: the "real" world is merely an illusion that we must endure until, in death, we are finally permitted to enter the eternal world of which, at present, we can only dream. It is that kingdom of death, the timeless world of the mythic contest between Good and Evil, between Adam and Lilith, that the mirror represents.

The realm behind the mirror continues to provide the scene in romances from Lewis Carroll through George MacDonald down to James Branch Cabell. In *Something about Eve* (1927), however, the mirror-realm is reduced to a single episode.[78] When Gerald arrives in the land of Dersam he goes to the Temple, where he sees the Sacred Mirror of Caer Omn. Without preliminaries he passes through a

[78] *Something about Eve: A Comedy of Fig-Leaves* (1927; rpt. New York: Robert M. McBride, 1929), pp. 67–98 (Part IV: "The Book of Dersam").

"warmish golden mist" into the realm of the mirror, which turns out, as in MacDonald's *Lilith,* to be a kingdom of myth, where he sees many heroes from the realm of poetry: Prometheus, Solomon, Odysseus, Faust. Stepping back out of the mirror, Gerald is released from its magic, only to be enraptured by Evervan of the Mirror, who comes out of "the gold glowing of the sacred mirror." But he resists her allure and exorcises her with "the old runes of common-sense." Evervan is transformed through the stages of womanhood back into the womb. Then everything else in the land of Dersam, including the people and the temple, enters the magic mirror and vanishes into the realm of poetry and myth. "Caer Omn was gone: the land of Dersam was a ruined land without inhabitants. Afterwards the pale glass blinked seven times like summer lightning, and the mirror was not there." In Cabell's romance the symbolic magic mirror has become little more than a requisite, adding nothing to the meaning of the image as it was used by MacDonald. In that same decade, however, another work appeared that combined surrealism and irony to win a new dimension from the familiar image.

When Jean Cocteau's play, *Orphée* (1926) opens, Orpheus has virtually given up poetry in order to devote himself full-time to attempts to communicate with the spirit world through the medium of a horse that taps out messages.[79] Eurydice, jealous of the horse, obtains a lump of poisoned sugar from the witch, Aglaonice, who also happens to be Orpheus' chief competitor in poetry. When Orpheus goes to town to sign up for the coming All-Thrace poetry contest, Eurydice poisons the horse; but as a result of Aglaonice's trickery—a poisoned envelope in which Eurydice was to send her a message—she falls ill and dies. When her accomplice, the glazier Heurtebise, rushes off to fetch Orpheus, the room gets dark and the figure of Death, dressed in

[79] Cited according to the translation by John Savacool in Jean Cocteau, *The Infernal Machine and Other Plays* (Norfolk, Conn.: New Directions, 1963), pp. 97–150.

evening clothes and accompanied by two assistants in surgeons' uniforms, enters the room through the large mirror on the wall. Death dons a surgical gown and rubber gloves while her assistants operate various electrical instruments that they have brought along. After various manipulations—which involve the illusion-breaking trick of borrowing a watch from a member of the audience—they pack up their equipment again and walk back through the mirror, leaving behind a pair of rubber surgical gloves. The dead Eurydice is transformed into a dove, which flies off into space.

When Orpheus returns with Heurtebise to discover that Eurydice has been carried away by Death, he resolves to reclaim her from the underworld. Heurtebise advises him to put on the surgical gloves that Death has forgotten, for she will offer Orpheus a reward in return for them. Then Heurtebise leads Orpheus to the mirror, revealing to him the secret of secrets, which he—as a glazier—understands. "Mirrors are doors. It's through them that Death moves back and forth into life." Since the realm of death lies behind the mirror, anyone who looks at himself in a mirror can see Death at work there "like a swarm of bees storing up honey in a hive of glass." With the gloves on his hands, Orpheus passes through the mirror and disappears. Sometime later he emerges again, followed by Eurydice. He explains to Heurtebise that he had to make a pact with Death never to look at Eurydice again lest she be taken back to the underworld. But within a few minutes they quarrel, he looks at her, and she goes back into the mirror.

Shortly thereafter a frenzied mob of women, led by the Bacchantes and stirred up by Aglaonice, arrives outside Orpheus' house. When Orpheus goes out to speak to them, they cut off his head and hurl it back into the house. As the severed head cries out for help, Eurydice steps out of the mirror again. Taking his invisible body by the hand, she leads it through the mirror. A moment later the Commissioner enters and finds Heurtebise alone in the house with Orpheus' head. An eclipse of the sun has shifted public sympathy in favor of Orpheus, and the town is now crying for justice. Heurtebise is suspected of the crime. As the Commissioner interrogates him, Eurydice appears in the mirror again, urging Heurtebise to join her and Orpheus. Meanwhile, the decapitated head of Orpheus answers the Commissioner's questions, revealing that Heurtebise is none other than Cocteau himself. When the Commissioner leaves, Orpheus and Eurydice, guided by Heurtebise, re-enter the room through the mirror. After a prayer of thanks for their rescue from the devil, who had assumed the form of a horse, and expressing their gratitude for Heurtebise's (Cocteau's) guidance, they sit down at the table and drink a glass of wine as the curtain falls.

Orphée displays in exemplary form the principal characteristics of surrealism—notably, the rejection of rationalism and the appeal to the higher truth of dreams in a manner that insistently defies the rules of conventional realistic drama. As in Werfel's *Mirror-Man*, the magic mirror provides the central organizing image for the entire drama. Here, of course, we are not dealing with a double that emerges from the mirror: the mirror is a symbol for the realm of death, which the various figures enter and leave. In other words, Cocteau is exploiting one of the most primal superstitions concerning mirrors as the abode of spirits and souls. At the same time, to the extent that Heurtebise the glazier is identical with Cocteau the poet, the author seems to be implying that the realm beyond the looking glass is also the timeless realm of poetry—like the mirror-world into which the poet plunges to rediscover his past in Cocteau's subsequent film, *The Blood of a Poet*. But the seriousness of the image is disqualified by the irony of the play, which uses the image simply as a symbol with no suspension of disbelief in the supernatural.

Once writers (and their culture) reach the stage of playful and often parodistic exploitation of magic images—in other words, once the images have been fully disenchanted—the development seems to reach a stopping-point. Where can writers go but back to myth and folklore if the image is to be rejuvenated? This seems to be the conclusion reached by several recent literary "amis des miroirs." In his tale "Assirata, or The Enchanted Mirror"[80] Jean Louis Bouquet introduces a "society of curious spirits" who come together every Saturday to discuss archaeology, mythology, and the occult sciences. At one such meeting a member displays an ancient silver mirror contrived by a Cabalist, bearing an Aramaic inscription to the spirit Assirata: anyone who contemplates the mirror while invoking Assirata will see visions of distant or hidden things; but the reflection of the interrogator will remain forever engraved on the magic surface. The mirror is passed around, but no one notices anything remarkable until it reaches the hands of the young secretary of the society, a would-be poet named Ludovic. Ludovic becomes convinced that he perceives among the many figures in the misty depths of the mirror an image of himself in the costume of another age and speaking an unfamiliar language. Obsessed with the notion that the mirror will help him recover the powers of creativity that he possessed in his earlier incarnation, he implores the owner to sell the mirror to him. When this fails, he finally steals the mirror and leaves Paris, never to be heard of again—although the members of the society do attempt to conjure up his spirit once in the course of a séance.

Bouquet, a master of the modern supernatural tale, has provided various possibilities of interpretation. The doctor, the rationalist of the group, considers Ludovic's vision to be nothing more than an auto-suggestive hallucination produced by the legends surrounding the old mirror. Several other members, by nature disposed toward the supernatural, tend to accept a more marvelous explanation for his visions. Finally, an aged rabbinical scholar declares that Assirata is a malevolent spirit who presides over dreams and daydreams, flattering our vanity and consoling us with deceitful visions.

[80] "Assirata, ou Le Miroir enchanté," *Alastor ou Le Visage de feu* (Paris: Robert Marin, 1951), pp. 101–24.

"It is not the depths of the past that the mirror reflects. It is an interior abyss, the perpetual invasion route of the dark powers that desperately aspire to the domain of forms and substances and that can attain that state only through the collapse of your reason"—a view remarkably similar to the early romantic conception of the eternal battle between the conscious and the unconscious. In short, the author leaves his ending ambiguously suspended, and if Ludovic does indeed enter the mirror—in spirit, at least—he does so after his disappearance from the narrative.

Another modern author, however, uses the same Jewish folklore as the basis for a tale in which the heroine actually does enter the magic mirror. Isaac Bashevis Singer was influenced by the exotic romanticism of writers like Hoffmann, Poe, Gogol, and Dostoevsky. But he also conceded in a recent interview that he believes "absolutely" in the supernatural, which comes up so frequently in his writing "because it is always on my mind."[81] Singer says that it is perfectly natural to use the devil and his imps as images. "The fear of the supernatural is in everybody. And since we are all afraid of the supernatural, there is no reason why we shouldn't make use of it." Singer's story "The Mirror" (from *Gimpel the Fool*, 1957), which he regarded as important enough to convert in 1973 into his first play, has a rather sophisticated twist appropriate for the late form of any image: it is narrated from the point of view of the imp within the mirror.[82] But the basic motif is the familiar one of the vain woman who permits herself to be lured by the devil into the kingdom of death beyond the mirror.

The imp has installed himself in a mirror in order to tempt Zirel, a beautiful but vain young woman in the *shtetl* of Krashnik, who locks herself every day into the attic of her house in order to admire herself, nude, before the mirror.

[81] "Interview with Isaac Bashevis Singer," *The Paris Review*, 44 (1968), 53–73.

[82] Isaac Bashevis Singer, *Selected Short Stories*, ed. Irving Howe (New York: Modern Library, 1966), pp. 57–67.

The imp flatters and cajoles her until she agrees to enter the realm of the mirror where, he promises, she will "sit on Asmodeus' lap and plait tresses in his beard" while nibbling almonds and drinking porter. After performing a sequence of blasphemous rituals, Zirel is enabled to enter the mirror, and the imp does indeed carry her off to the kingdom of Asmodeus. But to her woe she discovers that it is quite different from her expectations. "In the vale of shadow which is known as the world everything is subject to change. But for us time stands still! Adam remains naked, Eve lustful, still in the act of being seduced by the serpent, Cain kills Abel . . . Job scratches at his sore-covered body. He will keep scratching until the end of time, but he will find no comfort." The imp delivers Zirel, who is tortured by devils. "Meanwhile generations come and go—Zirel follows Zirel, in a myriad of reflections—a myriad of mirrors."

We need, in conclusion, to make two points about these magic mirrors as symbols of another world. First, whether the world beyond the mirror is portrayed as good, bad, or merely different, it is characterized in every case by the quality of timeless spirituality that goes back to the most primitive folklore. It is the kingdom where Adam and Lilith still struggle, where Cain continues to slay Abel, where the mythic heroes reside, where nothing changes. Second, the penetrable mirror, though not so consistently as the doubling mirror, reveals several stages in the process of disenchantment. The image enters Macdonald's fantasies bearing clear associations of magic and the supernatural, which require the suspension of our disbelief. Lewis Carroll uses logic rather than imagination to create the delusions of his mirror world and then supplies us with a perfectly rational means of reconciling the seemingly supernatural with reason. Cocteau poetically ironizes the image that he places at the center of his drama. And Singer rounds the circle by returning the image to the mythic-religious realm where the belief in magic mirrors originated.

CHAPTER FIVE

The Implications of Iconology

In the preceding chapters we have been concerned with the cultural origins of three related magic images and with the history of their disenchantment as reflected in European literature of the past two hundred years. In the interest of clarity we found it useful to distinguish the three images according to the principal literary functions each fulfills (notably theme, motif, and symbol) and to classify each image according to the principal aspects it displays (e.g., as *genius loci, figura*, or *anima*). Our study has led us to examine roughly a hundred works in which magic images, at various stages in their disenchantment, play a conspicuous role. Although this list does not aspire to be iconographically exhaustive, it should be iconologically representative, including as it does some seventy writers from five different national literatures covering a period of two centuries. At this point we need to venture beyond our differentiating analysis to recapitulate those common elements that constitute certain larger patterns integrating all three images.

Insofar as animated statues, haunted portraits, and magic mirrors are supernatural—that is, phenomena that seemingly violate the laws of nature as they are understood at a given time in history—our study belongs to the general category of works on the supernatural in literature. Yet it differs from most of them in several important respects. To the extent that it is comparative in scope, it goes beyond those studies that limit themselves to a single national literature (e.g., *The Supernatural in Modern English Fiction*, or *Essai sur le merveilleux dans la littérature française depuis 1800*), and can thereby note characteristics that are generational or otherwise supranational in their implications. To the extent that it deals with works of different literary types, it goes beyond those studies that limit themselves to a single genre (e.g., the Gothic romance, the *Gespenstergeschichte*, the *conte fantastique*), and can thereby register shifts of images from one literary level to another. To the extent that it attempts to differentiate with iconographical precision among three magic images and to trace their histories separately, it differs from those studies that cite images simply as peripheral accessories to Gothic romances of fantastic tales and list them indiscriminately, as though there were no essential differences between magic mirrors, haunted portraits, and animated statues. Finally, to the extent that it is historical in approach and emphasizes the process of "disenchantment," it differs from those studies that deal in a more theoretical way with *das Unheimliche* or *le fantastique* or "the marvelous." In conclusion, it is appropriate to test from our different vantage point certain conclusions reached by other related studies and, at the same time, to examine the implications of our iconological approach. In full awareness of the limitations of our own method and texts, let us guard against the temptation of generalizing to a degree unwarranted by the material that has actually been analyzed here.

IT HAS long been recognized that the sensations variously labeled "uncanny" or "fantastic" or "marvelous" depend upon a certain relationship in the apprehension of what is real and what is unreal. In a Prefatory Note to "The Haunted and the Haunters" Bulwer Lytton observed: "It is just when elements of the marvellous are thus struggling between superstition and philosophy, that they fall by right to the domain of Art—the art of poet or tale-teller."[1] Peter Penzoldt, after surveying the views of H. P. Lovecraft, M. R.

[1] Edward Bulwer Lytton, *A Strange Story* (Philadelphia: Lippincott, 1888), p. 348.

James, and other masters of horror fiction, concludes that "all stories of the supernatural are tales of fear that play on our doubt whether what we maintain to be pure imagination is not, after all, reality."[2] Roger Caillois, the *doyen* of French students of the supernatural, asserts that "in the fantastic, the supernatural appears as a rupture of the universal coherence. The prodigy becomes a prohibited and menacing act of aggression, which shatters the stability of a world whose laws had hitherto been regarded as rigorous and immutable."[3] The most systematic attempt to come to grips with the question has been undertaken by Tzvetan Todorov in his *Introduction to the Fantastic in Literature*. Todorov defines the fantastic as the hesitation experienced by someone who acknowledges only natural laws and who is suddenly confronted with an event that is seemingly supernatural.[4] If the fictional character overcomes this uncertainty to conclude that the laws of nature suffice to explain the prodigy, then we are dealing not with the fantastic but with what Todorov, borrowing a term from Freud, calls "the uncanny" (*l'étrange, das Unheimliche*). If, on the other hand,

[2] *The Supernatural in Fiction* (London: Peter Nevill, 1952), p. 9.

[3] "L'Image fantastique: De la féerie à la science-fiction," in *Images, Images: Essais sur le rôle et les pouvoirs de l'imagination*, by Roger Caillois (Paris: José Corti, 1966), p. 16. Caillois' theory has been developed, with particular reference to Piranesi and Jules Verne, by Lars Gustafsson, "Über das Phantastische in der Literatur," in *Utopien: Essays*, trans. Hanns Grössel (Munich: Hanser, 1970), pp. 9–25.

[4] *Introduction à la littérature fantastique* (Paris: Seuil, 1970), p. 29: "Le fantastique, c'est l'hésitation éprouvée par un être qui ne connaît que les lois naturelles, face à un événement en apparence surnatural." Todorov's book has been translated by Richard Howard under the title: *The Fantastic: A Structural Approach to a Literary Genre* (Cleveland: Press of Case Western Reserve Univ., 1973). Eric S. Rabkin, *The Fantastic in Literature* (Princeton, N.J.: Princeton Univ. Press, 1976), has approached the phenomenon (almost exclusively in English literature) with wholly different criteria. Specifically, Rabkin (p. 118) challenges Todorov's notion of "hesitation"; but his discussion of the point is too brief to be persuasive.

natural laws cannot account for the phenomenon, then we are in the realm of "the marvelous" (*le merveilleux*). Todorov's approach, in its logical rigor and elegant simplicity, goes far beyond all other attempts to analyze this important impulse of nineteenth-century literature. Being purely theoretical, however, it lacks any historical dimension. Our study suggests a different way of approaching Todorov's three "genres" (which might more appropriately be called "modes").

In all three chapters we observed four distinct stages in the process that we have called disenchantment. In each case an image enters literature around 1800 bearing ancient magical associations which are accepted by the conventions of the fiction: in *The Castle of Otranto* the portrait actually walks; in Goethe's *Faust* the mirror is truly catoptromantic; in Tom Moore's "The Ring" the statue literally comes to life. The following thirty years produced a conspicuous shift in attitude. Scott, Hawthorne, Gogol, Mérimée, and their contemporaries resort to a variety of narrative devices that leave open the possibility of a rational explanation for seemingly supernatural occurrences even though the "magic" is never explicitly denied. A generation later the situation has changed yet again. Zola, Henry James, Stevenson, and Rodenbach do not even entertain the question of "magic": what seems to be supernatural always turns out to have a clearly rational explanation, usually an internalized psychological one. These three stages, which correspond with considerable precision to Todorov's three "genres," suggest the need for two modifications.

First, in contrast to Todorov's, our analysis of the process of disenchantment indicates that the three categories are not synchronic "genres" or modes but reactions to the supernatural that can best be understood in a diachronic sequence. An example from a different cultural realm should make the point clear. At the beginning of the nineteenth century there were two established methods of interpreting the "miracles" of the Bible.[5] For hundreds of years biblical exegesis had been dominated by "supernaturalism," which assumed that all the miracles occurred quite literally as represented in the Bible—from the creation of the world to the resurrection of Jesus. In the course of the eighteenth century there emerged a competing school of "thoroughgoing rationalism." According to these rationalists, every miracle in the Bible is susceptible of a perfectly natural explanation: the angels were meteorites, the voice of God thunder in the distance; Jesus fed the multitudes from stores of food hidden in caves by his "secret" disciples; the miraculous healings amounted to psychosomatic cures; the resurrection was nothing but the reappearance of Jesus, who had been taken from the cross drugged and living, and restored to health; and so forth. By the time David Friedrich Strauss published his epoch-making *Life of Jesus* in 1835, many thoughtful people found the improbabilities of a super-subtle rationalism at least as farfetched as the implausibilities of a naive supernaturalism. Strauss took a compromise position between the supernatural and the rational schools: according to him the New Testament is simply not reliable enough to provide satisfactory documentary evidence for any events in the life of Jesus, supernatural or otherwise. The so-called miracles can be explained in part as literary interpolations by the gospelists, inserted in an effort to make the life of Jesus consistent with expectations about the Messiah in the Old Testament. At the same time, Strauss concedes that Jesus might well have possessed some extraordinary "magnetic" powers of healing that would account for other seeming miracles. By mid-century a new generation of historically sophisticated Bible critics had lost patience with Strauss's ambivalence. Arguing that "miracle" was not a question worthy of serious discussion and discounting its possibility

[5] For this paragraph see Albert Schweitzer, *The Quest of the Historical Jesus*, trans. from 1st ed. of 1906 by W. Montgomery (1910; rpt. New York: Macmillan, 1968).

in any form, these theologians turned their attention from the life of Jesus to the early Christian community in an attempt to understand the consciousness that required the belief in miracles.

If we step back and look for structural parallels between these attitudes toward biblical miracles and contemporary responses to the supernatural in fiction, we can easily detect precise generational analogies. The belief in biblical miracle by the "supernatural" school corresponds to the acceptance of magic images—either credulous or by convention—among many German and English writers around 1800; "thoroughgoing rationalism" provides a counterpart to the *surnaturel expliqué* of Mrs. Radcliffe and other practitioners of the Gothic romance. Strauss's attempt to achieve a compromise between the rational and the supernatural interpretations bears a close generational resemblance to the fictional stance of Mérimée, Gogol, Hawthorne, and other writers of the thirties and forties, who exploited the effects of the supernatural while leaving room in every case for a rational explanation. Finally, the skeptical historicists, who deny the possibility of miracle while attempting to comprehend the consciousness of those who believe, are evidently the intellectual contemporaries of Henry James, Maupassant, and Rodenbach, who investigate the psychology of credulous iconomaniacs without suggesting for an instant that anything supernatural really takes place.

These striking generational parallels between literature and theology imply that Todorov's categories are not timeless "genres" that can be taken out of their historical context but stages that emerge in a necessary and irreversible sequence in response to specific cultural circumstances.[6] We can go a step further. Although these stages emerge in a strict historical sequence, they do not disappear when a new stage prevails. According to a principle that might be called the Conservation of Cultural Energy, they remain in exist-

[6] It goes without saying that similar generational analogies can be ascertained in other fields as well, notably in science and philosophy.

ence as fictional or intellectual possibilities. (Obviously, many people still believe literally in the miracles of the Bible, some reject them altogether, and still others rationalize them.) This fact accounts for the fourth stage in the process of disenchantment, which often involves a reanimation of the disenchanted images by transposition into a literary form where the marvelous can still be taken literally: parody (e.g., Anstey, *The Tinted Venus*, or De Morgan, *A Likely Story*), horror fiction (e.g., Mrs. Nesbit's "The Ebony Frame"), or fantasy (e.g., Werfel's *Mirror-Man*). Other works continue to exploit the ambiguity characteristic of the fantastic: Böll leaves us, in the curious religious ambiance of his novel, suspended in a state of inconclusiveness regarding the epiphany of the Virgin on the television screen. Still other works ultimately resolve the appearance of the supernatural to the uncanny (e.g., Hesse's *Steppenwolf*). In the twentieth century, in other words, it is accurate to speak of the synchronicity of various "genres" of the supernatural; but we must remind ourselves that these "genres" or modes emerged in the course of the nineteenth century in a fixed sequence that reflects the history of culture and ideas.[7]

The discovery of a historical sequence suggests the need for a second modification of existing theory. Our study of magic images has borne out a generalization advanced by many students of the supernatural: that the obsession with the supernatural is a reasonably persistent trait in the history of mankind.[8] At the same time, its occurrence in literature

[7] In this connection see Leonard B. Meyer, *Music, the Arts, and Ideas: Patterns and Predictions in Twentieth-Century Culture* (Chicago: Univ. of Chicago Press, 1967), p. 235: "Evidence presented in the preceding chapters indicates that the arts have entered a period in which multiplicity of styles and techniques, attitudes and ideologies, will coexist for a considerable period of time."

[8] Dorothy Scarborough, *The Supernatural in Modern English Fiction* (New York: Putnam, 1917); Penzoldt, *The Supernatural in Fiction*, pp. 3–4; Edith Birkhead, *The Tale of Terror*, pp. 1–15 and pp. 221–28; Siegbert S. Prawer, *The 'Uncanny' in Literature: An Apology for its Investigation* (London: Westfield College, 1965), pp. 23–24.

neither is so steady as some writers have suggested; nor does it occur in isolated and unpredictable spurts, as is implied by other writers who deal with such temporally limited genres as the Gothic romance or the French *conte fantastique*. What our study—comparative in focus, transgeneric in scope, historical in approach—has shown would seem to be rather obvious: the interest in the supernatural—at least during the two centuries when it has played a significant role in European and American fiction—occurs in regular waves.

If we visualize a chronological table of the texts discussed, it is immediately apparent that the first period of high density occurs in the years from roughly 1795 to 1815. This corresponds to the findings of other scholars. If we discount *The Castle of Otranto* as an early anomaly, we find that the supernatural was first introduced programmatically into English literature by Lewis in *The Monk* (1796), a book conspicuously inspired by contemporary treatments of the supernatural in German literature.[9] French scholars regard the period from 1830 to 1850 as the high-point of literature of the fantastic in France, pointing out that the term "fantastique" became fashionable around 1830 following the translation of E.T.A. Hoffmann's tales.[10] Our study not only confirms that conclusion; it goes on to show that the same decades represent a period of high density in Germany, England, Russia, and the United States as well. In other words, the vogue of the supernatural just before mid-century is not national but cosmopolitan in its appeal. Following a notable ebbing of interest during the fifties and sixties—we found only three works, all British, between *The House of the*

[9] Karl S. Guthke, *Englische Vorromantik und deutscher Sturm und Drang: M. G. Lewis' Stellung in der Geschichte der deutsch-englischen Literaturbeziehungen*, Palaestra, vol. 223 (Göttingen: Vandenhoeck & Ruprecht, 1958).

[10] Pierre-Georges Castex, *Le Conte fantastique en France de Nodier à Maupassant* (Paris: José Corti, 1951), pp. 64–68.

Seven Gables (1851) and *Venus in Furs* (1870)—the next two decades produced another wave of high literary density.

These three principal waves, each lasting about twenty years, correspond almost exactly to the first three stages of disenchantment that we have defined. Each level of achievement is followed by a period of reassessment, during which no significant advances are made. Then a new generation of writers reanimates the old images with new meanings that are consistent with contemporary cultural attitudes. But these conclusions concerning the cultural wave-movement, which leads from the marvelous through the fantastic to the uncanny, now confront us with another question. For our statistical games—and in literary history and criticism, statistics can never be more than a game—are of value only to the extent that they generate intelligent questions. In this case: what factors account for these fluctuations?

IN THE first sentence of his essay "Witches, and Other Night-Fears" (1821), Charles Lamb cautioned that "we are too hasty when we set down our ancestors in the gross for fools, for the monstrous inconsistencies (as they seem to us) involved in their need of witchcraft."[11] At the other end of the same decade, in his *Letters on Demonology and Witchcraft* (1830), Sir Walter Scott echoed this opinion. Speaking of man's "predisposition to believe in supernatural occurrences," Scott writes that "mankind, from a very early period, have their minds prepared for such events by the consciousness of the existence of a spiritual world. . . . The abstract possibility of apparitions must be admitted by every one who believes in a Deity, and his superintending omnipotence."[12] These assessments have been borne out by our investigations. In all three cases we had occasion to note that the belief in magic images derived originally from a primitive belief in the material origin of the soul; that is,

[11] Rpt. in *Elia* (1823).

[12] Quoted from 2nd ed. (London: John Murray, 1831), p. 46.

it arose in a religious context. This fundamental belief underlies the magic associated with the three images that we considered.[13] But the matter does not stop there.

It was not mere credulity or ignorance or superstition that prompted perfectly intelligent people of earlier times to accept supernatural phenomena. They were often encouraged by sorcerers and priests who, for reasons of their own, used trickery to create the illusion that the statue could move, that the portrait could weep, that the mirror could reveal hidden truths. This kind of chicanery is not restricted to the past, as we have seen, and it is not limited to images of the soul, of course. To take an entirely different example, it was believed for centuries—from early Christian times down to the middle of the eighteenth century—that the stone known as the carbuncle possessed the power of glowing in the dark. Because of this endogenous power, which called to mind the biblical *lux in tenebris*, it soon became one of the common symbols for Jesus Christ.[14] From classical antiquity through the Middle Ages down to the Renaissance many otherwise reliable witnesses recorded the fact that they had seen such carbuncles with their own eyes. We now understand some of the means by which the delusion was achieved. In his *Naturalis historia* (Bk. 37) Pliny the Elder relates that certain charlatans, in order to mystify the people, soak

[13] This study has focused on the three images suggested by Cocteau's film; it has dealt only peripherally with the closely related image of the autonomous shadow, which occurs less frequently than the other images and which overlaps to an appreciable extent with the image of the mirror-reflection. Any study that concerned itself with the shadow would need to consider, among other texts: Goethe's "Fairy Tale"; Chamisso's *Peter Schlemihl*; H. C. Andersen's "The Shadow"; Poe's "Shadow: A Parable"; Judith Gautier's *Le Dragon impérial*; Oscar Wilde's "The Fisherman and His Soul"; Hofmannsthal's *The Woman without a Shadow*; Stanislaw Przybyszewski, *The Visitors*. In this connection see Otto Rank, *The Double*; and Jerzy Peterkiewicz, "Cast in Glass and Shadow," *New Literary History*, 5 (1974), 353–61.

[14] For this paragraph see Theodore Ziolkowski, "Der Karfunkelstein," *Euphorion*, 55 (1961), 297–326.

garnets (that is, carbuncles) in vinegar for fourteen days, whereupon the stones shine of their own power for as many months. According to an alchemistic tract from the fourth century A.D., priests treated certain stones with the phosphorescent organs of various sea animals in order to impress visitors to the temples with glowing stones. In view of such practices, it is hardly surprising that so many witnesses reported in good faith that they had seen such wonders. By analogy, given the various devices by means of which a statue could be made to perform, it is not astonishing that writers from William of Malmesbury to Robert Burton proclaimed their faith in that particular marvel.

Given the attested medieval faith in magic images, it was perfectly natural for writers of the late eighteenth and early nineteenth centuries, when they introduced these wonders into their works, to locate their narratives in those more credulous times. Speaking of *The Castle of Otranto*, Sir Walter Scott observed, "Romantic narrative is of two kinds,—that which, being in itself possible, may be matter of belief at any period; and that which, though held impossible by more enlightened ages, was yet consonant with the faith of earlier times."[15] Contrasting Walpole's methods favorably with the farfetched rationalizations of Mrs. Radcliffe, Scott states that "Ghosts and witches, and the whole tenets of superstition, having once, and at no late period, been matter of universal belief, warranted by legal authority, it would seem no great stretch upon the reader's credulity to require him, while reading of what his ancestors did, to credit for the time what those ancestors devoutly believed in."[16] If we recall the early examples from each of our three chapters, we find that they are almost always set in the Middle Ages or Reformation—from *Heinrich von Ofterdingen* and Tieck's *Genoveva* to Tom Moore's "The Ring," Southey's "The Pious Painter," and Goethe's *Faust*. All these works belong

[15] *Lives of Eminent Novelists and Dramatists*, new ed. (London, 1887), p. 541.

[16] *Lives of Eminent Novelists*, p. 568.

to the category that Todorov would call the marvelous, because the supernatural occurs in a fictional context that makes it possible to be taken wholly for granted.

But we need to go a step further. The paradox has often been noted that literary interest in the supernatural—in contrast to the perennial belief that survives in folklore, superstition, and fairy tales—is a product of the Enlightenment. How did this happen? In their effort to dispel beliefs they considered foolish, the thinkers of the eighteenth century produced scores of volumes on the supernatural. In an early study entitled "The Dreams of a Visionary, Interpreted by the Dreams of Metaphysics" (1766), Kant arrived at the rather inconclusive opinion that the ultimate solution to problems of the supernatural is not accessible within the limits of human reason and that the matter in any case is not worthy of serious consideration.[17] But other Enlightenment propagandists were less measured in their critiques. In England there appeared a series of anonymous chapbooks whose titles leave no room for doubt concerning their aim:[18]

> *An Antidote to Superstition: Or, A Cure for those Weak Minds which are Troubled with the Fear of Ghosts & Witches, or who Tremble at the Consequences of Inauspicious Dreams or Bad Omens;*
> *Visits from the World of Spirits, being a Collection of Facts relating to the Appearances of Ghosts, Spectres, and Apparitions: To which is prefixed, the Best Cure for Imaginary Terrors.*

The German rationalists were no less zealous in their attacks.[19] We find *Scriptural and Rational Thoughts about*

[17] "Träume eines Geistersehers, erläutert durch Träume der Metaphysik," in *Werke in zehn Bänden*, ed. Wilhelm Weischedel (Wiesbaden: Insel, 1960), II, 918–89.

[18] Titles cited according to Parson, *Witchcraft and Demonology in Scott's Fiction*, pp. 4–5.

[19] See Klaus Kanzog, "Gespenstergeschichte," in *Reallexikon der deutschen Literaturgeschichte*, ed. Werner Kohlschmidt and Wolfgang Mohr, 2nd ed. (Berlin: De Gruyter, 1958), I, 573–76.

Ghosts (Caroli Bohemi, *Schrifftmässige u. vernünfftige Gedanken von Gespenstern*, 1731) as well as J. H. Jung-Stilling's famous *Theory of Spirit-Lore, in a Natural, Rational, and Scriptural Response to the Question: What must be believed and not believed about Presentiments, Visions, and Apparitions* (1808). The French did not lag behind.[20] Jean-Baptiste Thiers discussed *Superstitions anciennes et modernes, préjugés vulgaires qui ont induit les peuples à des usages et à des pratiques contraires à la religion* (1733–36), and Jean-Baptiste Fiard bemoaned *La France trompée par les magiciens et les démonolâtres du dix-huitième siècle, fait démonstré par les faits* (1803).

Now, evidence of this sort needs to be interpreted carefully. First, the prevalence of such works proves that the belief in the supernatural was still quite widespread during the Age of Reason. Otherwise there would be no need for such fervent protests. The supernatural wonders that characterize many of the earliest works we have discussed no doubt found a credulous audience among many of their readers. In addition, these very texts made more easily accessible a mass of lore that had previously been buried in learned compendia or passed along by oral tradition.

Second, faith in the supernatural must be undermined before the sensation of the fantastic can emerge. As long as the cultural context accepts the supernatural, the appropriate form of response is the marvelous. The fantastic occurs only when that faith has been called into sufficient question for doubt, hesitation, and ambivalence to exist.[21] Rational skepticism turns out, paradoxically, to be a necessary condition for the very disease it set out to cure. Our study of the haunted portrait provided the most vivid example. The

[20] Titles cited according to Louis Vax, *La Séduction de l'étrange: Étude sur la littérature fantastique* (Paris: Presses universitaires de France, 1965), pp. 267–68.

[21] Vax, *La Séduction de l'étrange*, pp. 163–64; Maurice Lévy, *Le Roman "gothique" anglais, 1764–1824*, Publications de la Faculté des Lettres et Sciences Humaines de Toulouse, Série A, Tome 9 (Toulouse: Maurice Espic, 1968), pp. 615–16.

literary popularity of the portrait as *figura* and as *anima* did not emerge until the image had been disenchanted by numerous parodies.

Third, once the supernatural was liberated by rationalism, its literary usefulness soon became evident. It is a critical commonplace that the supernatural long functioned as a literary surrogate for the still forbidden subjects of sex and eroticism.[22] It is hardly an accident that the horror story thrived in a Victorian England that so notoriously repressed its sexuality. More specifically, the theme of Venus and the Ring is explicitly sexual in its implications whenever it occurs—from William of Malmesbury through the German romantic writers down to Anthony Burgess. In addition, it has been widely remarked that the supernatural provided a hint of the numinous in a skeptical age whose religious belief had been destroyed by the Enlightenment.[23] Our own studies have demonstrated that all three magic images, which emerged originally from a specifically religious context, show a marked tendency to return to that context when their meaning has been exhausted by rationalization and parody.

In short, various possible explanations account for the revival of the supernatural toward the end of the Age of Reason and clarify the attractiveness of ancient magic images for writers of the period. But the circumstances of reception vary from age to age. Many writers of the next generation, to be sure—Scott, Hoffmann, Gautier, Nerval, Poe, Le Fanu, and others—had a more than playful or lit-

[22] This conviction underlies Freud's essay "The 'Uncanny,'" *Collected Papers*, trans. Joan Riviere, IV (London: Hogarth, 1925), 368–407; Eino Railo, *The Haunted Castle*, pp. 267–81; Mario Praz, *The Romantic Agony*, trans. Angus Davidson (1933; rpt. New York: Meridian, 1956); Penzoldt, *The Supernatural in Fiction*, pp. 146–91; Vax, *La Séduction de l'étrange*, pp. 49–52.

[23] Castex, *Le Conte fantastique*, p. 15; Caillois, "L'Image fantastique," pp. 28–30; Varma, *The Gothic Flame*, pp. 206–31 ("Quest of the Numinous"); and Marcel Schneider, *La Littérature fantastique en France* (Paris: Fayard, 1964), p. 406: "c'est la forme que revêt le sens du mystère et du sacré dans les périodes de trouble et de scepticisme."

erary or symbolic relationship to the supernatural.[24] Mérimée was not just joking when he responded to an inquiry whether or not the statue actually killed Alphonse by saying: "Goodness, child, I have no idea!" Beyond this ambivalence in the face of the supernatural, however, each generation found contemporary scientific justifications for its use of the supernatural in literature—justifications that accorded to the magic images a status that was not purely symbolic. During the first decades of the nineteenth century, for instance, the widely prevalent *Naturphilosophie*, with elements appropriated from mesmerism, galvanism, Schelling's philosophy, and various other sources, provided a theoretical basis for the belief in the animation of the inanimate. It is this new tendency to justify the supernatural by scientific explanation that distinguishes the writers of the thirties and forties from the Gothic romancers around 1800, and that facilitated the development of the attitude that Todorov calls the fantastic.[25] It is noteworthy that, as the marvelous gives way to the fantastic, the preferred settings for the fiction also change. Remote times and exotic places are suitable for the marvelous; but the ambiguity that characterizes the fantastic is most readily maintained in the familiar present. As a result, the works of Gogol, Mérimée, Hawthorne, and their contemporaries most often take place in the present or the recent historical past.

It is also worth stressing an obvious characteristic of our three images that made them more attractive to nineteenth-century writers of the fantastic than the wraiths, specters, and other insubstantial apparitions that Clara Reeve held to be more plausible than walking portraits. They have an incontestable existence in everyday reality. The writer does not need to conjure up the supernatural image; it is already there, ready to be manipulated by the power of imagination like the Venus of Ille or the portrait of the evil money-lender in Gogol's tale.

[24] Vax, *La Séduction de l'étrange*, pp. 160–61.
[25] Castex, *Le Conte fantastique*, pp. 57–58.

The third wave of interest in the supernatural is the heir of the second in its eagerness to justify the supernatural by means of theory: the spiritualism that fascinated Henry James, the electro-magnetism that obsessed Maupassant, the occultism and the theosophy that passed for science in the last decades of the century. But the distinguishing characteristic of this generation was principally the new interest in psychology, which informs the stories of Henry James, Rodenbach, Stevenson, Maupassant, Briusov, and others. All external "scientific" justifications are reduced in importance in comparison with the internalization of motivation that underlies almost all portrayals of the supernatural in the last decades of the century.[26]

The main point is this: whenever there is a revival of interest in the supernatural, we should look for the cultural factors that account for that revival. The image may remain constant; but the justification shifts from one generation to the next. Sometimes the use of the magic images is purely playful, especially in the twentieth century: it would be quite wrong-headed to look for any scientific justification for the magic mirrors in the works of Hesse or Cocteau. At other times we find a more serious rationale for their occurrence. The religious context that informs the images in the works of Barrett, Böll, and Singer is at least an indirect reflection of the revival of interest in religion during the past two decades. If we ignore these cultural and generational differences, we run the risk of misinterpreting images and seeing similarities where none exist. But if we observe them, then our material permits us to draw certain cautious conclusions regarding their broader cultural implications.[27]

[26] Castex, *Le Conte fantastique*, pp. 111–12.

[27] Here I am in sympathy with Prawer, *The 'Uncanny' in Literature*, p. 19: "An awareness of historical and social processes will illuminate at every turn the form in which the uncanny confronts us in a given period of literature." I disagree with Penzoldt, *The Supernatural in Fiction*, pp. 148–49, who believes that the tale of horror "has an entirely individual origin" and therefore has no reliable implications regarding the society from which it originated.

OUR STUDY has shown that all three images are essentially multivalent. The penetrable mirror can symbolize the realm of death (Cocteau's *Orphée*), timeless myth (MacDonald's *Lilith*), or an inverted reality (Lewis Carroll's *Through the Looking Glass*). The haunted portrait can be benevolent (De Morgan, *A Likely Story*), malevolent (Gogol, "The Portrait"), or simply morose (Walpole, *The Castle of Otranto*). The animated statue can act as a fierce avenger (as in the legend of Don Juan) or a gentle consoler (as in the legends concerning statues of the Virgin Mary). Yet certain general tendencies connect these images in larger patterns.

First, it seems apparent that images in their capacity as theme are more closely defined by specific parameters of meaning than in their function as motif or symbol. Although the image of the walking statue is multivalent as a motif, in its hypostasis as Venus it is almost invariably associated with the conflict between paganism and Christianity, a conflict inherent in the theme from William of Malmesbury to Anthony Burgess. Given the British overture and the British finale of the theme, it is striking that seven of the first ten purely literary examples we encountered were not British but German. Why should this theme have had such a particular appeal for German writers at the beginning of the nineteenth century? The reasons may presumably be sought in the associations that the theme bears. The generation of 1810–40 was heir to two strong cultural traditions: the revival of classical pagan antiquity associated with such venerable names as Winckelmann, Lessing, and Goethe; and the revival of the Christian Middle Ages that marked German romanticism. The legend of Venus and the Ring embodied more vividly than any other literary theme the problem of "clashing myths" these writers inherited. Should they follow the fateful lure of pagan beauty or the solemn challenge of Christian responsibility? The relative neglect of the theme on the other side of the Rhine suggests that this conflict between Hellene and Nazarene was less compelling in

France. There, a revolutionary idealism disappointed by political developments of the post-Napoleonic era had focused its attention on other problems: notably the crass materialism that was driving out republican values.[28] This difference of emphasis between the cultural concerns of Germany and France is highlighted by the fact that Mérimée played down the conflict between paganism and Christianity and stated the theme in such a way as to reveal the characteristically French concern: the conflict between primitive passion and an exhausted, materialistic civilization. At the same time, it could be argued that the intellectual detachment with which he appropriated the theme and divested it of its old associations enabled Mérimée to give it a more effective literary treatment than could his German contemporaries, in whose works the message is often so obtrusive that it spoils the tale. It is perfectly consistent with these national differences that the most significant German treatment of the theme is not a work of fiction but Heine's essay.

Although the obsession with a particular image can sometimes betray national concerns, all three images are occasionally permeated simultaneously by the same cultural energies, exposing the preoccupations of certain literary generations that transcend national boundaries. Their problematic fear of the corrupting power of art reveals that Poe, Hawthorne, Nerval, and Gogol are contemporaries who stand at an equal remove from the German romanticism that inspired them and who have grown equally skeptical of romanticism's idealizing view of "Art." Similarly, the fascination with madness that pervades the works of Maupassant, Rodenbach, Stevenson, Briusov, and others betrays an obsessive concern of a later generation that had just dis-

[28] Castex, *Le Conte fantastique*, p. 400. This is not to suggest, of course, that the tension between Christianity and neo-Hellenism did not exist in France. But it is particularly in Germany, where the romantic tendencies emerged more sharply than elsewhere in Europe, that we can observe what E. M. Butler called "the tyranny of Greece over Germany" and the ensuing "clash" of myths.

covered psychology. Literary history can produce very strange bedfellows indeed. The young Henry James and Sacher-Masoch make an unlikely couple, yet their internalizing treatment of the Venus theme points to a generational similarity that transcends their different sources in Mérimée and Heine. The elder Henry James and J. E. Poritzky, who presumably never heard of each other, turn out to share the curious notion that the present haunts the past. Heinrich Böll, William E. Barrett, and Isaac Bashevis Singer, representing different religious backgrounds, nevertheless feel what seems to be a common generational need to relocate magic images in the religious context from which they originally emerged.

Our three chapters have displayed one overarching pattern that suggests a final important cultural implication. The theme of Venus and the Ring reached its peak of perfection around 1837 with the works of Heine and Mérimée; it then virtually disappeared for thirty years. When it reappeared it received two further interesting treatments at the hands of Sacher-Masoch and Henry James before it was trivialized in ghost stories and parodies. At the same time, the image of the magic mirror, which initially was limited almost completely to its rather mechanical catoptromantic function, suddenly around 1840 began to provide the basis for a number of major literary works involving doubles. What accounts for the sudden exhaustion of one image, which had been immensely popular for three decades, and the simultaneous emergence of a different one, which had hitherto been quite conventional when it occurred? If we glance at the history of the haunted portrait for comparative purposes, we note an equally striking shift in the thirties: up to that point the dominant aspect of the image had been the *genius loci*; now suddenly, with the generation of Gogol, Poe, and Hawthorne, the portrait as *anima* becomes the characteristic aspect.

The common fact linking the images that prevailed until about 1835 is that they all represent a threat to the individual from the outside. The statue intrudes into the marriage of the hero and his bride; the portrait of the ancestor steps out of its frame and intercedes in the affairs of the family; the catoptromantic mirror reveals truths that affect the life of the individual, most often balefully. If we now search for the common denominator among the images that come to the fore at mid-century, we note that the doubling mirror and the portrait as *anima* represent a threat to the individual from within: the double in the portrait or in the mirror is not something external and alien, but a repressed aspect of the individual's own personality (e.g., William Wilson and Dorian Gray). Why did this striking shift occur?

It is a commonplace of cultural history that political unrest often reanimates superstition and belief in the supernatural.[29] More specifically, students of the Gothic romance, the *Schauerroman*, the *roman noir*, have noted that many of its attributes—the tyrannical villain who threatens the young hero and heroine, the secret society that manipulates the figures of the plot, the ghostly powers that influence the action—represent the fear of a whimsical and unpredictable authority that dominated the later eighteenth and early nineteenth centuries—not just, or even principally the fear of monarchy, but even more of the revolutionary directorate and the Napoleonic dictatorship.[30] Just as the crumbling castle symbolizes the crumbling order of pre-revolutionary Europe, the portrait figure represents the attempts of that dissolving past to continue to exercise its authority over the youth of the present. If these theories are correct, then the magic images that threaten from without embody the fears of an age that is still accustomed to look into the external world for its anxieties. The threat could be relocated within the individual only when political circumstances had relaxed in such a way that the threat of external oppression was re-

[29] Parsons, *Witchcraft and Demonology in Scott's Fiction*, pp. 2–3.

[30] Prawer, *The 'Uncanny' in Literature*, pp. 19–20; Railo, *The Haunted Castle*, p. 299 and pp. 311–14; Lévy, *Le Roman "gothique" anglais*, pp. 608–13; Varma, *The Gothic Flame*, pp. 216–19.

duced, a development that took place in the course of the nineteenth century.

The shift from an apprehension of a threat from without to a threat from within, which reflects contemporary political circumstances, also corresponds to the development of scientific thought in the nineteenth century. Scientists, thinkers, and writers of the immediate post-Enlightenment were fascinated by the newly discovered powers of the unconscious that exerted such a profound influence on "rational" man. During the early decades of the century, however, these unconscious powers were still thought to be external. Schelling explained them as "nature" striving upward toward consciousness. According to Mesmer, the unconscious was a force or fluid emanating from one person and affecting the mind of another. In both cases psychological phenomena were considered to be the effect of essentially external causes —a conception aptly exemplified by a statue that intrudes upon our lives or a portrait that climbs out of its frame. As psychological theory grew more sophisticated, it was gradually realized that the same effects could better be explained as manifestations of the individual psyche; it was not necessary to resort to external forces to provide an explanation. When it became desirable to find adequate literary images to express this new intellectual paradigm, the mirror double and the portrait as *anima* were readily at hand. It was simply necessary to revaluate the conventional image.

In short, a culture's choice of its representative images can tell us a great deal about the central concerns of that culture. In this case, the choice around 1840 reveals a pronounced shift in the location of existential anxiety from without to within. Of course, the process does not stop at that point. In the first place, as the originally justifying meaning is withdrawn from any particular image (e.g., the portrait as *genius loci*), the image remains in literature according to the law of Conservation of Cultural Energy; but it is usually reduced in literary status, becoming, for instance, a figure in a parody or a ghost story. The ancestral portrait, which in *The Castle of Otranto* still bears the burden of the past and its responsibilities, is revealed in *The House of the Seven Gables* to be an ineffectual "odious picture," and degenerates in "The Judge's House" into a malevolent rodent. By analogy, Heine's Grecian marble and Mérimée's Roman bronze are reduced to cheap Sicilian plaster in Burgess' parody of Venus and the Ring.

In the second place, the threat from within is merely a transitional phase in cultural history, whose final hectic stages we see in the works of Rodenbach and Briusov. If the image that comes out of the portrait or the mirror is characteristic of the nineteenth century and its obsession with the unconscious—first as a threat from without and then as a threat from within—the typical image of the twentieth century is the portrait or mirror that is penetrated by a figure from this world—in the works of MacDonald, Carroll, James, Cocteau, Hesse, Cabell, Singer, and others. This shift helps to explain the disappearance of the Venus theme: for the statue, unlike the mirror and the painting, can only represent a threat from without; it has no world or context of its own that the individual can enter. (In the single case when a figure enters the "field" of a sculpture, in E. M. Forster's story "The Classical Annex," the effect is explicitly comic.)

It would be an oversimplification to conclude that the act of entering the painting or the realm behind the mirror is simply an effort to escape this world and its various threats.[31] If we scrutinize those worlds behind the mirror in

[31] Friends of the fantastic object to the reproach of escapism. See Marcel Schneider, *La Littérature fantastique en France*, pp. 406–07: "Evasion, oui, dans le sens où l'on s'évade d'une prison pour trouver cette liberté que la littérature soumise à la science, à l'Eglise et à l'Etat ne nous donnent pas." Or Penzoldt, *The Supernatural in Fiction*, p. 254: "It is pointless to discard weird fiction with such slogans as 'escapism,' or to reproach the tellers of weird tales with their apparent lack of interest in problems of actuality and so-called reality. The fact is simply that they deal with realities deeper and more ancient than those apparent."

all their variety, we realize that they do not always symbolize an appealing alternative to reality in this world. The common impulse motivating these heroes who enter mirrors and portraits would seem to be the impulse to explore other worlds and other dimensions, in contrast to the self-exploration represented by the doubling mirror and the portrait as *anima*. In any case, the three magic images reveal a remarkable similarity in their cultural implications. The portrait that climbs out of its frame and the walking statue appeal to the imagination of a society concerned with threats from without—political, social, scientific. The portrait as *anima* and the doubling mirror reveal the preoccupations of a society that has been relieved of its principal fears of external danger and that now devotes itself to the exploration of its own consciousness. Finally, the man who climbs into the mirror or the picture frame comes from a society that has transcended exploration of the individual psyche, out of weariness or even horror at what it has found, and that turns instead to investigate other worlds: either new modes of consciousness or new realms of life. Can it be chance that these aspects of the various images emerged on the eve of the age of consciousness-expanding drugs and space exploration?

THE STUDY of magic images produces certain interesting cultural implications; it also suggests other implications that are purely literary. If our conclusions up to this point have borne out the historian's view that "iconography serves as a constant auxiliary to the history of ideas,"[32] the following remarks stem from the conviction that iconology can serve as a valuable auxiliary to the theory of literature. It has frequently been observed that the realm of the fantastic is predominantly fiction, not poetry or drama.[33] Among the works

[32] Jean Seznec, *The Survival of the Pagan Gods: The Mythological Tradition and Its Place in Renaissance Humanism and Art*, trans. Barbara F. Sessions (1953; rpt. New York: Harper Torchbook, 1961), p. 7.

[33] Todorov, *Introduction à la littérature fantastique*, p. 65; Hubert

we considered, about three-quarters were novels and stories, and only one quarter were poems, plays, operas, and films. We can go even further. All the poems and dramatic works —from Goethe's *Faust* and Tom Moore's "The Ring" to D'Annunzio's *La Pisanelle* and Cocteau's *Orphée*—take their magic wholly for granted and locate the action in a time and place in which the supernatural and the marvelous are accepted as a convention. This means, in turn, that these works never progress beyond the stage that Todorov calls the marvelous; they never break loose to that attitude of ambivalence or hesitation between the rational and the supernatural that characterizes the fantastic. The main reason for this generic affinity is not technical but theoretical. Performances of *Don Giovanni*, *Ruddigore*, *The Student of Prague*, or Korngold's *Die tote Stadt* prove that opera and film have long been able to handle the appearance of the supernatural as a technical problem. The crucial point is this: the experience of the fantastic takes place in the mind. The moment a painting is actually said by the author of the poem to move, or the moment the mirror image actually steps out of the mirror in the film, all ambivalence is destroyed. When the statue of the *commendatore* arrives at Don Giovanni's house, we simply suspend our disbelief and settle down to enjoy their duet. It is only in the mind that we can savor that moment of ambivalence or hesitation, and the literary mode whose action takes place exclusively in the mind is narrative fiction.

For this reason the narrative stance is immensely important. Often we find a first-person narrator, for the sense of ambiguity can most easily be maintained if the report is filtered through the consciousness of the person who is actually experiencing doubts. In works in which the marvelous is taken for granted by participants and readers alike—e.g., the various poems or *The Castle of Otranto*—the narrative

---

Matthey, *Essai sur le merveilleux dans la littérature française depuis 1800* (Paris: Payot, 1915), pp. 259–71.

can be recounted by a third-person narrator. Yet it is an oversimplification to say that the first person is *per se* the mode of the fantastic.[34] Further discriminations need to be made. First, several works—e.g., Gogol's "The Portrait" and Wilde's *Dorian Gray*—manage to maintain the sense of ambiguity even through a third-person narrator. In these cases the author takes up a narrative stance that is quite close to the consciousness of his hero: we experience the animated portrait through Chertkov's eyes and through Dorian's imagination. Scott even brings off the feat of suggesting ambiguity at two removes: he reports supernatural experiences that have been related to him by sources (his Aunt Margaret and Mrs. Anna Seward) who did not, themselves, claim to be firsthand witnesses. So the first person is by no means the necessary narrative stance for the fantastic.

Indeed, the first person can even undermine the fantastic: this happens frequently in works that turn out to be "uncanny" rather than fantastic, as is the case in Maupassant's "The Horla" or Briusov's "In the Mirror." In both cases we realize very quickly—long before the allegedly supernatural event occurs—that we are dealing with unreliable narrators who are mentally deranged. As a result, we do not share the attitude of ambivalence that they experience; rather, we witness their dilemma and come to understand how delusions regarding the supernatural can take hold of an over-agitated mind.

Finally, even in those cases in which the first person is used to establish the sense of hesitancy it is necessary to discriminate.[35] There is a vast rhetorical difference between the

[34] As does Todorov, *Introduction à la littérature fantastique*, p. 87: "Dans les histoires fantastiques, le narrateur dit habituellement 'je': c'est un fait empirique que l'on peut vérifier facilement." My own count does not verify this "fact."

[35] Note the sane position of S. S. Prawer, *The 'Uncanny' in Literature*, pp. 9–10: "Much depends, too, on the kind of reflecting consciousness that the author interposes between himself and his readers. . . ."

worldly skepticism of Mérimée's narrator in "The Venus of Ille" and the disturbed ponderings of William Wilson in Poe's tale, between the unquestioning credulity of the narrator of MacDonald's *Lilith* and the drugged consciousness of Hesse's Harry Haller. In short, the narrative point of view determines the effect of the tale, ranging from the marvelous to the comical. But detailed examination of specific works suggests that there is no rule of thumb governing the choice of a specific point of view. Our study simply confirms what common sense dictates: that the grand simplifications of theory must always be submitted for verification to a close scrutiny of the text.

Three-quarters of our texts consist of narrative, in contrast to poetry or drama, and most of the narrative, in turn (in a ratio of two to one), falls into the category of short fiction: tale, short story, *conte*, novella. There would seem to be at least two reasons for this preference of shorter forms of fiction over longer forms. First, the intrusion of the supernatural into everyday reality—whether from within or without, whether real or presumed—constitutes a moment of crisis. What matters is not the duration but the intensity of the experience. In fact, repetition in such cases easily leads to burlesque effects (e.g., Anstey, *The Tinted Venus*).[36] Of course, in romances that take their magic for granted—*Through the Looking Glass, Lilith, Something about Eve*—the author can employ longer forms. We simply enter a fictional universe that takes the supernatural for granted; once we pass through the looking glass there is no confusion between reality and the supernatural at all. Otherwise, however, authors favor the shorter form that culminates in a single or isolated instance of intrusion: the Venus of Ille walks only a single time, Gogol's portrait comes out of its frame only once, William Wilson encounters his double only at a few crucial moments in his life. As the marvelous gives

[36] Penzoldt, *The Supernatural in Fiction*, p. 254: "The short tale of the supernatural is best suited to modern taste, for its brevity strains our scepticism less than the longer forms."

way to the fantastic and then to the uncanny, depictions of the moment of intrusion are replaced increasingly by analysis of the consciousness of the supposed witness.

There is a second reason for the priority of the short form over longer forms of fiction. The intrusion of the supernatural into a world governed by rational laws of nature is one of the most violent acts of chaos imaginable, an offense to reason and order. If such an intrusion is to be fictionally acceptable, it must be presented in a context that embodies reason and order. Otherwise the chaos would be both aesthetically unsatisfactory and morally depressing. Among the various literary forms, the shorter forms of fiction—novella and short story—have long been regarded as models of aesthetic form. Since they exemplify order, they can afford to incorporate instances of chaos as fleeting moments of crisis. The order of the narrative itself—in contrast to the generally looser order of longer forms like the novel—functions as a consolation in the face of the chaos depicted within the story. If we recall the works in their chronological sequence, we note that the earliest works involving magic images tend to be longer fictions or poetry because, as representatives of the marvelous, they take the supernatural for granted. With the stories of E.T.A. Hoffmann a conspicuous change takes place. Hoffmann was the first writer to introduce the supernatural into the everyday life of contemporary Europe rather than into some remote past or exotic present. Moreover, Hoffmann perfected the novella as the appropriate mode for the representation of this new "fantastic" treatment of the supernatural, establishing a tradition that dominated the works in all three categories for thirty years. After 1850 the short fiction does not disappear, of course; it is immensely important in works that fall into the category of the uncanny (Maupassant, Briusov, Rodenbach, Stevenson, and others). But as the ambiguity that characterizes the classic short stories of the fantastic gradually gives way to other concerns—e.g., the symbolic romance of MacDonald and Lewis Carroll, the allegorical fiction of Oscar Wilde, the psychological investigations of Zola and James, the surrealistic exuberances of Cocteau and Hesse—the longer forms begin to emerge in importance again. It is perhaps symptomatic of this trend that the examples since World War I include other forms—operas, films, plays, and novels—because at the fourth stage of disenchantment, as we have seen, the various modes and aspects begin to exist synchronically. In other words, generalizations about the generic affinity of the supernatural need to be carefully qualified: it looks very much as though the short story is the most suitable form for the supernatural only at the specific stage of the fantastic.

MacDonald's *Lilith* begins and ends in a library. This fact, along with the prominence of books and libraries in so many other works we have considered, suggests a final conclusion implicit in our material: the essential literariness of literature of the supernatural. Although the preference for a particular image may reflect a national or generational concern, it is apparent that the works we have considered derive their basic material more often from other literary works than from "life." This statement is most obviously true with reference to a theme such as Venus and the Ring. A writer simply does not invent this theme or discover it in the world surrounding him: he finds it in books and libraries. Often the text contains a reference to the source of the theme: Apel cites William of Malmesbury, Heine refers to Kornmann, Mérimée acknowledges a source but sends the scholar off on a wild-goose chase, Burgess alludes to Robert Burton, and so forth. But the literary provenance of these images is evident even when no specific source is cited, for—to put it most simply—writers are not likely to encounter walking statues, haunted portraits, and magic mirrors in their everyday experience.[37] As a result, as we moved chronologically

[37] See Todorov, *Introduction à la littérature fantastique*, pp. 86–87: "Si le fantastique se sert sans cesse des figures rhétoriques, c'est qu'il y a trouvé son origine. Le surnaturel naît du langage. . . ." See also Vax, *La Séduction de l'étrange*, pp. 28–29.

from text to text, it was easy to establish lines of continuity—in the interest not so much of demonstrating "influence" as, rather, of tracing the history of the images themselves. But it should be obvious that this "history" exists, at least during the past two hundred years, exclusively in literature.

These thoughts on the literariness of literature bring us to the point at which we can hazard a response to the question with which our study began: the source of the images that open Cocteau's film, *The Blood of a Poet*. Cocteau, it will be recalled, maintained that the images emerged from the darkness of his blood, and that he recovered them by "letting down within me a diving bell like the one that they let down into the sea, to great depths." However, our iconological considerations persuade us to agree with Shklovsky that there is a more probable source than these profundities of the collective unconscious. The portrait that comes to life, the animated statue, and the magic mirror are three of the most common images not only in folklore and legend but in nineteenth- and twentieth-century literature. It seems far more likely that Cocteau was lowering the bathysphere of his imagination into the sea of literary tradition rather than into the sanguinary waters of his psyche and that the images sprang from the pages of books on his library shelf rather than from "the great darkness of the human body."

This conclusion regarding the literary origin of the images seems all the more reasonable when we recall that the Gothic romances through which they entered European literature enjoyed a conspicuous revival in France during the twenties and thirties. In his first Surrealist Manifesto (1924) André Breton heralded Lewis' *The Monk* as an example of the "marvelous" that was needed to revitalize modern literature.[38] In 1931, just when Cocteau completed his film, Antonin Artaud published his "re-telling" of *The Monk*. It is likely that Cocteau knew of this much-publicized undertaking during the preceding years when Artaud was working on

[38] André Breton, *Manifestes du surréalisme* (Paris: Gallimard, 1965), p. 24.

his adaptation; in any case, he reviewed it enthusiastically immediately upon its publication.[39] The general fascination the Gothic romance held for the generation of surrealists is indicated by the fact that Breton cited *The Castle of Otranto* as a model of the "automatic writing" that he recommended to his own peers.[40] In 1943 Eluard wrote the preface to a translation of Walpole's novel, and twenty years later Dali provided the illustrations for yet another translation of the same work. Breton himself prefaced a translation of *Melmoth the Wanderer* in 1954. To think that Cocteau could have remained unaffected by the enthusiasm that generated these tokens of interest from 1924 on strains the credulity at least as much as walking statues or talking portraits do.

It could be argued, in fact, that the three magic images have such an immediate impact at the beginning of Cocteau's film precisely because they were by that time more or less conventional. Some of the images that occur in subsequent scenes, after the poet enters the realm behind the mirror, are more private and hence less accessible—at least to viewers unfamiliar with Cocteau's earlier works. But Cocteau eases the viewer into the world of his film quite gently through the mediation of familiar images that summon up specific expectations and responses, conditioned by a century and a half of literature.

These three images, common though they are, almost never occur in the same literary text. (The single exception we noted was the brief and purely humorous passage in Hawthorne's story, "Dr. Heidegger's Experiment.") As we have seen, each has its own history and characteristic contexts. The fact that Cocteau can introduce all three of them within the first few minutes of the film indicates that the images have reached a point in their own history at which, liberated from the contexts and associations that normally govern them, they are free to be playfully assembled in new and

[39] *Nouvelle Revue Française*, 36 (May 1931), 764–66.

[40] "Limites non frontières du Surréalisme," *Nouvelle Revue Française*, 48 (February 1937), 210–11.

surprising configurations. For even though the images themselves are familiar, the configuration is startingly original. In other words, the process of disenchantment is complete. The three images that originated in the primitive consciousness as projections of the human soul and that made their way through pagan and medieval superstition into eighteenth- and nineteenth-century literature bearing supernatural associations, have been disencumbered by rationalization and psychological internalization of the last vestiges of their ancient meaning. It is perhaps nothing less than a modern miracle if these disenchanted images still retain so much literary vigor that they can be conjured up again and again to provide a fleeting touch of magic for our disenchanted world.

Index

LIBRARY OF CONGRESS CATALOGING IN PUBLICATION DATA

Ziolkowski, Theodore.
Disenchanted images.

Includes index.
1. Magic in literature. 2. Symbolism in literature.
3. Demythologization (Literature) I. Title.
PN56.M3Z5 809 76–45917
ISBN 0–691–06334–6